Modes of Discipline

The Bucknell Studies in Eighteenth-Century Literature and Culture

The Bucknell Studies in Eighteenth-Century Literature and Culture aims to publish challenging, new eighteenth-century scholarship. Of particular interest is critical, historical, and interdisciplinary work that is interestingly and intelligently theorized, and that broadens and refines the conception of the field. At the same time, the series remains open to all theoretical perspectives and different kinds of scholarship. While the focus of the series is the literature, history, arts, and culture (including art, architecture, music, travel, and history of science, medicine, and law) of the long eighteenth century in Britain and Europe, the series is also interested in scholarship that establishes relationships with other geographies, literatures, and cultures of the period 1660–1830.

Titles in This Series

Tanya Caldwell, *Time to Begin Anew: Dryden's* Georgics *and* Aeneis

Mita Choudhury, *Interculturalism and Resistance in the London Theatre, 1660–1800: Identity, Performance, Empire*

James Cruise, *Governing Consumption: Needs and Wants, Suspended Characters, and the "Origins" of Eighteenth-Century English Novels*

Edward Jacobs, *Accidental Migrations: An Archaeology of Gothic Discourse*

Regina Hewitt, ed., *Orthodoxy and Heresy in Eighteenth-Century Society*

Deborah Kennedy, *Helen Maria Williams and the Age of Revolution*

Chris Mounsey, *Christopher Smart: Clown of God*

Chris Mounsey, ed., *Presenting Gender*

Laura Rosenthal and Mita Choudhury, eds., *Monstrous Dreams of Reason*

Philip Smallwood, ed., *Johnson Re-Visioned: Looking Before and After*

Sarah Jordon, *Anxieties of Idleness*

Lisa Wood, *Modes of Discipline*

http://www.departments.bucknell.edu/univ._press

Modes of Discipline

Women, Conservatism, and the Novel after the French Revolution

Lisa Wood

Lewisburg
Bucknell University Press
London: Associated University Presses

Associated University Presses
2010 Eastpark Boulevard
Cranbury, NJ 08512

Associated University Presses
16 Barter Street
London WC1A 2AH, England

Associated University Presses
P.O. Box 338, Port Credit
Mississauga, Ontario
Canada L5G 4L8

The paper used in this publication meets the requirements of the American National Standard for Permanence of Paper for Printed Library Materials Z39.48-1984.

Library of Congress Cataloging-in-Publication Data

Wood, Lisa, 1964–
Modes of discipline : women, conservatism, and the novel after the French Revolution / Lisa Wood.
p. cm. — (Bucknell studies in eighteenth-century literature and culture)
Includes bibliographical references and index.
ISBN 0-8387-5527-5
1. English fiction—18th century—History and criticism. 2. France—History—Revolution, 1789–1799—Literature and the revolution. 3. Women and literature—Great Britain—History—19th century. 4. Women and literature—Great Britain—History—18th century. 5. English fiction—Women authors—History and criticism. 6. Conservatism—Great Britain—History—19th century. 7. Conservatism—Great Britain—History—18th Century. 8. English fiction—19th century—History and criticism. 9. France—History—Revolution, 1789–1799—Influence. 10. Conservatism in literature. I. Title. II. Series.

PR858.F7 W66 2003
823′.509358—dc21 2002074416

PRINTED IN THE UNITED STATES OF AMERICA

Contents

Acknowledgments

THIS PROJECT WAS NURTURED BY A NUMBER OF PEOPLE OVER THE course of its development. Many thanks to Rusty Shteir for warm collegiality and guidance, and to Susan Sniader Lanser, Ian Balfour, Betty Sabiston, Lorna Erwin, and John Lennox, whose thoughtful suggestions guided this study toward its final form. Mary, David, Stepan, and Evan Wood have been warmly supportive and acute critics, while Kate Lum, Julie Cairnie, and Victor Shea have been intellectual companions and great friends. Gisela Argyle's suggestions and support helped smooth the final stages of this project, and conversations with Donna Andrew, Gary Kelly, Bill Westfall, and Bill Whitla clarified central issues. The librarians at the Osborne Collection of Early Children's Books in Toronto offered informed advice and friendly help, the staff at the British Library were kind and efficient during several visits there, and the John W. Graham Library at the University of Toronto provided a peaceful setting for final revisions. I am grateful to the Government of Ontario and York University, whose financial support enabled significant portions of my research. I also thank Greg Clingham and Bucknell University Press for their support of this project.

I would like to acknowledge *English Studies in Canada* for permission to include in chapter 5 portions of my essay "'This Maze of History and Fiction': Conservatism, Genre, and the Problem of Domestic Freedom in Jane West's *Alicia de Lacy*" (*English Studies in Canada* 23, no. 2 [June 1997]: 125–40), and also *Tulsa Studies in Women's Literature* for permission to incorporate portions of "Bachelors and 'Old Maids': Anti-Revolutionary British Women Writers and Narrative Authority After the French Revolution" (forthcoming) into chapter 3.

I dedicate this work to David, whose emotional and intellectual support has, in so many ways, made this work possible, and to Jonathan Tristram, for the astonishing joy he has brought.

Modes of Discipline

1

Poison or Pudding? Women, Antirevolutionary Didacticism, and the Novel

> The rage for novels does not decrease; and, though I by no means think them the best vehicles for 'the words of sound doctrine'; yet, while the enemies of our church and state continue to pour their poison into unwary ears through this channel, it behoves the friends of our establishments to convey an antidote by the same course; especially as those who are most likely to be infected by false principles, will not search for a refutation of them in profound and scientific compositions.
>
> Jane West, *The Infidel Father* (1802)

JANE WEST FOLLOWED HER OWN ADVICE: IN ADDITION TO MORAL poetry and drama, and moralistic conduct books, she published eight didactic novels over the course of her long writing career (1786–1827). For West, fiction provided a way to challenge what she called "the alarming relaxation of principle that too surely discriminates a declining age," thus her fictional as well as her overtly didactic texts are concerned less with literary effect than with conveying and enforcing a conformist moral message.[1] The antirevolutionary novel became, for her, a bulwark against revolutionary threats from without and within Britain. West was not unique. A significant number of novels published in Britain during the post-French Revolutionary period were both didactic and conservative, united by the explicit purpose of protecting the British people from revolutionary contagion; of these, the majority were written by women. How did women in these turbulent years use the novel form to promote an antirevolutionary message? Their project took various, often surprising, forms, as they attempted to mold the structures of a variety of novelistic genres to a propagandistic purpose. The different shapes their narratives took, and the challenges and problems produced in the attempt to combine the novel form with a didactic message, are my primary objects of exploration in this study.

The period spanning the years from 1793 to 1815 was perhaps the most tolerant of overt didacticism in the history of British fiction. This was in part due to the widely-held fear of the spread of revolutionary sentiment to Britain after the French Revolution. The promotion of antirevolutionary lessons became one of the critical criteria used by periodicals for judging the "value" of novels, especially for female readers, and conservative didactic texts were widely read and well-received by the reading public. Didacticism provided the means for women to conceive of themselves as writers, the rationale for the act of writing, and the basic form of the text produced. This study focuses on the brief historical moment when the popular and critical appeal of novels by women, and of didacticism, was at its peak. What Gary Kelly has called the "remasculinization" of culture during the early decades of the nineteenth century was coincident with the increased professionalization of novel writing, the decrease of didacticism as a criterion of literary value, and a shift toward the aesthetic as the means by which to measure a novel's worth. While novels remained "ideological," in the sense that they were produced within and promoted specific ideologies, their didactic element became obscured by an increasingly overt emphasis on form and narrative.[2] My focus here, then, is on the "rhetoric" of explicitly didactic fiction from a generation of novelists for whom the conflicts between "telling" and "showing," "realism" and "intrusion" did not exist.

The writers I deal with in this study were resolutely and unapologetically oppositional and didactic, both in their fictional and nonfictional writing. As Doris Y. Kadish notes, the French Revolution effected a politicization of nonpolitical discourse that had no precedent; the events of 1789–92 in France produced "a profound social and historical fear that novelists seek to mediate through symbolic expression."[3] In many cases, therefore, the stated purpose and catalyst for writing was a perceived political necessity. Hannah More's first project in fiction writing, for instance, the Cheap Repository Tracts (1795–98), was instituted with the explicit aim of combating the effects on the working classes of Thomas Paine's *Rights of Man* (1791–92). Laetitia Matilda Hawkins's *Letters on the Female Mind* (1793) specifically responded to Helen Maria Williams's *Letters Written in France* (1790) and *Letters From France* (1792). Elizabeth Hamilton takes Mary Hays's *Memoirs of Emma Courtney* (1796) and William Godwin's *Memoirs of the Author of "The Rights of Woman"* (1798) as her objects of attack in *Memoirs of Modern Philosophers*

(1800).[4] For the most part, in keeping with their ideology of separately gendered spheres, antirevolutionary women positioned themselves in relation to revolutionary women writers, such as Hays, Wollstonecraft, and Williams. Their engagement with them was an effort to control the spread of revolutionary ideas in Britain, and took a number of related forms: a struggle over gender and class ideologies; a debate over the meaning of central terms and concepts, such as "rights"; and conflict over the parameters and form of the novel.

The novel, more than any other literary genre, was used to promote the ideas of radicals and moderates as well as antirevolutionaries. The facility with which the form could be adapted to seemingly contradictory political uses was the source of much concern for writers of a variety of political stances; the conservative Jane West worried that the novel genre could convey revolutionary ideas, while in her literary reviews the radical Mary Wollstonecraft critiqued the models of femininity promoted by sentimental novels. Many women conservatives openly declared their discomfort with the novel form, and utilized prefaces and digressions within their texts to explore issues of moral and formal coherence. In her *Strictures on the Modern System of Female Education*, Hannah More states her suspicion of the genre and the messages she believes it to promote: "the corruption occasioned by these books has spread so wide, and descended so low," she complains, that "among milliners, mantua-makers, and other trades where numbers work together, the labour of one girl is frequently sacrificed that she may be spared to read those mischievous books to the others." This blanket criticism applied especially to French and German productions, but also to the many popular novels published in Britain during the 1790s. More's concern is both with the "pernicious" doctrines conveyed by novels, and with the disruption of industry entailed in their consumption. Laetitia Matilda Hawkins takes the opportunity of "speaking aside" in the preface to her novel, *The Countess and Gertrude*, to inform the reader that one of her main concerns is the practice of reading novels to servants, after which she carefully assures the reader that her narrative is more true than "invention." "A story," she explains, "was necessary to connect the circumstances and recommend them to attention." Hawkins attempts to solve both the formal and moral problems raised by the novel form by insisting on the truth of her narrative: "We narrate—we do not create," comments the narrator in an early chapter. The reactionary *Anti-Jacobin Review and Magazine*, in apparent response to these disclaimers by Hawkins, refers to the text as "[t]his performance, which we are sure the fair author will not consent to have called a novel."[5] Implicitly acknowledging that a generic choice is an ideological choice, these writers were determined to dissociate their productions from the problematic form of the novel.

This deep ambivalence about the novel genre is evident in West's peroration on the "rage for novels" at the head of this chapter, with its alarmist metaphors of poison and infection. West's discourse in this passage serves to underscore the nonliterary function of her text—its role as "antidote"—and the seriousness with which she represented her antirevolutionary cause. By West's account, the act of reading novels is inherently dangerous, not only to the individual, but to "church and state," "our establishments," and, by extension, the nation. The reader, "unwary" and vulnerable, is infantilized by this argument. Like Hamlet's sleeping father, whose murder provides the pretext to West's metaphor, the reader is easily overcome by a wakeful antagonist. If we follow this allusion, the "enemies of our church and state" are aligned with the usurping Claudius, while the reader is positioned with the wronged legitimate monarch. By corrupting the reading public through fiction, this passage suggests, revolutionary novelists attack legitimate British power structures, undermining the security of the nation as a whole.

The language of West's account is not unusual in antirevolutionary writing of this period. A year later, in a review of West's novels, the *Anti-Jacobin Review and Magazine* parrots the words of its subject: "We have had frequent occasion to lament that the species of literary composition, unhappily most in vogue in the present degenerate times, and which has, therefore, been rendered by the sceptical, schismatical, and disaffected writers of the age, a vehicle for the promulgation of every false, bad, and vicious principle, that can corrupt the heart or contaminate the mind of the present and of the rising generation, has not sufficiently occupied the attention of authors who are both willing and able to counteract the pernicious effects of the mental poison thus copiously administered." In a similar vein, Hannah More acknowledges the pleasure of reading, and the real problem facing antirevolutionary propagandists, when she writes of her Cheap Repository Tracts: "Dry morality will not answer the end, for we must bear in mind that it is a pleasant poison to which we must find an antidote." Mary Brunton provides a further example of this rhetoric in her 1814 preface to *Discipline*, where she comments: "The appetite for fiction is indeed universal, and has unfortunately been made the occasion of conveying poison of every description into the youthful mind. Why must the antidote be confined to such forms as are sure to be rejected by those who need it the most?"[6]

The rhetoric of corruption, contamination, and poison works to pathologize the novel in these texts, and to construct a pervasive antirevolutionary model of literary consumption as negative. Yet West and her conservative contemporaries agree that the "vehicles" that convey the "poison" of radical philosophy also provide the best method for countering revolutionary theory. The counterrevolutionary project will be effected, by this logic, not through the cessation of consumption, but through the purification of the product consumed.

At least one radical, Anna Letitia Barbauld, uses the metaphor of poison to refute anti-Jacobin attacks on the genre: "Though a great deal of trash is every season poured out upon the public by the English presses, yet in general our novels are not vicious; the food has neither flavour nor nourishment, but at least it is not *poisoned*." In this passage Barbauld combines two metaphors that helped to organize late-eighteenth-century conceptualizations of the effects of reading: literature as food and as poison. Jane West employs the former to recuperate her novel-writing project. At the beginning of *The Infidel Father*, the narrator explains that her books, in contrast to "high-seasoned French and German cookery," are "a little old English fare, dressed in a plain style, and, if not more *piquant*, at least more *wholesome*, than those outlandish farragoes." The patriotic morality underlying this culinary figure is repeated in the introduction to *The Loyalists*, in which the book is described as "plain old English food," while the act of writing is also described in terms of food in a letter in 1811: "It is often a relief, when writing a long work, to take off the mind to another; and a line of poetry and prose intermingled will make a sort of layer pudding, which I think excellent food." In general, "moral" books are a "wholesome nutriment" to satisfy the "cravings" of the new middle-class reading public.[7] The suggestion that the same food, when properly prepared, can be rendered wholesome helped to justify West's use of a genre that so easily could be spoiled by the excessive "seasoning" of foreign theories. This reconceptualization of her texts through metaphor helps to explain the mechanism whereby a morally and artistically suspect genre could become the preeminent "vehicle" of antirevolutionary didacticism in this period.

These writers, then, chose the novel in large part because it was expedient. It gave them potential access to a large reading audience, and the genre fulfilled at least one half of the eighteenth-century *utile et dulce* formula. The domestic novel, with its teleological trajectory toward sexual and material rewards, provided a form and a readership for writers hoping to reach young women in particular. Entertainment promised access to readers who might not necessarily read a didactic tract. In a letter to Jane West on the subject of a conduct book she intended to write, Bishop Percy points to the habitual purchaser of conduct manuals and didactic texts: "Your intended 'Letters to a Young Man on his Entrance into Life,' &c. will I doubt not . . . be a favourite present for parents and guardians." Percy's comment gives no suggestion that the parental present is actually consumed by the recipient. He goes on to suggest that West continue to utilize the novel form for practical reasons: "as example interests more than precept, I should scarce expect your monitory letters will have so extensive a circulation as your instructive narratives."[8] Hannah More makes a similar argument about popular literature in *Coelebs in Search of a Wife*: "Let us then endeavour to allure our youth of fashion from the low pleasures of the dissolute; to snatch them not only from the destruction of the gaming-table, but from the excesses of the dining-table, by inviting them to an elegant delight that is safe, and especially by enlarging the range of pure mental pleasure." According to Barbauld, novels had a "very strong effect in infusing principles and moral feelings," and the fact that "every body" read them gave the form considerable ideological power. She concludes: "let me make the novels of a country, and let who will make the systems." Describing this exploitation of novels for moral and political purposes, Robert A. Colby notes that "religious educators like Mrs. Barbauld and Hannah More appropriated fiction to their purposes in something like the way in which early Christianity adapted pagan ceremonies."[9]

Behind all of these statements about fiction is a free-market model of literary consumption in which consumer demand determines the form of the product. Yet the frequent apologies and justifications for the use of the genre raise the question of how the popular "vehicle" was modified to make it an acceptable method of transmitting "the words of sound doctrine"; or, in West's culinary terms, how it was made digestible. In general, the novels I examine here are characterized by an excess of strategies designed to limit meaning. Unlike Jane Austen, whose narratorial "indirection" allows for various contradictory readings of her novels, West and other writers of antirevolutionary didactic fiction strove toward a single meaning and complete closure (which helps to explain why these novels never scrambled into the canon, and why now, when we value subtlety and multiplicity in fiction, they remain relatively unread). Narrative voice, plot, character, prefatorial material, and even style, are constructed to produce a repetition of the didactic "message" promoted by the text, on several narrative levels.

Narrative excess, however, even of techniques designed to provide closure, opens space for textual disruption. Language itself, as twentieth-century linguistics and literary criticism has indicated, is radically unstable, and the tenuous connection of signifier and signified is destabilized by multiple forces. As Bakhtin has argued, language is dialogic, drawing meaning from the social context in which speaker and addressee are positioned. The goal of monologism is thus inevitably unachievable. "Even in those places where the author's voice seems at first glance to be unitary and consistent, direct and unmediatedly intentional," Bakhtin argues, "beneath that smooth single-languaged surface we can nevertheless uncover prose's three-dimensionality, its profound speech diversity, which enters the project of style and is its determining factor." Though my main focus is on the "authoritarian" function of didactic literature, the narrative I tell here can be read in another way: as the struggle for narrative containment and closure (in an effort to improve an inadequate "vehicle") against the tendency of prose fiction toward *heteroglossia*, to use Bakhtin's term for the process by which language resists uniformity, becoming, in practice, multiple "languages."[10] The novel, as West, More, and Brunton worried, was not a perfect form for transmitting didactic messages; yet, as West intimates, it was the best vehicle available to them in the "battle" to counteract revolutionary "poison."

Many of the writers I deal with in this study appear only (if at all) on the periphery of literary scholarship. Very few of their texts are still in print, and they appear only rarely on course syllabi, circumstances that are, of course, connected. In positioning this range of mostly obscure writers at the center of a study of this kind I am not making a bid for their canonization. Rather, taking a cultural studies approach, I attempt to avoid the issue of literary "value" inherent in the concept of canonicity, reading these texts instead as "artifacts" intimately entwined with the culture that produced them. By analyzing these novels in this way, I am able to complicate our understanding of the relationships among women, writing, power, and politics during the Romantic period. Yet the issue of canonicity is still important, because it is precisely the operations of canonization, and shifting standards of literary value, that have relegated these writers, for the most part, to several photocopied pages in the middle of course kits for innovative women's studies and English courses.

"There is no such thing as a moral or immoral book," wrote Oscar Wilde, with characteristic witty certainty, in his preface to *The Picture of Dorian Gray*. "Books are well written, or badly written. That is all." This statement demonstrates one of the standards of literary value that worked to exclude the writers I examine in this study. As Marilyn Butler justly claims, "[n]o English novels before or since have been so unremittingly ethical as the conservative novels of the generation following 1790." Yet during the nineteenth century the novel became progressively more concerned with aesthetics than morality. While critics of the 1790s would endorse a novel for its obvious and irreproachable morality, later theorists of the novel, like Henry James in the 1880s, identified a "conscious moral purpose" as inimical to the "art of fiction." For Edgar Allan Poe, "the heresy of *The Didactic*" "accomplished more in the corruption of our Poetical Literature than all its other enemies combined," and he advocates instead the "poem written solely for the poem's sake." In these readings, form takes consistent precedence to didactic morality. This position reaches its critical apotheosis in the New Critics, whose "intentional fallacy" makes analysis of didactic fiction impossible.[11]

Similarly, poststructuralist criticism devalorizes the didactic—which depends on the transmission of a clear and single message—through its emphasis on plurality of meaning, self- and multiple-referentiality, and the "free play" of the signifier. By devaluing overtly didactic elements in fiction, these critics effectively locate conservative writing beyond the limits of the acceptably "literary." Raman Selden notes that there is "a tendency among recent critics to treat polyphonic and other kinds of 'plural' text as normative rather than as eccentric; that is, they treat them as more truly literary than more univocal (monologic) kinds of writing." It is important that we recognize, therefore, that critics such as Bakhtin and Barthes "are indicating *preferences* which arise from their own social and ideological predispositions." Susan Rubin Suleiman concurs: "Modern criticism has been tremendously wary of any literary work that 'means to say something' (that has a 'message')," and rejects the "communicative" function of language for texts that seek to "multiply meaning or to 'pulverize' it." D. A. Miller notes the focus in novel criticism on how a text's "ideological projects" are disrupted "by the disseminal operations of language, narrative, or desire," rather than on "what this text mundanely 'wants to say.'"[12] In a hierarchy of literary value in which form, ambiguity, and subversion are privileged over communication, didactic antirevolutionary writers are necessarily inferior; their absence from literary history is unlikely to be noticed, let alone questioned.

The writers I examine here have also been notably absent from traditional scholarship of the Romantic period. One of the only ways antirevolutionary novels have conventionally been addressed by critics of this period is as "influences" on more canonical writers. Jane West's influence on Jane Austen has been a particularly fertile subject for scholars. Martin Melander, Kenneth L. Moler, Valerie Grosvenor Myer, Colin Pedley, and J. M. S. Tompkins, all address this issue. Bonnie Nelson has explored West's influence on Keats's "Ode to a Nightingale." These studies help to show that the generally obscure novelists I focus on here had an effect on the work of more canonical writers, yet they do little to show how the original writers engaged with their own literary and social environment.

The absence of antirevolutionary writers from the literary history of the Romantic period has much to do with how we have conventionally defined "Romanticism." In its purest sense, the term "Romantic" was developed retrospectively to describe the work of a group of artists and writers in Europe, who, at the beginning of the nineteenth century, developed a style in opposition to the neoclassicism of the Enlightenment. The Romantic aesthetic involved an attempt to represent, visually or linguistically, what Wordsworth famously describes as "men in a state of vivid sensation." In their aesthetic commitment to foregrounding emotive extremes, Romantics challenged neoclassical ideals of purity, balance, and formal harmony, with results that caused a reconceptualization of the purpose of art. Still art "with a purpose" (to use Robert A. Colby's term), Romantic writing and art was intended to stimulate the imagination of the viewer or reader, reproducing in him (or her, though the implied consumer of most Romantic art is male) emotions and excitement. By this process, Wordsworth concludes optimistically in his 1800 preface to the *Lyrical Ballads*, "the understanding of the being to whom we address ourselves . . . must necessarily be in some degree enlightened, his taste exalted, and his affections ameliorated."[13] Emotion and imagination, coupled with individualism, become privileged within the Romantic conception of the purpose of art, and the relationship between art and the self.

One of the earliest uses of the term "Romantic" in a literary sense was Friedrich Schlegel's in the *Athenaeum* in 1798, where he defined it as "progressive universal poetry."[14] This description is a useful one. In spite of its predilection for the Gothic, Romanticism was predominantly a modern movement that responded to the widespread social and economic changes occurring across Europe and North America. The shift to a capitalist economy, the Industrial Revolution, the revolutions in the United States and France, the growing influence of the bourgeoisie, were all occurrences that stimulated Romantic responses. In this modern, "progressive," engagement with the social world around them, many Romantic writers became involved, to some extent, with radical political movements. Byron, of course, was active in the Greek war for independence from Turkey, while Wordsworth, Blake, Coleridge, and Southey, among others, were vocal supporters of the French Revolution. Concurrent with this endorsement of radical politics, Romantics posited alternative forms of spirituality, which challenged or modified the tenets of the established Christian church. Religion was conceived of as a personal relationship between an individual and a God who was increasingly represented as pantheistic. The emphasis shifted from the submissive faith and good works promoted by the Church of England, to the experience of personal spiritual transcendence, often through exposure to the sublime in nature.

This model of the "Romantic ideology," promoted by such critics as Harold Bloom and M. H. Abrams, ensures that the writers I examine here cannot be accommodated under the rubric of "Romanticism."[15] In fact, very few writers of the period can be defined as "Romantic" in this sense, since the term, as it is used in English studies, is intended to describe the work of only a few poets: Wordsworth, Coleridge, Blake, Byron, Keats, and Shelley. Antirevolutionary writers who promoted political, social, religious, and literary conformity, rejected individualism in favor of community, and valued Christian virtues such as temperance, modesty, and submission over imagination and emotion, could more aptly be described as "anti-Romantics" according to this model. As women writers, they are almost necessarily excluded, since the values of Romanticism—individualism, solitude, passion, imagination, nonconformity—tend to conflict with prevalent ideologies of femininity of the period, or the material circumstances of women's lives. Much work has been done recently to extend the conceptual boundaries of the term "Romantic" beyond the parameters of the "Romantic ideology" promoted by earlier scholars: Anne Mellor's *Romanticism and Gender* describes a "feminine Romanticism" coexisting with the canonized masculine tradition; Gary Kelly enlarges the scope of "Romantic" writing in *English Fiction of the Romantic Period*, to include fiction across a wide range of genres; *Romanticism and Feminism*, edited by Mellor, *Romantic Women Writers: Voices and Countervoices*, edited by Paula R. Feldman and Theresa M. Kelley, Joel Haefner and Carol Shiner Wilson's *Re-Visioning Romanticism: British Women Writers, 1776–1837*, and *At the Limits of Romanticism: Essays in Cultural, Feminist, and Materialist Criticism*, edited by Mary Favret and Nicola Watson, are collections of essays that question the masculinist tradition in Romantic criticism, and interrogate both traditional critical approaches to Romanticism and the conceptual boundaries of the term, creating room within the concept for other writers of the period.[16] None of these critical rereadings offers a convincing reason to include the writers I study here under the rubric "Romantic"; they were morally, politically, and stylistically opposed to the basic principles of even a revised Romanticism. Extending "Romanticism" to include these writers may simply erode the effectiveness of the term by stretching it too far beyond what it was originally intended to designate. As Georg Lukács commented long ago, "then the physiognomy of Romanticism, in the proper, narrow sense, becomes blurred."[17] Yet this critical work has made it possible to reexamine, as I do here, writers who do not fit comfortably within the category, and to analyze the ways in which the concepts of Romanticism were debated and contested after the French Revolution.

Feminist literary historians have begun, in recent years, the important job of reconfiguring the landscape of literary history to include formerly excluded women writers. Jane Spencer's *The Rise of the Woman Novelist*, Marilyn Butler's *Romantics, Rebels and Reactionaries*, Dale Spender's introduction to Pandora Press's (now defunct) Mothers of the Novel series, *Mothers of the Novel: 100 Good Women Writers before Jane Austen*, Janet Todd's *The Sign of Angellica*, and J. M. S. Tompkins's classic *The Popular Novel in England, 1770–1800* all contribute to a new history of the long eighteenth century, in which women are shown to be an active part of a thriving literary community. In general, feminist literary history has been legitimately interested in reclaiming proto-feminist voices, like Mary Wollstonecraft and Mary Hays, or writers like Jane Austen, whose subtle treatment of political and feminist issues allows a reading in terms of their resistance to patriarchy. The first wave of feminist criticism of the Romantic period, beginning in the 1970s, focused on recuperating these voices above others, in an attempt to establish a feminist history of literary "foremothers." Read in these terms, Jane West's significance to feminist history is much less obvious than Mary Wollstonecraft's. Revolutionary and feminist writers continue to be more compelling than conservatives for many critics of this period, especially in the attempt to analyze the contributions made by women to gender and social history. Antirevolutionary writers, in comparison, seem to fulfill the purely negative function of obstructing progress, and to epitomize an antifeminist acceptance of repressive patriarchal ideologies. Susan Pederson, for instance, reads Hannah More as an agent of patriarchal middle-class oppression, Eleanor Ty's *Unsex'd Revolutionaries* shows that Hannah More and Jane West internalize a dominant "masculine code," which is reproduced in their fiction, and Beth Kowaleski-

Wallace examines the ways in which More is engaged in "patriarchal complicity" as a result of her relationships with her father and father figures.[18] While not inaccurate, in the sense that these writers did support existing institutions, including a patriarchal social structure, this approach may obscure the complexity of conservatism, and the variations in the ways in which women speaking from an antirevolutionary position related to social and political power structures.

Another approach to these writers is to read them for the ways in which they subvert, counter, or manipulate patriarchal norms. Thus, in *Women, Writing, and Revolution* Gary Kelly foregrounds Elizabeth Hamilton's "counterrevolutionary feminism," Ty, in her recent study, *Empowering the Feminine,* focuses on the ways in which West's texts work toward this empowerment, and Christine Krueger, usefully placing Hannah More within the context of female evangelical preachers, notes the writer's "Christian feminism." Eve Tavor Bannet, similarly, reads writers like Hannah More, Mary Brunton, and Jane West as feminist "Matriarchs," to differentiate them from the "Egalitarian" feminists represented by Wollstonecraft and Hays. Gerald Newman unequivocally labels More, with other Evangelicals, a "subversive." These studies contribute substantially to a more complex understanding of these writers' social, political, and ideological positions, by offering a suggestion of the ways in which a single writer may hold contradictory positions—or, at least, positions that seem to us in retrospect contradictory—simultaneously. As April London points out, "seemingly incompatible strands of orthodox and iconoclastic opinion can comfortably, and sometimes creatively, coexist in a single work," and any reading of the writers of this period must take this into consideration.[19]

This study aims to complement and contribute to the body of scholarly criticism on women's writing of this period, by developing a more nuanced and complex understanding of the nonfeminist, conservative aspects of the work of antirevolutionary women writers. I acknowledge their overtly political didactic purpose, and foreground it as a way of re-visioning its effect on their work, and its relationship to the social and cultural context in which their novels were produced. Rather than reading for subversions of patriarchal imperatives, I look at the form and substance of their antirevolutionary writing, examining the implications of a political purpose for literary form, and the ways in which the didactic intent is complicated by the gender of the author. To this end, I position these writers within the broader context of antirevolutionary writing by women, and conservative writing more generally. Reading West, More, and their contemporaries against this larger historical and literary backdrop foregrounds their engagement, through fiction, in the political arena, as well as the literary and ideological connections and differences among the writers themselves. What such a rereading suggests is that the terms "feminist" and "antifeminist" may not be the most useful in describing these writers. Rather, reading them according to the approach I propose here can help us to understand the ways in which they engaged critically with contemporary conservative theories in order to produce a gendered politics, a feminine (but nonfeminist) discursive space within the broader field of post-Revolutionary conservatism.

Another way to reconsider writing by conservative women is to rethink the functioning of ideology within a social structure. Feminist and Marxist criticisms have focused almost exclusively on the negative functions of dominant ideologies: identifying in cultural objects (such as novels) the means for the reproduction of ideology and thus of inequitable social formations. This is a valid approach to the interpretation of history, however, I would like to suggest a complementary approach that examines both the ways in which ideology may reproduce inequities, and the ways in which it serves what Frederic Jameson calls a "Utopian" social function. In his conclusion to *The Political Unconscious*, Jameson argues that the purview of Marxist literary criticism must be expanded, and imagines a new approach to ideological criticism, "which can no longer be content with its demystifying vocation to unmask and to demonstrate the ways in which a cultural artifact fulfills a specific ideological mission, in legitimating a given power structure, in perpetuating and reproducing the latter, and in generating specific forms of false consciousness. . . . It must not cease to practice this essentially negative hermeneutic function . . . but must also seek, through and beyond this demonstration of the instrumental function of a given cultural object, to project its simultaneously Utopian power as the symbolic affirmation of a specific historical and class form of collective unity."[20] My reading attempts to accommodate these dual concerns, acknowledging both the repressiveness and the inclusiveness of conservatism, particularly as it is manifested in writing by women.

This approach entails an acknowledgment that women did not, and do not, always act, think, or write, in ways that support my own political position. My first encounter with Hannah More's *Strictures on the Modern System of Female Education*, which struck me initially as antifeminist to the point of misogyny, challenged me to confront my own ideology of femininity, which assumed a "natural" connection between being female and being feminist. What I have come to realize over the course of my research is what the editors of *Women and Right-Wing Movements: Indian Experiences*, writing in a very different context, also conclude: "Feminist convictions are not given or inherent in women, after all." This troubling conclusion provided the impetus for my subsequent research into women who supported conservative, often, by modern Western standards, repressive, models of femininity and class. *Women and Right-Wing Movements* represents an alternative route in feminist historical research, which focuses not on how women resisted dominant, often destructive and repressive discourses, but on how they were and are implicated in right-wing social movements. Focusing on the extreme political right, Kathleen Blee's disturbing *Women of the Klan: Racism and Gender in the 1920s* carries out a revisionist project in this vein. Her analysis shows that women were not simply accepted in the Ku Klux Klan, but that their activities were the basis of many of the Klan's real successes: their "poison squads" were responsible, Blee argues, for most of the acts of social ostracism that occurred, the ruin of businesses, and the effective social exile of non-"whites."[21] Claudia Koonz's earlier work on female Nazis (*Mothers in the Fatherland*) effects a similar rereading, writing women into history in ways that we may rather not acknowledge. Women are not necessarily liberal, any more than they are naturally feminist. Nor are they naturally gentle or maternal, as the recent brutal murder in Victoria, British Columbia, of a young teenager by a group of her female schoolmates attests. These examples move far from my subject in this study; the writers I focus on were proponents of a model of domestic femininity that was maternal, nonviolent, and retiring. Yet it is important to acknowledge that women are products of their historical context, and femininity at any given historical moment is highly complex and constituted by a range of ideological, social, cultural, and economic influences. Work that attempts to understand these multiple forces is a legitimate avenue of feminist inquiry. By foregrounding only those qualities we find most compatible with our current political position, we deny women the status of full historical subjects.

This topic is also strangely current at the beginning of the twenty-first century. The 1990s in North America witnessed a swing to the political right, and women have been a part of the change. In the United States, religious fundamentalism and conservative politics have promoted a "return" to mythical "family values" based on a conventional nuclear family and a model of domesticity that demands a stay-at-home mother. Well-heeled and well-educated young conservative Christian women—nicknamed "Bible belles"—promote "sacred motherhood" and "joy in submission" to their husbands and fathers. In Canada, the group Real Women upholds a model of domestic femininity against the advances of women in the workplace.[22] The context has changed and some of the issues are new, but this "neoconservatism" articulates many of the same concerns and uses the same forms of rhetoric as the antirevolutionary writers of the period I study here. Scholarly analysis is one of the important ways we can begin to understand this phenomenon. By examining the didactic fiction of antirevolutionary women writers, I attempt to understand their relationship to the conservative debates of their time. This seems particularly important two hundred years later, as women continue to be both subjects and agents in the practice of conservatism.

* * *

Most of the writers I examine here are of Mary Wollstonecraft's (1759–98) immediate generation; one, Laetitia Matilda Hawkins (1759–1835), was born in the same year as Wollstonecraft, while two, Jane West (1758–1852) and Elizabeth Hamilton (1758–1816), were born the previous year. (On the radical side, Mary Hays was born a year later in 1760.) Hannah More was born fourteen years earlier (1745–1833), making her the eldest of the group, while Mary Brunton and Jane Porter are by far the youngest, born in 1778 and 1776 respectively (Brunton died in 1818, and Porter in 1850). The coincidence of Wollstonecraft's birth year with these others suggests that the "war of ideas" between radicals and reactionaries was in many ways a phenomenon of a single generation; in this case, women who were in their thirties in the 1790s. Only Brunton, however, with her retrospect as the youngest of these writers, articulates a sense of community among them, when she acknowledges literary debts to More, and speaks admiringly of Jane West and Jane Porter.[23]

Despite the similarities in their antirevolutionary projects these writers differ from each other on a number of levels. Two of the group, Hannah More and Mary Brunton, are establishment Evangelicals, and my reading of their work identifies the central role that a "religion of the heart" takes. In these novels, the antirevolutionary project is affected by a religious didactic purpose in ways that both support and destabilize the former. The Evangelicalism of More and Brunton differs geographically and nationally; More was associated with the "Clapham Sect" of London Evangelicals, while Brunton was linked, through marriage to a clergyman, to the Church of Scotland. Two other writers, Jane West and Jane Porter, uphold central principles of Evangelicalism in their novels, without explicitly adhering to Evangelical sects within the established church. West, in particular, differs from the Anglican Evangelicals on the matter of abolitionism; while Evangelicals like More fought the slave trade, West, in an effort to deflect criticism from the actions of the British government, rationalizes it.[24] The writers also differ in their national and class locations. Two were Scottish (Brunton and Porter), one an Irish woman who grew up in Scotland and England (Hamilton), and the rest were English. Yet even within these apparently clear categories there are shades of difference. Brunton spent all of her life in Scotland, but Porter moved to London as a child with her mother, whose circle included the Bluestockings More and Anna Laetitia Barbauld. Elizabeth Hamilton was born in Ireland but moved to Scotland at the age of six. She spent the 1790s in London and finally settled in Edinburgh in 1804. Hannah More grew up in Bristol but spent the years of her young womanhood in London, associating with the Bluestockings and major literary figures of the day, including Samuel Johnson and David Garrick. Jane West was born in London but spent her life after the age of eleven in Northamptonshire, later becoming the wife of a yeoman farmer. Laetitia Matilda Hawkins was a lifelong Londoner. It is difficult to characterize the productions of these writers as Scottish, or English, or Irish, though their nationality helped, in some cases, to determine the setting and form of their novels. Hamilton, Porter, and Brunton incorporated elements of the "regional tale" in their writing, and Brunton in particular fought against prevalent English prejudice against the Scots and Scotland. Porter began, before Walter Scott, to write the national literature of Scotland, with the production of *The Scottish Chiefs* (1810), based on events in Scottish history.

These writers positioned themselves in specific and unique ways in relation to the ideological and political power structures of late-eighteenth and early-nineteenth-century Britain. Several of them, in particular Jane West, Hannah More, Elizabeth Hamilton, and Laetitia Matilda Hawkins, aligned themselves closely, in their nonfictional and fictional writing, with the dominant conservatism exemplified by Pitt's Whig party in Parliament, and used this alignment to support their interventions in discussions around gender, class, and "philosophy" (meaning revolutionary political and social theory). Yet each of these writers also occupied the gendered position of a woman writer of the period, with its attendant and well-documented restrictions, and became themselves, as domestic women, their own critical object. The implications of this dual positioning for their fiction are varied, and I trace them in the following chapters. I begin by examining the characteristics of antirevolutionary writing of the 1790s. Chapter 2 places this group of antirevolutionary women writers within their political context, and explores the complexity of their relationship to "mainstream" conservatism. Writers like Jane West and Hannah More were neither subversively feminist, nor submissively accepting of the conservative theory promoted by thinkers like Edmund Burke. Rather, they positioned themselves very carefully in relation to prominent conservative theorists and public figures, and reconfigured conservative rhetoric and form to fit their own antirevolutionary agendas. In chapter 3 I sketch a taxonomy of the antirevolutionary novel, and propose a model for analyzing the functioning of antirevolutionary novelistic propaganda. Reading this type of text as an "authoritarian" genre (Susan Rubin Suleiman's term in *Authoritarian Fictions*), I focus on the formal elements that constitute an antirevolutionary text.

My focus in the next two chapters is on narration. The devotion of two chapters to one narratological category reflects my conviction that narration or "voice" is the location of several key issues and problems in the particular novelistic form I examine here. As Susan Sniader Lanser argues, "voice" is the site at which feminist criticism (with its interpretation of the term as political empowerment) and narratology (in which "voice" is an analytical term describing narration) intersect. The female voice or narrator becomes, in Lanser's argument, the "site of ideological tension made visible in textual practice."[25] Chapter 4 acknowledges that in practice an "authoritarian" voice is difficult to establish and maintain, if the writer is both female and concerned to support conservative social and gender models (which are intertwined in antirevolutionary social theory). Hannah More, Elizabeth Hamilton, and Jane West engaged in different (and variously successful) strategies to achieve the narrative authority necessary to an effective antirevolutionary text, while placing cautious limits on female voice. Chapter 5 examines changes in narration over the early years of the nineteenth century, and the consequent implications for an authoritative, female, didactic voice. Through a close analysis of novels by Jane West and Laetitia Matilda Hawkins, this chapter reinterprets the standard assumption about changes in narrative voice over this period (that the progressive trend toward a distant, omniscient, third-person narrator represents a conservative shift), and shows that the adoption of a distant narrative voice in many ways worked to undermine the effectiveness of the didactic antirevolutionary novel.

I conclude this study by tracing changes in the antirevolutionary novel by women during the early years of the nineteenth century, when the development of new types of narrative began to alter both the form and the social position of the novel as genre. Chapter 6 analyzes one of these new genres as it was adapted by antirevolutionary writers. In *Coelebs in Search of a Wife* (1808), Hannah More pioneered what has been called the "Evangelical novel," a form that combines fiction with Evangelical religious doctrine and social policy. Mary Brunton, building on the considerable success of *Coelebs*, developed what has been termed the "Evangelical romance," which combines the religious concerns of More's novel with the plot and subject matter of romance. For both of these writers, religious observance is closely linked to social behavior, and the Evangelical "lesson" of each text is inculcated as much through an insistence on appropriate gender and class roles as it is through sermonizing. Thus, I examine the ways in which both masculinity and femininity are represented in each of these Evangelical genres, specifically in relation to the domestic sphere, and show how gender ideology becomes a means for representing a conservative ideal of British nationhood. Chapter 7 deals with the historical fiction of Jane West and Jane Porter, both of whom were early experimenters in the field. Starting from the assumption (laid out by Nicola Watson in *Revolution and the Form of the British Novel*) that historical fiction is well-adapted to promoting a conservative social message, I examine the ways in which West's hybridization of the historical novel with the domestic novel and the romance enables the expansion of gender roles and identities within a still conservative social model. What this analysis across genres and decades allows is a representation of the antirevolutionary novel as heterogeneous, multiplicitous in form and style, and responsive to changes in the social and literary context, as writers worked toward producing a vehicle that effectively carried the antidote to the "pleasant poison" of revolution.

A Note on Terminology

> Not a few of the evils of the present day arise from a new and perverted application of terms.
>
> Hannah More, *Strictures on the Modern System of Female Education*

One of the prominent trends in eighteenth-century studies is an interrogation of critical and political terminology, and a rethinking of epistemological categories that previous critics and historians have taken for granted. This approach echoes eighteenth-century concerns around the stability of signification, which is the focus of anxiety in fictional and political writing by women. The meaning of particular words—such as "liberal," "sensibility," "patriotism," and "rights"—became, for them, the ground against which political concerns were debated. Appropriately, then, I ask a terminological question: what is an accurate adjective to describe the writers I bring together in this study? I use three terms throughout: "antirevolutionary," "counterrevolutionary," and "conservative." All three are problematic, and their usage requires some explanation. I use "antirevolutionary" and "counterrevolutionary" primarily because of their clarity as descriptors. All of the writers I examine were opposed to the revolution in France, and to manifestations of revolutionary sentiment or activity in Britain, which they believed threatened existing institutions. These manifestations were not necessarily openly political, nor were antirevolutionary responses; as many critics have indicated, the ideological conflict between revolution and antirevolution took place on a variety of cultural levels, including—most importantly for my purposes here—the literary. When I use the term "antirevolutionary," then, I intend it to mean this broader form of opposition to revolutionary theory, across a range of genres and discourses.

I use the term "conservative" in part for its breadth—unlike "antirevolutionary" it implies a political position that has broad cultural significance. Yet there are complications around this term as well, which demand explanation. While modern scholars regularly use the term "conservative" to refer to a particular political stance of the late eighteenth century,[26] the word as it is used in political discourse today did not, at that time, exist. According to the *Oxford English Dictionary*, "conservative" did not gain widespread usage as a descriptor of a political stance or set of political beliefs until the 1840s. Like "feminism," then, it is applied anachronistically, and therefore demands careful definition and explanation. Women writers like West, More, and Hamilton certainly would not have chosen "conservative" to describe their political positions: "loyalist," perhaps, to Church and King, as West uses it in her 1812 novel, *The Loyalists* (Linda Colley uses this term effectively in *Britons: Forging the Nation*, her historical account of political conformity in the eighteenth century); maybe "orthodox" or "conformist" in opinion and (especially religious) belief; certainly "correct" in its eighteenth-century sense of "proper" or "conventional"; and "anti-Jacobin" in their opposition to things French and revolutionary. I have not used any of these terms as a general descriptor, however, primarily because they are unwieldy and limited in their signification; instead, I intend "conservative" to be understood as subsuming these descriptors, and containing their various meanings. The word "conservative" was utilized in the late eighteenth century as a "preservative," "characterized by a tendency to preserve or keep intact or unchanged." This definition certainly contributed to the word's later signification as a political position. I would like to revive and exploit this meaning of the word, as the central component and ideological basis of the conservatism I explore in this study. Emily Lorraine de Montluzin uses the term in this way in her study of the *Anti-Jacobin Review and Magazine*: "conservative" designates "those persons who supported the established order in church and state—that is, monarchy, hierarchy, privilege, property, religious orthodoxy, and an unreformed Parliament."[27] Like de Montluzin's, my understanding of "conservative" is broad and multivalent.

Terminology also proves difficult when discussing this particular period in history and literature. Using "Romantic" to describe the period covered by this study is problematic because of the term's specificity, especially in a study that deals with essentially non-Romantic texts. The writers I discuss here, as I have argued, opposed Romanticism on many levels, both literary and political. Following literary convention, therefore, and calling this the "Romantic period" effectively excludes the very subject of my study. How then to find a term that is accurate and yet not unwieldy? Mitzi Myers's use of "Georgian" covers too broad a chronological area, since, strictly speaking, I deal here only with the reign of one George and the regency of a second; "postrevolutionary" is simultaneously too vague and too narrow, and has no clear chronological boundaries. For simplicity's sake, however, I retain some of these difficult terms, while acknowledging their problematic nature. I use "Romantic" to designate the literary period, rather than the writing I examine, simply because it provides a widely understood shorthand for "the period spanning the end of the eighteenth century and the first decades of the nineteenth." "Postrevolutionary" also remains, referring to the long period between the beginning of the French Revolution and the end of the Napoleonic Wars.

2

Women, Late-Eighteenth-Century Conservatism, and the "Proper Place" of Burke

> There were always dissenting voices: and it is right and proper that they should emerge loud and clear from the historical record and that we acknowledge them. But we should not let them drown out the other, *apparently* more conventional voices.
>
> Linda Colley, *Britons*

LOYAL CONFORMISTS FAR OUTNUMBERED REVOLUTIONARIES AND radicals at the end of the eighteenth century, though the latter have received the lion's share of critical attention. Similarly, many more literary texts were produced during the period that supported the status quo—"things as they are"—than challenged the established power structures. The historical dominance of Romantic literature—especially poetry—in the canon of British literature has until recently obscured this fact. In reality, women formed a part of a large community of conservative writers who were engaged in a common project to combat the spread of revolutionary philosophy in Britain. The conservative establishment, while it actively attempted to circumscribe writing that challenged orthodoxy, easily accommodated writing by women in an antirevolutionary cause, and promoted female agency in the implementation of conservative social practice. Women writers engaged actively in the production of antirevolutionary propaganda, in an effort to mobilize, morally and physically, the population of Britain. Ultimately, they helped to complete the postrevolutionary ideological shift toward conservatism that occurred during the early years of the nineteenth century. How, then, did British antirevolutionary women writers position themselves in relation to broader antirevolutionary discourses within their culture? And how did they construct the conservatism they promote in their writing? This chapter examines the ways in which women used conservatism as a political tool in their writing, and how they were in conversation with some of the more overtly political voices of their period, such as Edmund Burke, who takes a central position in studies of women's writing of this period.

1790s conservatism comprised a complex set of values, and women's relationships to it were equally complex. A wide range of movements, theories, theorists, and writers can be drawn under the umbrella of counterrevolution, and the conflicts and ambiguities among these defy essentialization. Conservatism during this period was hardly a homogeneous category, nor does the term adequately explain some of the apparent anomalies that appear in the writing of these women, and in their lives. It does, however, describe their overarching political and literary project: they perceived and constructed themselves as engaged in a process of political and social conservation or preservation. "Our task," wrote Jane West in 1801, neatly formulating her conservative position, "is, not to acquire, but to maintain; to preserve, not to erect." Hannah More, as epigrammatically, comments: "Nothing is right, which is not in its right place." Their statements clearly illustrate the central characteristic of the conservatism I explore in this study: a firm belief in the efficacy and justice of existing social institutions, which are not only "naturalized," but are directly supported by the will of an establishment God. As West points out, using her preferred rhetorical technique of analogy, the "law of distinction and degree" is proven by the rotation of the planets, as well as by the hierarchy established within Heaven itself, which is clearly described in scripture.[1] The major lines of "distinction" are drawn by West along class boundaries, between genders, and at the perimeter of nation (both geographical and ideological).

In the aftermath of the French Revolution, this model of conservatism gained a more urgent dimension. In 1805, Hannah More described the condition of Europe in this way: "We live [in a time] in which law has lost its force, rank its distinction, and order its existence; in which ancient institutions are dissolving, and new powers, of undescribed character, and unheard of pretension, are involving Europe in contests and convulsions, of which no human foresight can anticipate the end." This apocalyptic vision is based on a firm conception of an "order" that controls the functioning of nations, international relations, and the preeminent relationship between humans, nation, and God. As West puts it in her urgently patriotic *Elegy on the Death of the Right Honourable Edmund Burke* (1797), "Order's sacred Laws / Direct the Movements of the vast Machine."[2] During the revolutionary decade it became the duty of patriotic British citizens to defend the current, "traditional," structure of the social formation, with its distinctions and ranks, against the forces of dissolution and democracy, and it became the self-appointed job of conservative writers to promote that duty in print. What conservative writers construct as "tradition" is at least partially simply that, however: a construction for rhetorical and political purposes. Like the 1990s American conservatives who promoted a tradition of "family values" that had no real basis in historical fact, conservative women writers of the 1790s juxtaposed modern values with those of a semi-fictitious past, in an effort to devalue the former. The "traditional" values invoked by More, West, and others, however, were often in fact reformist values that developed in conjunction with a mid-eighteenth-century increase in the influence of the middle ranks.

Scholars have long noted the ideological shift that occurred near the turn of the seventeenth century, with literary critics identifying Jeremy Collier's attack on contemporary drama on moral and religious grounds, *A Short View of the Immorality and Profaneness of the English Stage* (1698), as the definitive marker of the end of the Restoration period. During the early years of the eighteenth century, Addison and Steele's *Spectator* and *Tatler* worked to establish a new definition of taste, based on a combination of gentry and middle-class ideals, while plays such as George Lillo's *The London Merchant* (1731) and Richard Steele's *The Conscious Lovers* (1722) showed a new tolerance of the formerly ridiculed merchant figure. Ian Watt's *Rise of the Novel* links the development of the new genre with the growth, greater influence, and better education of the middle ranks, and in spite of problems with the teleology and exclusiveness of Watt's account of the generic "rise," this connection remains relevant. In general, early-eighteenth-century literary texts began to reflect and promote a range of values more closely connected to the concerns and material conditions of the middle class, rather than the aristocracy. These texts privileged a new and antiaristocratic definition of virtue, which centered on respectability, responsibility, and a constellation of other ideals that span both the public and the private spheres: utility, industry, fair play, thrift, honesty, and sobriety. In *The Origins of the English Novel*, Michael McKeon reads the development of this new model of virtue as "progressive," in opposition to a "conservative" aristocratic model of virtue that was linked to the persistence in literature of the Romance form. As Gerald Newman has argued, the reconceptualization of virtue developed in response to a middle-class dissatisfaction with traditional aristocratic behaviors and beliefs, which privileged luxury, "continental" values, French taste, and European thought.[3] Among "a broad and expanding generational cohort of sensitive and 'socially conscious' intellectuals dating from the 1740s," argues

Newman, "we find an intensifying, in some cases a nearly obsessive—an 'agitated and agitating'—concern with national decline and with the need for thorough moral regeneration." This concern became particularly acute during the second half of the century. As Linda Colley argues, "the argument that a patrician degeneracy was subverting Britain . . . ran through a great deal of otherwise conservative middle-class comment" in the 1780s. Donna Andrew, analyzing the changing representation of the demi-rep in print culture during the mid to late eighteenth century, notes a significant change in the portrayal of the aristocrat/mistress relationship in the popular *Town and Country Magazine* during the 1780s. Whereas these liaisons were previously tolerated, or represented as a mild failing—often in both partners—by the 1780s the magazine's gossipy reports are marked by a growing intolerance. By 1786, Andrew concludes, "[p]eople were beginning to think that their governors should have qualities of character of a personal sort, of a sort that extra-marital liaisons undercut."[4]

It seems clear that, by the late decades of the eighteenth century, new conceptions of virtue, informed by middle-class sensibilities and values, were rapidly developing into the norm. Leonore Davidoff and Catherine Hall, in *Family Fortunes: Men and Women of the English Middle Class, 1780–1850*, follow the bourgeois reform of the ideology of virtue to its ascendancy in the early nineteenth century, when business virtues became closely aligned with the concept of "manliness," and "piety, domesticity, a proper sense of responsibility about business . . . were the attributes of the new man." Hannah More, writing to a working-class audience in the 1790s, conflates Christian values and bourgeois business ethics in her exemplary female character Betty Brown, who does not cheat, "impose bad goods on false pretences," or "put off bad money for good." "To break these rules," her middle-class benefactor informs her, "will be your chief temptation. God will mark how you behave under them, and will reward or punish you accordingly." Theories of domesticity are closely tied to this new class-based construction of virtue. As bourgeois business ethics became conflated with personal and religious virtues, the relationship between the public and private spheres was reconfigured. As Davidoff and Hall argue, the defining mark of this change in British society was a commitment in the middle ranks "to an imperative moral code and the reworking of their domestic world into a proper setting for its practice." In response to changing models of both domesticity and virtue, the upper classes underwent a process of reform designed to legitimize their continuing political dominance. This process is evidenced in the transformation of the monarchy to a domestic model, and in a propaganda system that emphasized in George III "his morality, his domesticity, his taste outside of ceremonial occasions for the simple life generously defined."[5] The growing importance of the private life of the public man brought the domestic sphere into the foreground, and lent greater social and ideological value to family relations and domestic activities.

This shift in focus toward the domestic foregrounded the role of middle-class women in British society and focused attention on virtue as a gendered category. For middle-class women throughout the century, chastity remained the defining characteristic of virtue, although this privileging of a "sexual virtue" became a subject for heated discussion by writers as diverse as Mary Wollstonecraft, Elizabeth Hamilton, Mary Hays, and Jane West in the 1790s. Novels, which became a forum for working out issues of gender and class for the middle class during the eighteenth century, came to valorize other elements of femininity during the mid-century, however. Richardson's wildly successful *Pamela* (1740) and *Clarissa* (1747–48) presented a type of heroine who could both reason and remain virtuous: a virtuous character became a matter of internal surveillance and rational resistance. Pamela, in particular, incorporated domestic, religious, and personal virtues, combining industriousness with piety, chastity, and reason, in a way that became a pattern for exemplary literature of the half century that followed the publication of the novel. When the conservatives of the 1790s refer to a more ideal, "traditional," form of femininity, they most often allude to this mid-century, reformist model. The fact that *Pamela* was read as subversive by some contemporaries (notably Henry Fielding) because of its heroine's transgression of class boundaries underlines the extent to which conservatives drew on both conformist and radical thought in their construction of late-century conservatism.

Ideologies of class, gender, religion, and nation are closely intertwined in antirevolutionary writing of this period. For, as Georg Lukács has noted, effective propaganda cannot narrowly restrict itself to its immediate catalyst, but must rather incorporate a range of discourses. Speaking of the propaganda produced to encourage mass enlistment during the Revolutionary wars, he argues: "It has to reveal the social content, the historical presuppositions and circumstances of the struggle, to connect up the war with the entire life and possibilities of the nation's development." Women writers took up this challenge on all of these levels; during the 1790s conservative women's domestic novels addressed the "social content" of the revolutionary struggle, while later historical fiction by writers like Jane West and Jane Porter placed the conflict in a historical framework. The writing of women conservatives after the French Revolution is explicitly presented as a deterrent to threats of anarchy and violence. In these texts, a number of conceptual categories are seen to be causally related: just as More's Betty Brown conflates Christian with class virtues, many writers associated the proper maintenance of the boundaries of class and gender with the protection of the state from external threats. As Jane West wrote in 1812, during a period of war and agitation by the working classes, the "domestic hearth" must act as a protection against "the wildest theories of democracy"; she concludes that "the exercise of the milder [i.e., feminine] virtues is imperiously called for in seasons of national alarm."[6]

This interarticulation of ideologies is played out in the domestic plots of novels of this period. Virtuous and religious femininity becomes, in these novels, the moral and practical prophylactic against revolutionary philosophy. If the heroine is seduced—as in West's *A Tale of the Times*—by the revolutionary and anarchic "systems" of the philosopher villain, the resulting social disorder is corrected only by her death. The seduction itself figures, at a domestic level, the penetration of French philosophy into the British social formation. The patriotic woman resists this penetration, by adhering to standards of modest and domestic femininity, and to the doctrines of the established national church. Femininity is thus intimately tied to the preservation of the state, the family, and the national church. The violent response to William Godwin's *Memoirs* of his recently deceased wife Mary Wollstonecraft (1798), is a practical result of this network of ideologies, which predominated in the conservative press. Godwin's frank relation of Wollstonecraft's experience (including sex out of wedlock and suicide attempts) is damning enough, but his attempt to vindicate Wollstonecraft by ascribing her actions to pure philosophical principles made a clear connection for the anti-Jacobins between revolutionary philosophy and what they interpreted as aberrant sexuality. "Such an individualistic, sentimental, antisocial and subversive portrait was a generous gift to conservatives, who made a great deal of it," notes Janet Todd.[7] The *Anti-Jacobin Review and Magazine*'s classification of Wollstonecraft under "Prostitute" in their 1798 index marks the review's explicit linkage of revolutionary philosophy with transgressive sexuality.

Despite their engagement in an antirevolutionary project of national defense, the conservatism represented by the writers in this study is far from unproblematic: as members of the middle ranks, who were concerned with the reformation of public manners and morals, they are inextricably associated with a movement for social change. Davidoff and

Hall have traced the development of this movement over the period between 1780 and 1850, untangling the various cultural threads that contributed to the *embourgeoisement* of British society. Of the middle class, they write: "In finding a cosmic and mundane place for themselves, no task was greater than that of definition and demarcation: of people, places, time and matter. The content and boundaries of categories were delineated by constant discussion, trial and negotiation."[8] The act of marking "distinction and degree," then, which is at the root of these writers' conservatism, is simultaneously a characteristic of their reformism.

Middle-class women were central players in the reform of British society, and they attempted to reconfigure models of gender and class by interrogating gender roles and redefining the domestic sphere. Both conservatives and radicals, as Mitzi Myers has argued, worked to dignify women's functions within the social formation. Thus, conventional female roles, such as motherhood and charity, are invested with increased importance within these writers' social philosophies. On the topic of women's social roles, it becomes clear that the opposition between revolutionaries and antirevolutionaries was not as clear as its conservative participants suggest. In "Reform or Ruin: 'A Revolution in Female Manners,'" Mitzi Myers argues the essential similarity of radical and conformist women writers around issues of gender. Hannah More and Mary Wollstonecraft, she notes, both promote a model of female spirituality that allows them to question prevailing recommendations for female education and activity: "If life is probationary, an education for immortality, then woman is not mere flesh for male consumption, not a being delimited by sexual attraction . . . but a creature of rationally educable mind and aspiring soul, a potent spiritual agent whose most exigent duties are personal improvement and social regeneration." This concept supports ideals of social activism for both More and Wollstonecraft, linking them with a range of women writers of various political positions who were engaged in reforming society "for women's benefit, suiting to their own needs the general middle-class protest against aristocratic license and inutility and inflecting bourgeois modes to fit the feminine sphere of endeavor."[9]

This project of reform was shared by women writers and activists who occupied a range of political positions, and the literature around female education and conduct shares many similarities, especially on the necessity for female "usefulness" and activity at a local level. An insistence on educational reform was the primary focus of women's writing on gender; criticism of an education that produced superficial "accomplishments," and the recommendation of training that suited women to an active role in the home and the community unites much of this writing. A variety of justifications are drawn on to support the prescription of a broader education: women's spiritual equality, their role as maternal educators, wifely companions, and domestic economists, as well as their developing influence within the local community through philanthropic activity. These justifications exist in conjunction with demands for female political equality in the writing of Mary Wollstonecraft, as well as with demands that women accept an inferior domestic and social position in the writing of Laetitia Matilda Hawkins, Hannah More, and Jane West. Darcy, in Jane Austen's *Pride and Prejudice,* articulates this shift in pedagogic priorities when he adds to Miss Bingley's conventional list of the attributes of an "accomplished woman" ("music, singing, drawing, dancing, and the modern languages . . . a certain something in her air and manner of walking, the tone of her voice, her address and expressions"): "All this she must possess . . . and to all this she must yet add something more substantial, in the improvement of her mind by extensive reading." This shared agenda is obliquely acknowledged in some conservative women's critiques of revolutionary writers; Jane West attempts a reasoned refutation of Wollstonecraft's *Vindication of the Rights of Woman* (unlike Hannah More, who refused to read it) in her *Letters to a Young Lady,* while Elizabeth Hamilton's *Memoirs of Modern Philosophers* agrees with certain aspects of Wollstonecraft's critique of female education, differing only on the issue of female equality.[10]

It is primarily on the issue of female equality that conservative women disagreed with Wollstonecraft and other women radicals. Since much antirevolutionary writing is based upon an ideology that creates analogies between a range of relationships within British society—the hierarchical relationship between monarch and subject, between classes, between God and humanity, clergy and congregation, adults and children, and men and women—a call for equality on any of these levels threatens the entire social formation by undermining hierarchy in one of its components. Wollstonecraft's plea for women's equality in her *Vindication of the Rights of Woman* must necessarily be rebutted, according to this logic; while her educational reforms may be applauded, her feminism must be exposed as "supereminent absurdity and audacity."[11] Because there is a coherence of interests on certain levels for middle-class women who espoused radically different politics, conservative women were careful to indicate the differences between their own proposals for educational reform, and the more revolutionary theories of their contemporaries.

Another area in which conservative and radical impulses coexist, and one with which women were intimately involved, is evangelicalism, which was comprised of a number of different grassroots movements. During the 1780s and '90s evangelicalism, which had been a strong but peripheral movement spearheaded by John Wesley and George Whitefield, became a significant force in establishment religion. By the early nineteenth century, evangelicalism became, as Boyd Hilton has argued in *The Age of Atonement*, the defining discourse of British capitalist and imperialist projects, as well as of British politics more broadly. This new religiosity permeates the social structure of the postrevolutionary period, and informs the writing, politics, and activities of women within the culture. The defining characteristic of this movement is that it emphasized the role of the "affections" in the practice of religion; what was most important was not simply a belief in the central doctrines of Christianity, but the "transforming influence in the heart" of those doctrines. Those "professed christians" who believe without feeling are described by William Wilberforce—probably the most influential figure in Church of England Evangelicalism—as suffering from a "palsy at the heart"; evangelicalism becomes a metaphorical cure for the "disease" of "languid" Christianity. One character in Hannah More's Evangelical novel, *Coelebs in Search of a Wife*, acts as spiritual "physician" who uses the Bible as her "receipt-book."[12]

To define the movement more accurately, all the forms of evangelicalism that proliferated during the eighteenth century, including establishment Evangelicalism, shared the following four characteristics (the terms are D. W. Bebbington's): "conversionism," a belief in the necessity for spiritual change, whether gradual or instantaneous; "activism," or "the expression of the gospel in effort"; "biblicism," the centrality of scripture in religious practice; and "crucicentrism," an emphasis on Christ's sacrifice for humanity, which is the basis for the doctrine of atonement Boyd Hilton describes as central to British social and political theory during the nineteenth century. To varying degrees, these religious priorities influenced all the sects of Protestant Christianity functioning in Britain during the late eighteenth century. The movement that most relates to the writers I deal with in this study, however, is Anglican Evangelicalism. This particular branch of evangelicalism was a response to widespread growth in grassroots movements such as Methodism, which were perceived to be drawing support away from the Church of England. Its central function was the reformation of establishment British Protestantism to a more "vital" state, which was conceived of as a return to the "primitive" church, and thus as a return to ancient tradition. Wilberforce argues that this reformed religion can compete with Methodism, as it is "the only one at all suited to make an impression upon the lower orders, by strongly interesting the passions of the human mind." The intellectual center of Anglican Evangelicalism was at Cambridge, around Professor of Theology Charles Simeon, who produced generations of clerics to disseminate establishment Evangelicalism across the British Isles. Engaging in a concerted effort to strengthen their influence, upper-middle-class Evangelicals raised money to provide financial assistance to young clerical students, and helped graduates to livings. (Patrick Brontë, father of Charlotte, Emily, and Anne, was one of the recipients of this Evangelical charity.) By these means, Anglican Evangelicals became the dominant voice within the Church of England by the late 1790s.[13]

The "Clapham Sect" of Anglican Evangelicals formulated the central imperatives of Anglican Evangelicalism near the turn of the century. Composed primarily of wealthy members of the middle class, this group had many connections among the middle and upper classes, and considerable influence within the established church. The members of the sect were, as one of Hannah More's biographers puts it, "public-spirited, influential, highly respected, well-to-do business and professional men, their wives and families, living comfortable lives in comfortable homes under the pastoral care of their spiritual guide, the wise and good father of the Society, John Venn, Vicar of Clapham." Along with Wilberforce and More, the group included banker and M.P. Henry Thornton; Charles Grant, M.P. and "Director of Directors of the East India Company and real Ruler of the East"; Zachary Macaulay, editor of the *Christian Observer*; Lord Teignmouth, Governor-General of India to 1802, and later president of the Bible Society (1804), among other wealthy or influential figures.[14] Between the 1780s and 1820 many Evangelicals were elected to the House of Commons; they became known as "Wilberforce's neutral party," or "the Saints," and by 1820 they numbered twenty-five to thirty members in an average year. Wilberforce "found himself the leader of a small coherent group, nearly all Tory but on moral issues virtually always belonging to no party but the Evangelical Party"; this group wielded considerable authority, especially with increasing Evangelical moral and political triumphs. As Hilton notes, Evangelicalism "was undoubtedly an important element in the mentality of the *haute bourgeoisie* that dominated British politics from 1784 to the 1840s." Through the influence of Evangelicals like Wilberforce and Thornton, "evangelicalism's distinctive middle-class piety fostered new concepts of public probity and national honour, based on ideals of oeconomy, frugality, professionalism, and financial rectitude."[15]

A similar shift in religious priorities occurred within the Church of Scotland, and during the early years of the nineteenth century it was divided into the "Moderate" and "Evangelical" parties. Like their Anglican counterparts, Church of Scotland Evangelicals stressed the importance of a revived, "vital" Protestantism, which was conceived of as a religion "of the heart." The two forms of Evangelicalism are also linked by their focus on "Christ's Atonement on the Cross," which provided the means for individual redemption, their belief in the "natural depravity" of humans, and the need for spiritual conversion, whether gradual or instantaneous.[16] Mary Brunton's *Discipline*, published in 1814, foregrounds these qualities in her heroine, who undergoes a gradual conversion from "nominal" to vital Christianity, and learns the importance of rigorous self-observation and "virtuous actions." The association of Evangelicalism with socially prominent Anglicans was paralleled in the Church of Scotland during the early decades of the century. As C. Duncan Rice notes: "By an extraordinary religious alchemy, these years saw the whole weight of the Scottish intellectual elite shift from the moderate party of the Old Kirk to the evangelical one."[17] The two national churches, therefore, underwent similar changes, with the remarkable rise in social and religious influence of Evangelical groups within their ranks.

Establishment Evangelicalism, like Methodism, provided many opportunities for women's involvement. Evangelicalism's emphasis on conversion valued female and male experience equally. The movement foregrounded characteristics that were traditionally ascribed to women; invoking a Christ-like model of human behavior, it privileged meekness and submission. The hero of Hannah More's *Coelebs in Search of a Wife*, for example, approves for everyone "meek and passive virtues which we all agreed were peculiarly Christian, and peculiarly feminine." The feeling heart, another central component of evangelical Christianity, was also more traditionally gendered female. Ann Braude argues: "During the eighteenth century, the rise of Evangelicalism enshrined a religious style that elevated qualities associated with femininity as normative. . . . The relative spiritual equality of the period produced remarkably similar accounts of the conversion experience from men and women—but both partook of qualities considered feminine." The new "religion of the heart," then, became a forum in which women could claim moral and spiritual, if not necessarily social, authority. As Christine Krueger has noted, evangelicalism also provided women with the means for resisting conventional power structures: "submission to the will of God often meant a break with temporal authorities," such as husbands or fathers, and therefore "gave women tremendous leverage."[18] The focus on conversion justified female activity in the community, since women became spiritually authorized to engage in the type of charitable education of the poor which was intended to lead to conversion. Middle-class women became active, like Hannah More, in teaching the poor to read scripture and perform functions suitable to their stations. "*Charity*," More argued, "*is the calling of a lady*," and her example and argument offered women an expanded sphere of activity. Visiting the poor, providing relief to the "deserving" and medicine to the sick, expanded middle-class women's nurturing role into the immediate community. This type of female involvement increased women's power and influence at the local level, particularly in the administration of their churches, and "extended the sphere of women's influence far beyond the home." This development authorized women writers' entrance into the more public sphere of religious publishing. Robin Reed Davis points out that during the early decades of the nineteenth century, women produced increasing numbers of religious tracts and articles; religious journalism offered to women a literary career that had become both lucrative and respectable.[19]

The Evangelical movement admits of at least two different historical interpretations: first, that it was a conservative movement designed to control the lower classes and to defend existing inequitable institutions; and secondly, that it was subversive of social order, and part of a broader middle-class revolution occurring over the course of the long eighteenth century. Gerald Newman, in *The Rise of English Nationalism*, positions Evangelicalism within a radical nationalist movement that was engaged in the reformation of the upper classes and the institution of middle-class values as hegemonic. Evangelicals, in this context, were "drastic moral and social revolutionaries" who did more to subvert than to uphold the social order: "*an extremely radical process was now working under cover of an extremely conservative one*."[20] By critiquing aristocratic manners and habits, Evangelicals opened the way for a critique of the aristocracy itself, and, as I have noted above, the aristocracy rose to the challenge by performing extensive internal reforms. Evangelicalism's role in empowering women within the church and the community also led to revolutionary changes in women's social function; as F. W. Prochaska and Anne Braude have argued, women's activities in the early

Evangelical movement paved the way for later feminist movements, such as the long battle for suffrage. Further, by promoting the literacy of the working classes, Evangelicalism offered access to revolutionary texts, as well as to the more didactic and religious publications distributed in the Sunday Schools.

Yet, even acknowledging the potential for radical change implied in Evangelical doctrine and practice, the movement must also be understood in terms of its potential for conservative social control. Anglican Evangelicalism adopted the innovative practices of nonconformist evangelical groups in large part in order to combat the inherent subversiveness in sects that placed themselves beyond the limits of establishment religion. The project of Church of England Evangelicals was one of restraint; its emphasis was on civil order as much as on moral and religious regeneration. This is evident in the frequent coupling of the two concepts in writings by Anglican Evangelicals. A central argument for vital Christianity in Wilberforce's *Practical View* claims that "it has graciously pleased the Supreme Being so to arrange the constitution of things, as to render the prevalence of true religion and of pure morality conducive to the well-being of states, and the preservation of civil order." Hannah More, more bluntly, argues that "there is something so safe and tranquillizing in Christian piety" that "it can hardly fail to promote, in the people, the ends of true policy"; she continues, the "virtuous are always the peacable." *The Christian Observer*, a monthly journal established in 1802 by Henry Venn, a founding member of the Clapham Sect, repeatedly confirms Anglican Evangelicalism's dual interest in "civil government and revealed religion." The preface to volume 1 claims: "We have no interests to serve but those of true Christianity: no schemes to prosecute, but those of making our fellow-creatures good subjects, and good Christians; teaching them to fear God and honour the King." The privileging of "good subjects" over "good Christians" in the first half of their "scheme," is inverted in the next, neatly illustrating the inseparability in Evangelical doctrine of religious and sociopolitical imperatives.[21]

Women's charitable didactic projects therefore served a double function: the poor and working classes, who were seen as a potential threat in the wake of the French Revolution, were taught the principles of Christianity in conjunction with the lessons of order and hierarchy. Evangelical texts for the working classes habitually link obedience to God with obedience to social superiors; insubordination becomes, therefore, a sacrilegious act, as well as a social challenge. Bebbington argues that the emphasis on conversion in evangelicalism served an important social function, since converts conformed to a bourgeois social ideal, worked hard, accepted their position, and in turn provided charity to the community. "The essence of 'practical Christianity' was to perform the duties of one's age, sex, and class without murmuring; murmuring was a sign of sin and infidelity which the godly had the plain duty to suppress," Davis points out. Hannah More places this project in a national context in her Cheap Repository Tract, "The Sunday School," when the exemplary Mrs. Jones asserts to a skeptic: "I, farmer, think that to teach good [i.e., Evangelical] principles to the lower classes, is the most likely way to save the country." Refuting Farmer Hoskins's worry that literacy will make his workers "fly in my face," Mrs. Jones counters that reading allows the working classes to know their duty; religion coupled with literacy thus becomes a form of social control. Ultimately, argues Davis: "The upper middle-class leaders of the Evangelical Party never confused spiritual equality with social equality." Their religious philanthropy and education were designed primarily to defend social inequality against theories of democracy.[22]

The Farmer Hoskins episode illustrates Anglican Evangelicalism's philosophy of religious and social order, as well as the suppressed (and legitimate) fear that the methods of religious education may become the means for working-class revolution. More's tale, predictably, validates Mrs. Jones's position by proving her correct; yet this ambiguity remained central to Evangelicalism. Anglican Evangelical texts, however, rarely admit the possibility of the misapplication of religious education, or of the doctrine of equality of souls. Even in writings aimed at their own middle-class members, such as the *Christian Observer* and Wilberforce's *Practical View*, these changes are understood solely as beneficial to the maintenance of a stringently hierarchical social order. The growth of Anglican Evangelicalism, like most historical episodes, is not simple or clear; it can be read as both conservative—in the sense that it attempted to restrain the influence of nonconformist sects, and to control the working classes through religious education—and as progressive—in the relative power it gives middle-class women, and in the vigorous education it advocates for girls and the working classes. I read it here in both these senses: socially conservative in intent and in many immediate effects, yet as providing the basis for progressive developments in women's rights and abolitionism, as well as contributing to the broader revolution that reformed British society and politics to a bourgeois model.

The fact that central cultural concepts relating to class, gender, and domesticity were in rapid flux during the late eighteenth century provides some explanation for the difficulty in identifying the precise cultural and political location of the conservative women writers I bring together in this study. Their texts are, in general, informed by developing middle-class constructs of virtue and gender, and their reform efforts cross class boundaries, making them a part of what Gary Kelly has called a "middle-class revolution." Yet they cannot be considered unproblematic members of an angry "revolutionary bourgeoisie." Rather, it is vitally important to determine varying ideological positions within the developing middle class itself. As Davidoff and Hall have emphasized, the middle class of the eighteenth century was not unified or homogeneous.[23] Membership within the class, and affirmation of its basic ideological imperatives, does not necessarily constitute revolutionary status. At the same time, the dual positioning of these writers as conservatives and as middle-class subjects produces a range of positions within conservatism as well. The extent to which each writer adheres to class values (for instance, around questions of the public responsibilities of the aristocracy) helps to determine the type of conservatism that forms the basis of her textual practice.

I have argued that the writers considered in this study constructed themselves as conservatives, as preservers of a traditional order, a concept that I proceeded to problematize. Yet, the figures of "order" and "tradition" should not be discarded entirely. As middle-class thought developed during the eighteenth century and influenced the dominant social theories of the later decades, traditional models gave way to the new, and a space was opened for the questioning of the entire structure of the social formation. Influenced by the work of French Enlightenment thinkers, and helped by the changing demographic of the British public, radical thought in England at the end of the century questioned the value of the aristocracy, the necessity for a social or domestic hierarchy, and for prevailing concepts of rank and gender. In opposition to this radical position, conservatives were, with Jane West, "[w]armly attached to the Cause of lawful Government, Subordination, and Property," supporting a truly traditional social formation, even as they promoted the moral reformation of its members. At the governmental level ideals of "tradition" were upheld, in the 1790s, by the dominant "Pittite" party. Originally one of the competing Whig factions, by the 1790s William Pitt's followers preferred the designation "Pittite," which differentiated them from the more radical Whig followers of Charles James Fox; by the 1820s they referred to themselves as "Tories." In describing the party's ties to traditional power structures during this period, one historian uses the term "Pittite" as a synonym for "conservative," "anti-Jacobin," "Tory," and "Church-and- King." As J. H. Plumb comments somewhat broadly, by the 1790s "the appellations Whig and Tory seem outworn symbols of a dead political fanaticism; for men of property it was enough to be a Pittite and an Englishman."[24] Edmund Burke became a Pitt supporter after Fox declared his approbation of the French Revolution in 1789. During the 1790s Pitt's party aligned itself with the established institutions, tradition, hierarchy, and order. In 1798, members of the party established the *Anti-Jacobin Review and Magazine* in order to promote these principles through the influential medium of print.

Conservatism in Print

Print culture played a significant role in the development and dissemination of conservative thought during the eighteenth century. In the 1790s, following the French Revolution, periodicals and pamphlets were regularly produced in an explicit effort to intervene in the political conflicts of the period. Theorists like Edmund Burke, reviewers in the *Anti-Jacobin Review and Magazine*, the *British Critic* and the *Gentleman's Magazine*, and novelists such as Isaac D'Israeli and Charles Lucas, advocated a stringent defense of "Things as They Are" in the face of revolutionary and radical challenge. As the *Gentleman's Magazine* commented in 1799: "The current of the times is set-in too strongly against revolutionary and jacobinical notions, for an author expressly to publish a formal vindication of them."[25] Indeed, by the time the *Anti-Jacobin* was established, it had become dangerous to vindicate "revolutionary and jacobinical notions" in print. The State Trials of 1794, in which leading members of radical corresponding societies were tried for treason, though failing to obtain convictions, indicated to radicals the potential dangers of engaging in political discussion—in clubs or in print. One of the more insidious outcomes of this event was the long-term suspension of *habeas corpus*. In Scotland, similar trials were more successful, with one radical being sentenced to lengthy transportation for circulating Paine's *Rights of Man*. The Two Acts of parliament in 1795 and 1796 eroded citizens' rights further, by extending the definition of treason from actions to speech and print, and by forbidding large public meetings. Unsuccessful French invasions in 1797 and 1798, the uprising of the United Irishmen in 1798, and mutinies in the British navy served to justify further extensions to the Two Acts in 1799, which worked to radically delimit the freedom of the press. In a study of periodicals of this period, Kenneth Graham notes a clear, and understandable, shift toward a more conservative tone by the end of the decade. Magazines like the *Anti-Jacobin*, therefore, spoke from a position of considerable authority backed up by the power of government.

Women consumed and contributed to conservative print culture, and their writing was both influenced by and constitutive of the broader social and political milieu. West and More both read and cited the *Anti-Jacobin* in their nonfictional prose; the *Anti-Jacobin* similarly commented positively on More, proclaiming her "amiable character," and supported lesser-known conservative voices, like the novelist Mary Ann Hanway, whose *Ellinor* was reviewed approvingly in 1799, and Laetitia Matilda Hawkins, whose *The Countess and Gertrude* was complimented for its "purest principles of morality" in 1813. The *British Critic* became the champion of Jane West: "Mrs. West ranks very highly among those moralists [including More and Sarah Trimmer] who have exerted their superior talents in checking the operation of modern philosophy."[26]

The *Anti-Jacobin Review and Magazine* is central to any discussion of conservatism in periodicals of this period, in that it was established as the vehicle of an ideological intervention in a very specific conflict; as its title makes clear, its aim was to combat "Jacobinism"—that is, revolutionary philosophy—in Britain. Thus, the magazine's general purpose is to critique the "Jacobin" journals—notably the *Monthly* and the *Critical* reviews—which "have been rendered the mere instruments of faction." By counteracting Jacobinism's "dangerous system," argues the *Anti-Jacobin*'s mandate, the magazine will restore "criticism to its original standard," that is, to a moral rather than aesthetic standard.[27] Reviews of novels, drama, journal articles, and political treatises, are submitted to a standardized critique, which reads for the moral "tendency," and which subordinates form to content. As the official voice of the anti-Jacobin movement, the *Anti-Jacobin* functioned both to authorize women's writing and to police its boundaries. Jane West and Elizabeth Hamilton were associated with anti-Jacobinism, attacking what they perceived to be French influences in English politics that encouraged revolution and the dismantling of social distinctions. West fits relatively unproblematically under the "anti-Jacobin" rubric, and her writing aligns closely with dominant anti-Jacobin principles. Her disapproval of "philosophers" and "democrats" is clearly stated in her conduct literature: the "systems" of these demonized thinkers, she argues, will lead to the loss of feminine virtue, the dissolution of class boundaries, and ultimately to the breakdown of British society as a coherent entity. Her novel, *A Tale of the Times*, written in the midst of anti-Jacobin reaction to political developments in France and Britain, dramatizes this process in the gradual decay of a marriage catalyzed by the intervention of a philosopher-villain based on William Godwin. In response, the *Anti-Jacobin* praises West as "vigilant in observation, and active in exertion, she openly braves their [religious and social order] enemies; boldly throws down the gauntlet to the philosophical sages, the Paines, the Godwins."[28] The *Anti-Jacobin*'s martial rhetoric figures West as a central and aggressive member in the anti-Jacobin cause, providing potent authorization for her engagement in literary polemic.

Hannah More also wrote strongly against Jacobin philosophy, arguing that "a spirit of independence, a revolutionary spirit" could cause the dissolution of society,[29] and satirizing the "New Philosophy" represented by Thomas Paine and the English Jacobins in two tracts: *Village Politics* (1792) and *The History of Mr. Fantom, the New-Fashioned Philosopher and his Man William* (1797). More's relationship to anti-Jacobinism was disrupted, however, near the turn of the century. Her involvement in the "Blagdon Controversy" (1800–1803), in which a Sunday School teacher appointed by her came under attack for teaching unorthodox religious views, drew the negative attention of the *Anti-Jacobin*. The ostensible object of criticism was More's perceived transgression of religious boundaries: Evangelicalism, which dangerously bordered dissenting sects like Methodism, was seen here to cross the boundary into "fanaticism." Two other major conservative journals, *The British Critic* and *The Christian Observer*, however, maintained their open support of More throughout the entire conflict, and helped to assure the subsequent strength of her moral and literary reputation.

The *Christian Observer* took up a contrary position to the *Anti-Jacobin*, yet nevertheless maintained a loyalist and conformist mandate. The impulse for founding the *Christian Observer* was less overtly political than that behind the *Anti-Jacobin*.[30] It was established in 1802 by Henry Venn in order to provide a mouthpiece for "genteel" Anglican Evangelicalism. "A monthly publication," he claims in his prospectus, "conducted upon the true principles of the Established Church, has been long desired by many of her members." Predictably, the journal's intention is to foster in its readers "sound theological knowledge" as well as piety and submission to "civil government"; a later volume sees as a central task of the journal "to inculcate sentiments of subordination, loyalty, and true patriotism." Less predictably, the "Conductors" of the publication "are determined to admit nothing harsh nor intemperate toward any sect of Christians," including the Calvinism and Methodism Anglican Evangelicalism was established to counter.[31] The editors espouse a "plain and practical religion," which demands attention to Christian good works and "self-examination" rather than controversy. This practical and "vital" religion demands "a spirit of forbearance and Christian Charity." Minimizing internal controversy, the Conductors argue, is necessary in order to strengthen the Christian church and its influence in a time of social and political upheaval. Their strategy to attain this goal is to correct "the mistakes and misapprehensions of writers on both sides of this endless controversy" by replacing them with Anglican Evangelical conceptions of "practical piety" and "Christian unity and peace."[32] The "Christian unity" the magazine proposes is therefore, on one hand, a construction intended to strengthen the established church by erasing differences between sects, and by subsuming nonconformist groups into a unified Anglican whole. On the other hand, the privileging of tolerance and religious moderation provides the basis for a resistance to widespread reactionary religious intolerance. The *Anti-Jacobin* states a typical point of view when it argues that Methodist preachers are "instruments of Jacobinism"; like other forms of nonconformity, religious unorthodoxy was regularly linked to political subversion.[33] The *Christian Observer*'s philosophy of tolerance destabilizes this rigid association.

Because the *Christian Observer* has a dual mandate—to promote both a revitalized establishment religion and a peaceful, nonrevolutionary population—it differs theoretically from magazines like the *Anti-Jacobin* that have a more narrowly political focus. An attack on the *Anti-Jacobin* appears in the March 1802 issue of the journal, in the regular "Review of Reviews" section, which was established to correct publications guilty of "disseminating doctrines subversive of all morality, and propagating tenets the most hostile to piety, order, and general happiness." That the *Anti-Jacobin* should find itself ranked with many of the publications it opposed, including the radical *Critical Review* and *Monthly Review*, is an unusual circumstance. Some explanation for this is apparent in the clear political motivation in the *Christian Observer*'s attack: the attack is positioned immediately before a lengthy defense of Hannah More's activities in the Blagdon controversy, which the *Anti-Jacobin* had condemned. The "Review of Reviews," then, prepares the reader for a positive interpretation of More's conduct by undermining her main detractors. The grounds for the attack, further, are religious. The editors and writers of the *Anti-Jacobin*, the *Christian Observer* argues, practice a "*political* religion," designed only to attain specific political ends, unlike the "spiritual religion" of Anglican Evangelicals.[34] While the reviewer is in sympathy with the political aims of the *Anti-Jacobin*, he does not accept that religion may be simply a means to a political end. Elsewhere throughout the *Christian Observer* religious and social order are similarly linked; with the difference that the link is constructed as natural rather than politic, and that social and religious order are equally privileged. The *Anti-Jacobin*'s main argument against More is a religious one: they argue that her evangelicalism is nonconformist, and that it is therefore politically subversive. The *Christian Observer* attempts to undermine this position by showing that the *Anti-Jacobin* itself is theologically unsound.

This incident suggests that conservatism was not a unified movement, nor, by extension, was conservative theory monolithic. While they shared an opposition to revolutionary political theory, the conservative journals could and did differ on local issues. In the case of the Blagdon Controversy, the site of difference is the interpretation of conventional Christianity. Both the *British Critic* and the *Christian Observer* position More's Evangelicalism within the Church of England and minimize her responsibility for her teachers' actions. The interarticulation of ideologies of gender, religion, and nation in the *Anti-Jacobin*, however, demands an even more rigid religious orthodoxy, since divergences from the established forms are potentially revolutionary. Further, the magazine's focus on print culture as the primary tool in the spread of philosophical contamination or cure foregrounds More as both a reformer and a prominent writer. As Mitzi Myers has argued, More's role as an influential public woman is centrally implicated in the *Anti-Jacobin*'s response to the Blagdon incident. By developing the "influence," which the *Anti-Jacobin* argues is women's proper political province, to the extent that she did, More posed a threat to conservative concepts of gender. The emergent Sunday School system that she worked to establish was subject to "alternative gender codings and to ambiguous definition as public or private, clerical or lay, sacred or polluted."[35] Worse, More's success suggested to the *Anti-Jacobin*'s writers the possibilities for female social and cultural power inherent in conservative theory itself. The *Anti-Jacobin*'s disciplinary voice, therefore, attempts to control potentially transgressive female "influence." Conservative journals like the *Anti-Jacobin* were active in policing the boundaries of politically acceptable writing, as well as in authorizing texts that they read as politically "unobjectionable." More's continued influence in print suggests that attempts at policing were not always entirely successful, primarily because of instability within the category of conservatism itself. While many writers and journals subscribed to a basic belief in the necessity of preserving established institutions, rank, and distinction, exactly how those traditions were to be preserved was a subject for debate. Conservative writers and publications adopted varying positions on issues, and altered those positions with a changing historical context. By 1813 a reviewer in the *Anti-Jacobin* concedes that More had "eminently distinguished herself as an able advocate for religion and morals."[36]

The *Christian Observer*'s intertwining of vital religion and genteel literature helped to establish the respectability of religious writing among the middle classes as well as the "fashionable world," and despite its initial mistrust of the genre (which was gradually dispelled after the publication of Hannah More's *Coelebs in Search of a Wife*), it prepared the way, stylistically and philosophically, for the religious novel. The Evangelicalism promoted by the *Christian Observer*, as well as evangelicalism more broadly, as Christine Krueger has compellingly argued, had a distinctive effect on women's writing in the nineteenth century. Women evangelical preachers of the eighteenth century adopted as one of their two principal discursive strategies an "ethos of simplicity" that was pragmatic at its base: "God revealed himself directly and plainly in scripture and in believers' lives, hence, the most effective means of evangelizing was to repeat the gospel truth in the simplest terms possible." Women preachers in particular "would also have wished to avoid the appearance of attracting attention to themselves as speakers."[37] For women conservatives, even those not directly associated with the evangelical movement, simplicity of language became, in the late eighteenth century, a philosophical choice; they privilege honesty, clarity, and humility of style over complexity and sophistication. Hannah More explicitly condemns the use of excess rhetorical figures, linking it to the potential problem of an uncontrolled imagination: "A habit of computing steadies the mind, and subdues the soarings of the imagination. It sobers the vagaries of trope and figure, substitutes truth for metaphor, and exactness for amplification." If truth and exactness oppose metaphor and amplification, simplicity of style becomes a moral imperative. Religious language especially must be simple to be effective. More's exemplary clergyman in *Coelebs in Search of a Wife* speaks in "plain language," and his preaching is characterized by "grave and majestic simplicity." In this case More is proposing as an example for the clergy what was already practice for antirevolutionary women writers. As Jane West notes: "it is not because I want powers for the terrific and romantic, that I continue to pursue the moral and probable."[38] Morality, probability, and simplicity become intertwined in a moral aesthetic governing the production of conservative women's texts. A "simple story" becomes not only a generic descriptor, but a mark of narrative honesty and morality. This simplicity helped to define a compelling discourse of conservatism which, combining elements of mainstream conservatism with evangelicalism and the "feminine" form of the domestic novel, was intended to speak to women.

Evangelical simplicity of style coincides with a number of cultural trends in Britain during the Romantic period. As Antony Easthope has noted, the dominant trend in canonical Romantic poetry was toward a form of "transparency" enabled by the use of "the bourgeois metre, iambic pentameter," and the rejection of the "rhetorical" poetry of the earlier eighteenth century. A philosophy of simplicity underlies the canonical seminal text of British Romantic poetic theory, Wordsworth's 1800 preface to the *Lyrical Ballads*. This trend is explained by Gerald Newman in terms of the development of an ideology of nation that began in the early eighteenth century. By mid-century, a new ideal of the national character which incorporated the concept of "sincerity," was disseminated in the work of bourgeois "artist-intellectuals." This ideal was deployed in opposition to supposed "French" sophistication, which was associated with the degenerate upper classes. The new middle-class ideal incorporated innocence, honesty, and moral independence, as well as "native" genius.[39] Michèle Cohen notes how this opposition of English sincerity to French sophistication enters the linguistic realm, producing a mistrust of sophisticated and worldly discourse, and a valorization of simple English speech. The Evangelical discourse of simplicity, then, dovetailed with more secular discourses of class and gender, and the various discursive strands are evident in the antirevolutionary writing I examine in this study.

In advocating Evangelical simplicity and delicacy of language, the *Christian Observer* sets itself in opposition to the more political *Anti-Jacobin*. The *Observer* condemns the *Anti-Jacobin* style specifically for its extremism, which, it acknowledges, may have been necessary when the journal was founded in 1798, but is no longer in 1802: "There was, however, even at this period [1798], a violence displayed in the work, beyond what is usually thought requisite in the support of truth; but the cause was important, and the occasion pressing." By its "violence" the *Anti-Jacobin* not only undermines the tone of "polite Literature," but contradicts the *Christian Observer*'s moral and religious anti-controversialist position; "if all this [violence of metaphor and invective] . . . is to be tolerated from persons, styling themselves the 'Guardians of polite Literature,' and Defenders of our Church," exclaims the reviewer, "who will not think that our polite Literature and our Orthodoxy deserve equal commiseration?" The *Anti-Jacobin*, while following the philosophical model of Edmund Burke, established a new style in conservative political writing. Marilyn Butler argues that the journal uses a satiric voice that counters Burke's "appeal to emotion": "A quite different anti-Jacobin manner was evolving, appropriate above all to satire: it was dry, cynical, detached, belittling to human greatness and to all rich insights, including the author's own."[40] While the philosophies behind the *Anti-Jacobin* were at least partially based on Burke's thinking, the tone is harsher and the language notably simpler than Burke's sprawling and sophisticated prose. The writers of the *Anti-Jacobin* use metaphor heavily, establishing bodies of imagery around medicine (often "poison," as I showed in chapter 1) and disease in order to describe what they perceive as the dangerous progress of revolutionary philosophy within the body politic. In its excess and dependence on analogy for rhetorical effect, this use of language is homologous to the satirical cartoons by Gillray that accompany the text.

Marilyn Butler has argued that the *Anti-Jacobin* style, with its detached cynicism, provided the tone for "reactionary novels" by women of the 1790s.[41] Yet very few women writers adopted the more excessive metaphors of the magazine, with the exception of Jane West, who used the *Anti-Jacobin*'s conventional figures of contamination and disease to describe revolutionary sentiment. These images are rare even in West's work, however, and her heavily didactic metaphors tend to draw on quite different bodies of imagery for their effect; religious and domestic metaphors are much more common, particularly those deriving from cooking and clothing. In general, women's novels avoided overtly political content and violent imagery, and instead encoded their "messages" in the form of the domestic novel. Women's antirevolutionary novels differ from the *Anti-Jacobin* in tone as well; satire, even when it is very prominent, as in Elizabeth Hamilton's *Memoirs of Modern Philosophers*, is subordinated to the domestic plot, or to the earnest moralizing of the narrator. If conservative women novelists took anything from the magazine, it is the simplicity—relative to Burke—of the *Anti-Jacobin* style, rather than the journal's overtly political focus, or "dry, cynical, detached" tone.

Though absent from most women's writing, the style of the *Anti-Jacobin* is apparent if we limit our focus strictly to anti-Jacobin novels. Anti-Jacobinism was promoted in novels by a range of writers, both male and female, and, as Gary Kelly points out, "there were others who adopted some Anti-Jacobin elements in novels with different objectives," simply because an anti-Jacobin message was both politic and popular with the reading public.[42] Anti-Jacobin novels responded directly to a perceived political crisis, and challenged revolutionary theory openly within the context of the novel, which makes them a subcategory of the broader antirevolutionary novel. Many anti-Jacobin novels use the figure of a Jacobin philosopher-villain who mouths revolutionary philosophy—often quoted directly from William Godwin or Mary Wollstonecraft—for personal, rather than altruistic or political, benefit. Jane West's villain, Fitzosborne, in *A Tale of the Times*, uses the philosophy of Godwin and Rousseau to seduce the married Geraldine Monteith. The French Vaurien (whose name means "worthless") in Isaac D'Israeli's novel of the same name (1797), is a free-floating instigator of revolution who has been forced to flee almost every country in Europe. His attempted seduction of the chaste Emily Balfour is shown to be analogous to his attempt to overcome Britain by terrorism and trickery. Elizabeth Hamilton's *Memoirs of Modern Philosophers* (1800) explicitly footnotes her text to show where the dialogue of her satiric philosopher characters—Bridgetina Botherim, Mr. Glib, Mr. Myope—is to be linked to Godwin's *Political Justice*, Wollstonecraft's *Vindication of the Rights of Woman*, and Mary Hays's *Memoirs of Emma Courtney* (the character of Bridgetina is a caricature of Hays). All of these novels incorporate philosophical dialogues and relatively "flat" characterization for satirical purposes. Gary Kelly has argued that this method of characterization draws on the "Character-book" tradition of La Bruyère and Butler.[43]

Despite their shared characteristics, anti-Jacobin novels by women tend to differ from those by men on one critical level: while anti-Jacobin philosophy is enacted, in all of these novels, through a domestic plot, those by men adhere more completely to the form of the satiric novel of ideas, rather than to domestic realism. In subtitling his novel *Vaurien*, "Sketches of the Times," D'Israeli argues he is choosing "the *form* rather than the *matter* of a novel." As "the most engaging and most instructive class of literature," the form of the novel provides an opportunity for the responsible writer to "trace and expose" "popular prejudices cruel in their effects."[44] In the concluding pages of his preface D'Israeli positions his work with *Joseph Andrews* and *Gil Blas*, rather than with antirevolutionary novels by women like Jane West and Elizabeth Hamilton. His negotiation of literary heritage in his preface suggests his literary approach: *Vaurien* provides "sketches" of aspects of London life, and of negative characters, as the protagonist, Charles Hamilton, a rural clergyman's son, comes in contact with them. While D'Israeli's central critique of Jacobinism is through the character of Vaurien himself, related critiques of the profligacy of the aristocracy, of the gullibility of the English people, of law, and of an absurd, emulative British revolutionary "philosophy," form the structure of the episodic narrative.

Halfway through the novel the appearance of the virtuous and vulnerable Emily Balfour introduces the "matter" of a domestic plot. D'Israeli closely ties the political to the domestic plot, and Charles's virtuous love for Emily is opposed to Vaurien's immoral lust. D'Israeli's interest in outlining the dangers of Jacobinism privileges the development of the character of Vaurien over that of Charles, the ostensible protagonist of the domestic plot. The most definitive indication that the domestic plot is subordinate to the social and political satire is in the conclusion of the narrative. The novel ends with Vaurien busily hatching plots on his way to Holland. Acting as a *deus ex machina,* he has cleared away the snares he has set for the young lovers, leaving open the possibility of their conventionally happy future. D'Israeli's plot imposes closure before a domestic novel would have; the final chapter of the novel neither hints at nor summarizes the reconciliation of Emily and Charles.[45] This plot structure, as well as the content of the novel, which, in simple terms of quantity, is heavily weighted toward the satiric novel of ideas, produces a text substantially different from most of the antirevolutionary novels written by women.

Charles Lucas's *Infernal Quixote* (1801) provides a similar profile. Like D'Israeli's novel, this one contrasts a virtuous country boy to a worldly villain (in this case an "infernal" one), whose characters are in part demonstrated through their treatment of women. Lord Marauder, the villain, seduces Emily by giving her Wollstonecraft's *Vindication of the Rights of Woman,* while the exemplary Wilson gives his young Fanny Hannah More's *Sacred Dramas.* The inevitable playing out of these plots—Emily's ruin and repentance, Fanny's late but happy marriage to Wilson—are didactic methods for contrasting two political systems and simultaneously instructing female behavior. Lucas is using strategies common to many antirevolutionary women's novels, yet he, like D'Israeli, subordinates the domestic plot to the political. Over half of the four-volume novel is dedicated to Marauder's plot as Jacobin arch-villain—he almost single-handedly incites and carries out the Irish rebellion of 1798—to the extent that after the narrative returns to Emily's domestic plot the narrator apologizes: "This digression from the main incidents of the history of Marauder is somewhat necessary to the general tenor of my subject: but the more regular account of the conduct of M'Ginnis [Marauder's Irish alter-ego] in Ireland is now resumed." This apology contrasts with one made by West in her historical novel,

The Loyalists (1812), in which the narrator apologizes for introducing historical details that draw the narrative away from the domestic plot.[46]

The types of plotlines and information privileged by male and female anti-Jacobin novelists differ. Even Elizabeth Hamilton who, like D'Israeli, used the "masculine" "learned quasi-novel" form (to use Gary Kelly's term),[47] focuses her political and social critique through the domestic plot, rather than utilizing it as an adjunct to the political plot. While I hesitate to draw an immovable, gendered line of distinction through the category of anti-Jacobin novels, my reading has suggested that this strong area of distinction exists. The difference in emphasis is explicable by a difference in focus, however; while men's novels were openly political, women's novels were more subtly so, and approached political issues through a number of ideologically related categories, such as gender, class, and domesticity. Women engaged with, developed, and modified the form of the anti-Jacobin novel, in the same way that they engaged with other forms within conservative print culture. The heterogeneous landscape of anti-revolutionary novels and periodicals provided the background against which they produced their politically engaged fiction.

The "Proper Place" of Burke

I have argued that women's antirevolutionary writing is based upon a network of linked cultural categories—religion, gender, class, and domesticity. Critics of Romantic women's writing have identified in the writing of Edmund Burke the source and justification for these linkages. Anne Mellor, in *Romanticism and Gender*, has produced a convincing argument for the influence of Burke on women writers across the political spectrum. According to her argument, Burke supplied women with a useful trope when he created, in his widely-read *Reflections on the Revolution in France* (1790), an analogical link between the family and the nation, and thus between the domestic and the political. As I have argued above, the importance of the domestic life of the public man had become an area of concern, even before Burke's tropic articulation of the public/private link, yet, while the family/nation analogy formed part of eighteenth-century (and earlier) political thought, Burke's formulation of the trope in the context of the French Revolution intensified and popularized the concept. What Mellor terms the "family-politic" trope functioned, she argues, as a basis for an expansion of the position and role of women in society. Mary Wollstonecraft, for example, could argue that the family-politic trope, which she refined to comprise the *egalitarian* family, provided the justification for both democracy and equality between the sexes. Romantic women writers in general, Mellor argues, used the trope to dignify their social roles, by privileging the domestic and idealizing the maternal. More broadly, she argues, many women writers of the period radically reconfigured domesticity itself by constructing an alternative "counter-public sphere": "They proclaimed the value of rational love, an ethic of care, and gender equality as a challenge both to a domestic ideology that would confine women within the home and to a capitalist laissez-faire system that would set the rights of the individual, free-will or rational choice, and an ethic of justice above the needs of the community as a whole."[48] Although Mellor is referring primarily to radical and moderate writers here, conservative women also utilized Burke's trope to expand their functions, emphasizing women's role in the community (especially charity), and privileging family and community as units in an ordered nation.

This metaphorical link between the domestic and the political also provided the basis for women's open politicization, in the radical politics and polemics of Wollstonecraft, Helen Maria Williams, and Mary Hays, as well as enabling the conservative commentary of writers like West and More. As Claudia Johnson puts it in *Jane Austen: Women, Politics, and the Novel*: "The reactionary ideology which evolved in England during the 1790s left a rich and paradoxical legacy: even as it required women to be amiably weak, retiring, and docile . . . it not only stimulated but also empowered women's commentary on political affairs."[49] The family-politic trope, which was essentially conservative at its origin, provided the conceptual tools for female politicization. Further, when traditional female functions became dignified through the idealization of the domestic sphere, this trope made possible an expansion of those functions: charity, especially as practiced by Evangelicals like Hannah More, legitimized female movement beyond the domestic, and became the justification for active and widespread political involvement. More's Sunday Schools in the Mendips, as well as her other charitable schemes, for instance, gave her broad influence, not only among the beneficiaries of her eleemosynary activity, but also in the admiring and supportive middle and upper classes. In short, once a link is made between the domestic and the political—the link not introduced, but made commonplace, by Burke—the political becomes, to a limited degree, open to the encroachments of the domestic.

Not all critics have presented Burke's influence on women and women writers in this positive light, however. In Eleanor Ty's *Unsex'd*

Revolutionaries, Burke becomes a representative of, and the central figure in, the Lacanian "Law of the Father," against which the five revolutionaries of the title define themselves. Ty reads Burke's family-politic trope as repressive, as a method whereby a conservative hegemony can control domestic, and, importantly, female relations and activity. Conservative women like West, she argues, "supported the Burkean paradigm of the domestic monarch." For Ty, Burke's trope forms the basis for a more rigid demarcation between the public and the private, and for more rigid gender definitions. By emphasizing the potentially negative effect of domestic misconduct, the conservative establishment could justify surveillance and control of the domestic sphere. Rather than empowering women, the family-politic trope becomes a means of oppression. Claudia Johnson also notes the connection between the political and the domestic, suggesting that conservative women followed Burke in their belief that national security was grounded in the morals of private individuals. "Following the outlines of Burkean 'plots,'" she argues, "the novels written in his shadow take the rights of parents over daughters, of husbands over wives, and the superiority of 'prejudices' favoring established modes of behavior to 'rational principles' dictating innovative social conduct as their basic starting points; feminine desire and illicit sex constitute their basic crises." The writing of conservative women, she argues, "dramatize[s] Burkean fictions," and therefore functions ideologically to enforce a social ideal, by constructing a "simpler world . . . where fathers are judicious and clergymen are pious; where the duties of daughters are clear, and where wives are either grave and good or petulant and power hungry; where villains and heroes occupy entirely different moral universes, and where right and wrong are mutually exclusive categories."[50]

The use of Burke by all of these critics is interesting because it further underlines the essential complexity of political categories during this period. That two apparently opposite interpretations of Burke's influence on women writers can be convincingly argued is because both positions are fair; the practical effect of this Burkean social model on women writers of the period was, often simultaneously, both enabling and constricting, depending upon their, and others', interpretation of its meaning. Part of this is due to the complicated political position of Burke himself. Burke, the arch-"conservative," was a Whig, not a Tory, and, historians have argued recently, subscribed to an agenda of reform that coexisted with his basic support of a creed of aristocratic government; indeed, one of the central arguments of his *Reflections on the Revolution in France* is that "[a] state without the means of some change is without the means of its conservation." James Conniff has argued in *The Useful Cobbler* that "Burke sought to reconcile a generally conservative outlook with an acceptance of the need for change through reform." Conniff's analysis repositions Burke politically by complicating our understanding of his thought, and by placing him within his eighteenth-century cultural context; it was only in the twentieth century, he points out, that Burke was labeled "conservative." Even after the French Revolution, and Burke's publication of his fervently loyalist *Reflections*, Conniff interprets Burke as a "gradualist" reformer, not merely a reactionary. At the time of the French Revolution, "Burke's basic message was that the old Whig faith of reform in detail combined with stability in essence was still valid." George Watson makes a similar point, arguing that Burke adhered to a central doctrine of Whiggism: "Reform that you may preserve." "Reform, after all," Watson claims, "has nothing to do with total change and a new start, since it arises out of a respect for the system that it seeks to improve."[51] If we accept Conniff and Watson's interpretation of Burke as essentially a conservative reformer, it is not surprising that non-radical and conservative women would find his work the source of inspiration, since it essentially aligns with their own doctrines of conservative reform. Rather than simply accepting a restrictive Burkean model of the family and the domestic sphere, women like West and More found support and justification in his writing for their own reformist agendas. His example enabled women's political discourse in this way, much as Mellor has argued his family-politic trope became the basis for the social and political engagement of women after the French Revolution.

The competing critical arguments about Burke's relationship to women writers open up a broader question: to what extent did conservative women replicate the thought, arguments, and philosophy of their male contemporaries? It oversimplifies these women's positions to assume that they were, in effect, unquestioning or unaware channels for Burke's social and political theory. At the same time, we cannot read hard-line conservatives like Jane West as utilizing his philosophy to the (potentially revolutionary) extent that Mellor suggests.[52] I would argue that conservative women's relationship to Burke was somewhere between these two extremes: while they easily accepted many of his basic premises, these writers were also in dialogue with his politics, and engaged critically with its arguments, adapting them to suit their own political projects.

Burke's name appears relatively rarely in the work of conservative women writers, though echoes of his arguments sound regularly throughout their work. Jane West is one of the few women conservatives who actually mentions Burke in her writing—not in her fiction, which rarely alludes directly to contemporary historical figures, but notably in her *Elegy on the Death of the Right Honourable Edmund Burke*, published in 1797. While the elegy appropriately focuses on Burke's life and achievements, its subtext is the complicated relationship between Burke and West, subject and elegist. West's enthusiastic portrait of Burke reveals both how she perceived his political contribution, and how she utilized his thought—and his character—in the production of her own texts and arguments. Rather than simply and clearly replicating Burkean philosophy, West engages with and transforms Burke's thought to produce a gendered politics, a feminine (but non-feminist) discursive space within the broader field of postrevolutionary conservatism.

The *Elegy* foregrounds Burke's patriotism, and the importance of his early antagonistic response to the French Revolution (personified as a "Fiend"):

> E'en while that Fiend, seductive, young, and gay,
> Yet pure from Slaughter, first withstood the Laws,
> He told the Horrors of her future Sway,
> And lifted Truth in Order's sacred Cause.[53]

Burke's defense of "Order" in the face of "Democracy's destructive Fires" (p. 7) is the basis for the speaker's exhortation: "Go—join the Host of Britain's mighty Dead" (p. 3). Burke, as West represents him, was a moderate, protecting "Liberty of British Birth" (p. 13) against both revolutionary sentiment and excessive monarchical and aristocratic power; or in the neoclassical discourse of the elegy: "His ported spear now menac'd Right Divine; / Now brav'd the shafts of Democratic Rage" (p. 14). Concomitant with this portrait of Burke as classical hero is a feminized portrait that constructs him as the domestic ideal of the family-politic trope; his home, West writes, "Glow[s] with the Radiance of Domestic Love" (p. 16), and she foregrounds his roles as "firm Friend," "fond Father," and "Husband ever kind" (p. 17). In short, he becomes a literary incarnation of that portion of his philosophy—the link between the domestic and the public spheres—that makes female political involvement possible.

West's poem moves from a discussion of Burke's political to his domestic virtues, and in her elegiac construction of his character the two are intertwined: he is simultaneously domestic and political. West creates a posthumous "Burke," who combines what she presents as both male and female attributes, and thus can stand, within her poem, as an exemplar for either gender. His moral androgyny is marked in the following stanza, in which he stands as both chivalric "champion" and feminized man:

> Daughters of Britain! let the grateful Tear
> Of kindred Worth your Champion's Ashes dew;
> His Breast, like your's, impassion'd and sincere,
> Glow'd with the Virtues he rever'd in you.
>
> (p. 15)

West's emphasis on Burke's "kindred Worth," and her suggestion that he shared the feminine qualities he revered in British womanhood, draws an analogy between him and the "Daughters of Britain" in the opening line of the stanza. Burke's value, the elegy argues, is in his successful coordination of the private and the public, the domestic and the political, the feminine and the masculine. As well as praising and repeating Burke's most basic political philosophies, West utilizes his public persona to promote a politicized ideal of domestic masculinity. Turning the family-politic trope on its maker, she insists on an equalizing moral reform: both men and women become the subjects of the politicized domestic sphere. This strategy makes strange bedfellows, and links West to Mary Wollstonecraft—whose *Vindication of the Rights of Woman* proposes moral reforms for both men and women, especially in domestic terms—in previously unexplored ways.

West's practice in her *Elegy* essentially refigures and reforms Burke's public image and his cultural importance, under the terms of her own reformist agenda. In a similar way, many women writers reworked the configurations of mainstream conservatism to produce a specifically feminine form of conservative and antirevolutionary discourse. Choice of genre provided one method of differentiation; the domestic novel, long associated with women as producers, consumers, and subject, became the dominant form of women's anti-revolutionary writing. As Ralph Cohen has remarked, "an author in making a generic choice involves himself in an ideological choice," and the choice of the domestic novel as a genre presented writers with a specific set of formal imperatives and problems.[54] Even as conservatism varies from writer to writer, so too does the use of form; chapter 3 will explore the shared and varied strategies that compose the discursive terrain of the antirevolutionary didactic novel by women.

3

Persuasive Fictions: The Novel Form of Conservatism

> I do not need to write for bread; and I would not write one volume, merely to gain the fame of Homer. A moral therefore is necessary for me; but where to get one on which to found a tale that will be readable, is the question. A *lofty* moral, too, is necessary to my style of thinking and writing; and really it is not easy to make such a one the groundwork of any story which novel readers will endure.
>
> Mary Brunton, letter to her brother, 27 October 1815

AS JANET TODD COMMENTS IN *THE SIGN OF ANGELLICA*, WOMEN'S novels after the French Revolution were designed primarily to teach a lesson rather than to reflect an artistic ideal: "Female art was resolutely *not* transcendental; ethics not aesthetics was its business." Didacticism is implicated in the texts of women of varying political stances, and coexists with or subsumes aestheticism. Novels, "cross-bred with the treatise on education," become vehicles to transmit moral or political messages, or "antidotes" to improper thinking, and, as Jane West comments candidly, (and the most inattentive of readers could infer), "the story is confessedly subordinate to this aim." This type of comment is common in prefaces and biographies of antirevolutionary women writers. Mary Brunton's biographer, for example, notes of her writing: "To its moral usefulness she uniformly paid much more regard than to its literary character." "Moral usefulness" claimed its place during this period alongside financial need as a stock explanation for women's literary activity. It is important, therefore, when considering this type of didactic text to avoid literary value judgments based on a post-Romantic ideal that privileges originality and individualism. As both Todd and Marilyn Butler have pointed out, the "value" of these texts was not in aesthetic superiority, but in the salutary effect they aimed to have on their readers; indeed, both originality and individualism were problematic concepts for conservative writers who promoted ideals of community (the "world") and conformity.[1]

Literary didacticism is often closely linked to discipline: a central lesson of conservative novels is self-discipline, while the narratives discipline their negative exemplary heroines, punishing them with dysphoric plotlines. In *Discipline and Punish,* Michel Foucault argues that during the late eighteenth century a change occurred in the exercise of monarchical and governmental power over criminals. This change is evidenced in the increasing emphasis on the rehabilitation of the transgressive subject, rather than on his or her punishment. During this period, Foucault argues, three "technologies of power" existed simultaneously: one is traditional monarchical vengeance, in which punishment is inscribed on the body through torture, and sovereign power is publicly demonstrated; the other two focus on reclaiming the criminal subject, either through instructive punishment, or "coercion," which reforms habits and behavior, instituting self-discipline.[2] In general, this last technology of power is most in evidence in didactic fiction, which takes as its focus the reform of both characters and readers, with the purpose of instilling self-discipline.

Jane West's self-described "remarkably pretty" children's book, *The Sorrows of Selfishness* (1802), however, moves beyond reformation, and reveals an otherwise obscured link between discipline and physical violence by bringing the juvenile reader's body into the text as the site of potential punishment. The narrator, Prudentia Homespun, comments: "When any young lady, under my own care, is so unfortunate as to be troubled with fits upon receiving any disappointment, I always take as large a bundle of birch twigs as I can grasp in my hand, and, binding it tight with a piece of string, I apply it with all my strength, till I bring her to her senses."[3] Here, the erring child's body is the site of punishment intended to reform her behavior: punishment becomes the means for reformation and the development of self-discipline, an internalization of the social codes that define "criminal" behavior. Here, criminality exists in an excess of inappropriate emotion ("fits"), a transgression of the boundaries of self-discipline, and of the moral and behavioral code, the dissemination of which is the purpose of the text. As it plays out Foucault's technologies of power on a personal and domestic level, West's "pretty" children's book clarifies the seriousness of her didactic agenda; while her domestic and historical novels attempt openly to effect behavioral and moral changes in the reader through exemplary plot trajectories, her children's literature underscores the violence at the root of her philosophy of moral reform, and the extent to which concepts of reform and punishment are linked within that philosophy.[4]

The "young lady" under discussion in this portion of West's narrative is the negative exemplar Susannah Richmore, but West's text generalizes, broadening the specific incident into a general lesson. The strategy of generalizing on the specific is, of course, typical of didactic texts, and could be said to be the defining characteristic of the genre as a whole. Many didactic writers of the Romantic period use the device regularly in their novels, often opening or concluding chapters with a broad moralistic rumination upon a narrative incident. Furthermore, each didactic narrative, in its entirety, is intended to provide a general lesson to the reader. Jane West's relatively interchangeable central characters are also interchangeable with her readers, by a logic of moral substitution: if the reader were to behave as the romantic Geraldine Powerscourt does in *A Tale of the Times*, for example, then her own plot trajectory would imitate the fictional character's tragic decline. As Susan Rubin Suleiman argues, the "persuasive effect" of this type of narrative "results from the virtual identification of the reader with the protagonist."[5] Thus, when the hypothetical "any young lady" of *The Sorrows of Selfishness* is beaten by the narrator, Prudentia Homespun, her uncomfortable position could be occupied by any reader who transgresses the moral boundaries set by the narrator. The generality of "any young lady" and the repetition inherent in "always" reinforce the menace of the threat.

I begin this chapter with West's punitive description in order to underscore the repressive and coercive aspects of didactic literature, especially in those texts by authors of reactionary politics. Texts like this one form a mechanism for social discipline that functions outside the institutional "system of carceral restraints or disciplinary injunctions," as D. A. Miller claims of the Victorian novel.[6] Didactic texts by radicals and moderates take a slightly different form: the didactic text remains coercive, in that it attempts to effect behavioral changes within its readers, but the punitive subtext is generally absent. Mary Wollstonecraft's benign and gentle Mrs. Mason, of her didactic children's book, *Original Tales* (1788), contrasts sharply with West's Homespun in this respect. The novels for adults and young women that form the bulk of the texts analyzed in this study follow a more sophisticated pattern, inculcating a moral message through a (highly codified) negative or positive exemplary narrative. Yet, underlying these texts, more or less obscured, is the threat of punishment, and the intention of coercion. The purpose of this chapter is to explore the ways in which conservative didactic texts are constructed to achieve their coercive end, and to provide a theoretical basis for more focused discussions of the formal and ideological elements of the genre in the following chapters.

Antirevolutionary Strategies

The antirevolutionary novels of this period provide a unique opportunity to study the form of the didactic novel in English. This is a result of two related circumstances. First, the novel had not, at this time, developed its post-Romantic anti-didacticism, and was still very close to its mid-eighteenth-century quest for generic respectability. Many of the women writers I examine here admired Samuel Richardson, who, as J. Paul Hunter has argued, spearheaded one of the movements toward novelistic respectability by emphasizing the didactic effects of his narratives. The second circumstance is the political situation, which authorized didactic literature as an essential component in the war effort. The didactic fiction written by conservative women after the French Revolution shares characteristics with the "authoritarian" *roman à thèse* described by Susan Rubin Suleiman in her study of the genre, *Authoritarian Fictions*, in spite of the fact that her main object of attention is the French "ideological novel" of the early twentieth century. In both cases, the narrative "is essentially teleological—it is determined by a specific end, which exists 'before' and 'above' the story." In order to promote a specific message, this genre aims ultimately to control meaning and to ensure narrative closure; as Michel Beaujour puts it, "the 'good' or righteous novel will therefore indulge in a lot of intratextual transcoding in order to eliminate ambiguity and therefore delimit the range of interpretation allowed to the reader." These texts are constructed to avoid ambiguity, and to discourage personal and idiosyncratic exegesis. As I shall argue later, the ambiguous nature of language, of women's place within conservatism, of politics, and of genre, makes a truly monological text an impossibility, yet the technical strategies of the conservative didactic novel produce narratives that come close to approximating the "single meaning and . . . total closure" described by Suleiman as characteristic of the aims of an ideological novel. Reader-oriented theory, narrowly defined, plays a necessary role in understanding the didactic novel. My focus here is on how narratives are constructed to produce particular moral effects in their readers; my attention, however, is on the narratee, the "encoded" or "implied," rather than historical, reader.[7] It is impossible to measure the effectiveness of these novels on readers; evidence of buying and reading patterns is lacking, nor is there any detailed record of contemporary readers' responses to the novels. When I speak of the "effectiveness" of an antirevolutionary novel, therefore, I am not referring to any measurable personal or social effect it may have had—rather, I limit my interpretation of success to the extent to which the narrative is able to limit meaning and to provide closure.

Didactic conservative fiction attempts to achieve this exemplary form of closure in a number of different ways. Most subtle is the use of embedded statements, such as "she knew then," or "she finally understood," which implicitly support the text's moral basis. More direct are value judgments that indicate the appropriate readerly response: "But, alas! [my mother's] too partial fondness overlooked in her darling the growth of that pernicious weed [pride], whose shade is deadly to every plant of celestial origin"; or, from Elizabeth Hamilton's *Cottagers of Glenburnie*: "Had Mrs. MacClarty been capable of reasoning, how would her soul have been wrung with remorse." Elsewhere the narrator's interpretive function interrupts the narration entirely, in digressive pauses that elaborate on the lessons to be drawn from a particular narrative event. Laetitia Matilda Hawkins, for example, takes an entire chapter to comment on the necessity of economy and renunciation in the battle against revolutionary philosophy, after her protagonist enters "society."[8]

In order for these strategies to be effective, however, the narrative voice must carry considerable authority. One of the ways this authority is achieved is through the establishment of what Suleiman calls a narratorial "ideological 'supersystem' that *puts in their proper place* the systems represented by the characters." The task of this ideological "supersystem" is to state, repeat, and reaffirm the lessons taught by the narrative. The "omniscient" narrator is arguably most effective at carrying out this task, since it carries greater authority and a semblance of objectivity. Conservative women, however, experimented with a range of narrative voices; their diverse strategies of narration worked toward the establishment of different forms of narratorial supersystem. Hannah More's protagonist in *Coelebs in Search of a Wife*, for example, acts literally as a judge, as he presents and explicitly ranks different stock feminine figures, from the hoyden to the learned lady. Narratorial authority is further strengthened through alignment with the didactic aims stated openly in the novels' prefatory material and notes. In West's *The Advantages of Education*, for example, the narrator states in the preface that she "wishes to convince them [girls], that it is but seldom that they will be called forth to perform high acts of heroic excellence, but that they will be daily required to exert those humble duties and social virtues, wherein the chief part of our merit and our happiness consists."[9] The aim of the story stated in advance in the authoritative context of a preface, it is the role of the narrator simply to remind the reader of it, and to point out how events serve as evidence to support the original premise.

Another strategy used by antirevolutionary women novelists to establish narratorial authority is the literary construction of what Gary Kelly has termed a "paternal chorus": authoritative mentorial figures within the novels who are paternalistic, if not actually male, and who speak in moral alignment with the narrator.[10] Dr. Orwell in Hamilton's *Memoirs of Modern Philosophers,* Mr. Stanley in More's *Coelebs,* Mr. Brudenell in West's *Infidel Father,* Mrs. Loveday in her *Ringrove,* and Miss Mortimer in Mary Brunton's *Discipline* are only a few examples of this ubiquitous strategy. The interventions of these characters mark them as both characters and narrators: their speech rarely contributes to the construction of plot or to character development. Most often, their speeches become set-pieces within chapters constructed around them; their narration of exemplary stories or their engagement in literary and moral criticism is their preeminent quality. The voices of these "paternal" figures support the narratorial voice, consolidating power and guiding interpretation.

Repetition is another strategy used in the conservative didactic novel to produce closure. The strategies to control moral interpretation described in the previous paragraphs are also, of course, strategies of repetition; the implied author, narrator, and paternal chorus are linked through complex and pervasive patterns of repetition. In addition, didactic novels occasionally incorporate subordinate narrative repetitions of central moral issues. Laetitia Matilda Hawkins uses footnotes to achieve this effect in *The Countess and Gertrude*; in the notes the narrator recounts stories from "real life" that support and reiterate the moral messages of the novel, and of the carefully explanatory didactic preface. Hamilton's *Cottagers of Glenburnie* uses embedded narratives to teach lessons; a housekeeper, for instance, who is guilty of drunkenness and slander, dies horribly in a fire.[11] West's *Gossip's Story* contains a lengthy interpolated "legendary tale" in verse, which repeats several of the moral lessons of the primary narrative: submission to authority, the valorization of (male) friendship over romantic love, virtue and piety over heroism, and simplicity over ostentation. *Ringrove,* West's final novel, incorporates improving tales by "Mrs. MacMendus," which similarly support morals promoted elsewhere in the narrative. The cumulative effect of these strategies is to produce a semantically overdetermined novel, in which the range of interpretations is limited.

One form of repetition is effected by the use of stock characters and plots. The domestic novel of the late eighteenth century was limited in terms of the plot trajectories available to writers, and the didactic novel was further limited by the necessity of teaching a particular lesson. As Daniel Defoe commented earlier in the century, plot was "in all Ages" central to the usefulness of literature; he claims that in his *Moll Flanders* "there is not a wicked Action in any Part of it, but is first or last rendered Unhappy and Unfortunate: There is not a superlative Villain brought upon the Stage, but either he is brought to an unhappy End, or brought to be a Penitent." In the tradition of Defoe's didacticism—which helped to form the novel as a genre—women writers of the period I am discussing here depended heavily on plot to inculcate particular morals. Jane West acknowledged this formal necessity in 1811, when, during the writing of *The Loyalists*, she commented in a letter to Bishop Percy: "As the plan of most of my former novels was to condemn what was wrong, I felt obliged by principle to give a melancholy termination; but, as in this my leading aim would be to recommend what is right, of course I must attach such a share of good fortune to correct principles as will induce imitation on worldly motives." Divergences from this imperative were risky, and to neglect to draw correct causal relations encouraged negative criticism, as this punitive review of *Liberality and Prejudice* by Eliza Coxe from the *Anti-Jacobin* illustrates: "If anything should tempt Mrs. Coxe to take up the pen again, we strenuously advise her, in the first place, to be fully prepared to assign a Christian motive for a good action."[12]

Plot types of this period are relatively formulaic, as critics since the late eighteenth century have noted. The *Gentleman's Magazine* complained in October 1808 that the contemporary novel constituted "a regular supply of sameness," and that "the incidents and plots of which Novels are composed must soon be exhausted (if indeed they be not exhausted already)." That novels were unoriginal in plot and presentation was the complaint of literary critics from the early 1790s to the late 1810s. More recently, Patricia Meyer Spacks has noted the prevalence, during this period, of the "sisters" plot, in which two female characters (not necessarily actual sisters) are contrasted—one plot dysphoric and one euphoric—in order to promote a moral lesson.[13] In this category belong several of Jane West's early novels, including *The Advantages of Education*, *A Gossip's Story*, and *The Infidel Father*, as well as Eliza Parsons's *Ellen and Julia*, and Jane Austen's *Sense and Sensibility*, which is a more subtly politicized narrative. (Anna Maria Porter published an interesting variation on this plot in her novel *Walsh Colville*, in which the contrast between two young men produces the moral lesson.) Nicola Watson has focused considerable attention on another stock plot, a commentary on Rousseau's *Nouvelle Héloïse* (1761), in which an adulterous or sexually promiscuous woman is ruined by her actions. This particular plot was refined to include those women who, like Geraldine Powerscourt in West's *A Tale of the Times*, are betrayed by a relatively minor social or behavioral error into rape or seduction. Elizabeth Hamilton's *Memoirs of Modern Philosophers* contains a subplot of this type, in the narrative of Julia Delmond, who is ruined by her susceptibility to "philosophical" discourse.

Other typical and related plots are the plot of education and the conversion narrative. The plot of education is intended to show the benefits of the "good" education, and takes a generally mildly transgressive heroine (like Gertrude in Hawkins's *The Countess and Gertrude* and Maria Williams in West's *The Advantages of Education*) through a program of education to a state of positive exemplarity. Austen's *Pride and Prejudice* and *Emma* are loosely based on this model, but the "indirection" of her discourse frustrates the assignment of didactic and political motives. Conversion narratives like Mary Brunton's *Discipline* and West's *Alicia de Lacy*, in which religious conversion is foregrounded, and the interior processes of moral and religious development provide the major "events" of the narrative, constitute a more spiritualized form of the education narrative. The popularity of this mainstream form of conversion narrative coincided, not surprisingly, with the rise of evangelicalism during the first decades of the nineteenth century. During this same time, the plots I have outlined above began occasionally to be combined with a historical plot or setting, by writers such as Jane Porter, Robert Bisset, Charles Lucas, and Jane West. In these novels, historical events generally serve as analogies for contemporary circumstances, and are made to teach a lesson about the problems of the "times." "However muffled up in a wide variety of nostalgic period costume," Nicola Watson comments, "these plots are all about the French Revolution, and would have been recognized as such by contemporaries."[14]

This range of plotlines serves to obscure a central and important similarity in plot among all of the antirevolutionary novels I explore here: each of these different forms of narrative is also a domestic novel, in that it is based upon a plot of courtship that makes explicit some of the text's central lessons. Marriage becomes the ground against which the instructive plot is played out; it is the mechanism by which a heroine is rewarded or punished, valorized or demonized; it is also the test by which a heroine's virtue is determined. The courtship plot was, of course, dominant in the eighteenth-century novel, and was, as Nancy Armstrong has argued in *Desire and Domestic Fiction*, highly politicized. Antirevolutionary novels, like earlier domestic novels such as *Pamela*, focus on women's role in achieving marital success. Unlike these earlier texts, however, the emphasis in the later novels is on female responsibility in achieving and maintaining this success, rather than on feminine vulnerability within a social system in which virtue is commodified. The antirevolutionary novel posits a civilized society threatened by foreign philosophy, in which a woman's marital choices become implicated in the national political struggle. The only true sexual threat in these novels is a lack of judgment on the woman's part. A simple alignment between moral exemplarity and a contented marriage therefore becomes possible; the moral message of the novel is reinforced by the heroine's success in marriage—which proves her moral fitness—and the existing system of gender relations can be shown to be appropriate, only dangerous to those who are badly educated.

Jane West's *A Gossip's Story* is typical in its use of the courtship plot for didactic purposes. In this novel the heroine, Louisa Dudley, proves her moral regularity by submitting to paternal authority, after which a benevolent Evangelical husband is bestowed on her. The plot demonstrates that, paradoxically, it is only through a complete submission to authority that a woman may achieve the relative freedom of a companionate marriage. This paradox is inscribed at the conclusion of *A Gossip's Story*, in a poetic epilogue ostensibly written by the exemplary, and therefore authoritative, Louisa. Stanza 2 of her poem constructs marriage in terms of its domestic restrictions, which are justified through an invocation of the powerful ideological categories of "reason" and "religion":

> The rose thrice hath bloom'd on the chaplet of May,
> Since I bow'd at the altar, and vow'd to *obey*;
> Talk not of *restrictions*, the *bond* I approve,
> 'Tis sanctioned by reason, religion, and love.

The final stanza of the poem, however, reinforces the text's ideal of a companionate marriage:

> Our boy at my bosom I cherish with pride,
> He calls to those duties we gladly divide;

> May he live when our limit of being is done,
> And our names and our virtues survive in our son.

The movement in the poem, from the language of restriction to an idealization of the companionate marriage, reproduces the female exemplar's movement from submission—to her father's and her husband's authority—to the ultimate reward of an egalitarian marriage. It is only through complete submission to authority, the "bond" mentioned in stanza 2, that Louisa achieves a good marriage. The novel's "sister" plot, conversely, demonstrates the negative marital plot of transgressive women: Louisa's "romantick" sister, Marianne, having chosen an inappropriate partner, experiences a loveless marriage, infertility, and social ostracism. These two plots, in varying but surprisingly similar form, are repeated across the range of novelistic subgenres that make up the didactic antirevolutionary novel of this period, and constitute a powerful means of persuasion. As Suleiman argues: "If the protagonist evolves toward a euphoric position, the reader is incited to follow him in the right direction: the protagonist's happiness is both a proof and a guarantee of the values he affirms. If the protagonist's story 'ends badly,' his failure also serves as a lesson or proof, but this time *a contrario*: the protagonist's fate allows the reader to perceive the wrong road without following it."[15]

The type of ideal marriage in these novels generally conforms to Lawrence Stone's definition of the eighteenth-century "companionate marriage," which is based on intellectual, emotional, and sexual compatibility, within the still hierarchical structure of the domestic sphere. Didactic antirevolutionary novels customarily critique a "romantick" attitude to marriage in women; in *A Gossip's Story* Louisa's negative sister Marianne expects a complete conformity of tastes with her husband, as well as consistent happiness. Despite this critique, however, the exemplary heroine who wishes only reasonable contentment is generally rewarded with a marriage that would have satisfied her romantic counterpart; the partners enjoy each other's company, rarely disagree, and the wife is respected for her intellectual as well as domestic capabilities. Susan Staves, in *Married Women's Separate Property,* challenges Stone's model, arguing that the apparent increase in women's freedom and influence within marriage was counterbalanced by a decrease in their actual property. "[W]hile the surface forms of Restoration married women's property rules appear to differ significantly from the surface forms of the rules at the beginning of the nineteenth century," Staves argues, "at a deeper level both share an underlying patriarchal structure."[16] These inequities are accepted by women's antirevolutionary novels, which are eager to reinforce two lessons: first, that women's errors in choosing a mate are the sole reasons for unhappy marriages (rather than social inequities); and secondly that virtuous behavior necessarily results in a comfortable marital situation.

One of the central problems with the use of plot for didactic effect was both theological and generic, and was articulated earlier in the century by Frances Sheridan in her novel of feminine distress, *Memoirs of Miss Sidney Bidulph* (1761). The "Editor's Introduction" describes a woman's criticism of the tragedy, *Douglas*, on the grounds that "the moral which it inculcates is a discouraging lesson, especially to youth; for the blooming hero of this story, though adorned with the highest virtues of humanity . . . is suddenly cut off by an untimely death, and that at a juncture too, when we might (morally speaking) say his virtues *ought* to have been rewarded." The response of the pious old lady who is her hostess provides the rationale for the narrative that follows. Her argument is that a simple model of reward for virtue is not only unrealistic ("the direct contrary is a truth, which everybody who has lived but a moderate number of years, must have been convinced of from their own observation"), but contrary to the lessons of Christianity, which teach practitioners to "look forward for an equal distribution of justice, to that place only, where (let our station be what it will) our lot is to be unchangeable." This is the argument of the Cheap Repository Tracts written by Hannah More in the 1790s in an effort to produce a contented and industrious working class. Her characters are rewarded by the approbation of middle-class mentors, by the religious satisfaction of penitence, and, sometimes, by modest material comfort. More attempts to direct the desires of the working classes toward the non-tangible rewards of Christianity, and away from the material property of the middle and upper classes. Similarly, in *The Sorrows of Selfishness*, Jane West states as her central argument the doctrine that "Man is born to sorrow, and affliction does him good."[17] The formal demands of the domestic novel, and the exigencies of didacticism, however, impose a narrative structure that concludes in material rewards—generally through marriage—at the conclusion of the plot, providing moral and formal closure.

The problem of material rewards is deeply rooted in class. The didactic novel of this period was closely aligned with the reforming middle class, as an anonymous reviewer in *Blackwood's Edinburgh Magazine* noted in 1819: "The manners and concerns of the middle classes have also been handled in works, which are not written like the highest novels, for the sake of recording the developements [sic] exhibited by the human mind, but which may be called moral novels; because they have generally a didactic purpose, relating to existing circumstances, and are meant to shew the causes of success or failure in life, or the ways in which happiness or misery is produced by the different management of the passions." Not only does this passage reveal the increasing devalorization of the didactic that occurred over this period, it also draws an explicit link between middle class "manners and concerns" and the "moral novel." (According to this review, working-class life is non-narratable, since: "In this class, the uniformity of occupations is such, as to destroy all variety in the developements [sic] of the mind.")[18] The *Blackwood's* reviewer identifies success or failure "in life" as the central concern of this genre, overlooking the writers' own anxiety that their texts teach a theological lesson that spans the boundary between this life and the next. Yet the reviewer is accurate in noting that these moral novels are unable to transcend the class-based values in which novelistic fiction of the eighteenth century is rooted. In chapter 2 I suggested the ways in which a range of value systems come together in the writing of conservative women of this period: religious, class, nation, and gender ideologies are mutually implicated, so that the middle-class value of industry (manifested in gendered forms) becomes a signifier of virtue, which is itself a mark of "true" religion, and consequently of patriotism. The entanglement of these ideologies demands a novelistic resolution that provides closure on each of these levels. If, then, a heroine like Louisa Dudley in *A Gossip's Story* is characterized (as many exemplary heroines are) by her industry, household economy, and prudence, the narrative must produce the "logical" closure by rewarding her with the financial as well as spiritual results of industry. Because of these ideological imperatives, and the form of the domestic novel they build on, conservative women writers had a limited novelistic vocabulary to utilize. With the exception of notable examples such as *Sidney Bidulph* and *Clarissa*, novels of the eighteenth century provided a fairly predictable model of rewards and punishments, and a codified system of moral rewards became a central characteristic of the conservative didactic novel of the Romantic period.

Form as Opposition

Many of the narrative elements I describe here are typical of the didactic novel across the political spectrum. It is important, therefore, to remember that antirevolutionary novels were written specifically as interventions in a political debate, and that antirevolutionary writers positioned themselves explicitly in opposition to revolutionary and radical women writers. This positioning affected not only the subject matter, but also the form of their narratives. While conservative women writers often argued openly against revolutionary philosophy, incorporating polemical passages in their conduct books and fiction, an important element of their resistance to it was at the level of literary form. As April London argues, "[c]onservative novels" of this period "mount their attacks on revolutionary politics less through direct reference to actual public event than through their own parodic versions of the representational conventions of radical narratives."[19] Antirevolutionary novels by women tended to emphasize the formal characteristics of conservatism, and engaged in political debate rarely: they reinterpreted revolutionary plots, used authoritative third-person narrators, sanitized their style to avoid excess (and therefore potentially revolutionary) rhetoric, and decentered the subjectivity of the protagonist, in an effort to counter the "poison" of revolutionary narratives.

In *Revolution and the Form of the British Novel,* Nicola Watson argues that the novels of revolutionary women are characterized by a privileging of individual experience and subjectivity. The letter, as the repository of personal voice, therefore carries revolutionary potential. The epistolary form not only provides a space for voicing the heroine's revolutionary desire, but valorizes the voice of an individual over that of the community. Antirevolutionary novels, in contrast, privilege consensus and community over individual experience. Antirevolutionary texts, as Watson notes, submit the personal voice in the form of the letter to the scrutiny of the community, producing a "policing" effect; private letters are intercepted and interpreted by authoritative figures within the community of the novel, as well as by the authoritative third-person narrator. Elizabeth Hamilton's *Memoirs of Modern Philosophers,* for example, highlights the sentimental (and therefore revolutionary) discourse of the personal letter by contrasting it to the third-person "reality" of the primary narrative; and Jane West, in *A Gossip's Story,* shows a young wife's private correspondence to be the catalyst for the decline of her marriage.[20] Antirevolutionary writers' regular (though by no means exclusive) use of a distant, third-person narrator, according to this argument, avoids the potential subversiveness of the personal voice, replacing it with an unidentified, conservative voice of authority.

The plots of antirevolutionary novels also attempt to contain the subversiveness of revolutionary plots. The revolutionary novels of the

1790s focus on individual experience, often pitting the protagonist against the world of custom and convention. William Godwin's *Things as They Are* (*Caleb Williams*) charts a servant's experience of injustice at the hands of an influential aristocrat, while Mary Wollstonecraft's *Maria; Or, the Wrongs of Woman* dramatizes more broadly the various systematic injustices against women in Britain. These didactic Jacobin plots are constructed to show the negative effects of the same "existing institutions" that antirevolutionaries are concerned to defend. Other Jacobin novels, like Robert Bage's *Hermsprong: or, Man as He Is Not,* show the positive social and personal effects of revolutionary philosophy. Bage's rational and benevolent hero (the ideal "man as he is not") upholds principles of democracy, revolution, and feminism, and the narrative confirms his political position by bringing his plot to a positive closure, and showing his rejection of the concept of "rank" to be appropriate (he is acquitted after throwing a baronet over a fence). Antirevolutionary novels, in contrast, construct plots in which submission to social order produces happiness, and legitimate power is wielded benevolently.

Gary Kelly, in his 1976 critical recuperation of didactic Jacobin novels, argues that these texts are constructed according to a "necessitarian" aesthetic: the Jacobins's belief, formulated in Godwin's *Political Justice,* that "'the characters of men originate in their external circumstances,' led them to consider the integration of character and plot as essential to the nature of the true novel." Because these novels are intended to teach a philosophical lesson, and, ultimately, to reform existing social institutions, they focus on the immediate effects of these institutions on their characters. For this reason, psychological realism became a central component of the Jacobin novel; by delineating the psychological effects of social circumstances, the Jacobin novel could "prove" the dangers of specific institutions and conventions.[21] An emphasis on personal psychological development is generally absent from antirevolutionary novels until the 1810s, when the Evangelical concerns of Mary Brunton foreground her protagonists' spiritual and moral progress (see chapter 6). Because of their refusal to attend to the emotional and psychological development of characters, antirevolutionary novels appear insubstantial by post-Romantic standards. There is no antirevolutionary *bildungsroman*; the exemplary protagonist's valorized qualities are generally established in early childhood in the home, and contact with the world (which in the *bildungsroman* is the catalyst for development) becomes an opportunity for the protagonist to resist corruption, rather than to gain experience. In general, antirevolutionary novels focus less on personal psychological and emotional development than on an individual's propriety of action within a social setting. The "characters of men [and women]" are shown to be a product of their family environment rather than their class or gender; responsibility for "character" is therefore transferred to the individual from the flawed society of the Jacobin novel.[22]

Elizabeth Hamilton's *Memoirs of Modern Philosophers* provides a useful example of how antirevolutionaries responded textually to revolutionary writing. Hamilton's text undertakes the exercise of refutation at three different levels. First, she uses the format of the fictional debate to discredit key revolutionary texts and concepts. In a central passage several of her characters debate the validity of Wollstonecraft's *Vindication of the Rights of Woman*; her exemplary characters indicate the points at which Wollstonecraft's argument is flawed, while a negative character ineptly defends it. Hamilton's second strategy is to use parody to mock central revolutionary texts; her ostensible "heroine," a cruel caricature of Mary Hays named Bridgetina Botherim, repeats the philosophy of Godwin (primarily drawn from *Political Justice*), Wollstonecraft, and Hays (especially her *Memoirs of Emma Courtney*) often verbatim, but also grotesquely exaggerated. Botherim's misinterpretation of these texts reframes radicalism as self-serving "innovation" which is socially harmful in its effects. As April London notes, this strategy "is intended to render the original ludicrous by a process of decontextualization that involves fracturing the coherence on which the affective unity of the source work depends."[23] Hamilton's third strategy is to rewrite the revolutionary novelistic plot according to a dysphoric model, which posits tragic or absurd outcomes to the implementation of revolutionary social theory. Nicola Watson has argued that Rousseau's plot of sensibility and female desire in *La Nouvelle Héloïse* became an allegory of revolutionary energy in the novels of radical women. Hamilton rewrites this plot to include a tragic conclusion that is closely linked to the heroine's philosophical beliefs: Julia, the focus of this plot, is seduced (and becomes pregnant) through her intellectual vanity, and by her adoption of principles of feminist equality.[24] Despite the assertion of Harriet, the exemplary heroine, that Julia can return to virtue, seduction leads inexorably to a penitent death.

The narrative of Julia's seduction and death incorporates attacks on specific radical writers, as well as on radical philosophy more generally. Julia is originally susceptible to the villain's advances because of her belief in the "*individuality* of affection" over social convention, a belief that echoes both Mary Hays's *Emma Courtney* and Godwin's *Memoirs of the Author of "The Rights of Woman"*. Hays's heroine attempts to align female desire and sensibility with reason and philosophy, arguing that it is rational to offer herself to the man she loves outside of marriage because, as Katherine Binhammer puts it, "the individuality of the affection, regardless of the custom of society and regardless of whether that affection is sanctioned by the laws of marriage, makes the sexual act pure."[25] Two years after the publication of Hays's novel, the grieving William Godwin wrote a revealing memoir of his recently deceased wife, Mary Wollstonecraft, and used the same rationale to defend her unconventional sexual behavior. By having her negative exemplary heroine die in circumstances similar to those of Mary Wollstonecraft (of a pregnancy-related illness), and by ascribing a similar motivation for sexual transgression, Hamilton marks the philosophy as negative, while at the same time using the (by then) notorious example of Wollstonecraft to support her polemic. Hamilton's antirevolutionary attack, then, is carried out at a number of narrative levels, and cannily invokes prevalent public outrage against specific radical figures in order to support her antirevolutionary message. Her strategies here are typical of the anti-Jacobin novel, and her practice, more generally, suggests the ways in which antirevolutionary women writers transformed radical forms into antirevolutionary "vehicles."

Making an Author: Morals and Marketability

"Selling" didacticism for consumption, as all of these strategies are designed to do, also involved literally selling novels, of course, and it would be a mistake to ignore the influence of economics on the form and fate of the didactic novel. During the late 1790s loyalism and conservatism gained discursive dominance, and novels were judged as much on their political and moral as on their literary merits. The most successful novels of the early nineteenth century were ones that made clear their alignment with the antirevolutionary position. It was common for reviewers to bestow praise on these grounds, in spite of technical and stylistic problems. The *Lady's Monthly Museum*, for example, noted that errors in Eliza Parsons's novels were due to haste, yet approved them for reading as "strictly moral."[26] Writers of anti-Jacobin and antirevolutionary novels had a greater chance of succeeding in the literary "marketplace" than writers on revolutionary or radical subjects, as public taste and government policy shifted toward the conservative. Writers like More and West made money on their publications (More, most dramatically, left a £30,000 estate at her death), as well as fulfilling their more explicit project of teaching antirevolutionary lessons. Others, like Eliza Parsons, seem to have made some attempt to capitalize on the shift in public taste. Parsons, a prolific writer (which may account for the many errors of grammar, logic, and style in her writing), had a documented need for money: she had eight children when her husband died of a stroke in the late 1780s. Always moral, though not necessarily instructive, Parsons's novels range from the conventionally didactic, in her now best-known antirevolutionary novels, *Woman as She Should Be* (1793), *Women as They Are* (1796), and *Ellen and Julia* (1793) to the Gothic in *The Mysterious Warning* (1796) and *The Castle of Wolfenbach* (1793) (two of Isabella Thorpe's "horrid" novels in *Northanger Abbey*).[27] Parsons's adoption of the conservative didactic form as one of a range of novelistic genres points to its popularity, and to her relentless search for the marketable. Conservative form and discourse sold. A didactic novel was not necessarily a simple reflection of the writer's political philosophy, nor was it written only to effect a political purpose; an important consideration in producing a novel was not just what it taught, but how the writer profited from it.

The marketability of these novels was, in many cases, based on the construction of the "author" as an authoritative figure. In the sense that this "author" does not correspond to a historical person, but is produced by discursive practices, we might think of it in terms of Foucault's "author function." Both writers and publishers worked to construct the figure who "authorized" works of moral and didactic fiction. Janet Todd has examined closely the ways in which women writers of the eighteenth century hung out the "signs" of their character and their femininity in order to make their writing acceptable. She argues that "the professional female author was by the late 1790s pretty much established in England," and that, therefore, there was no longer need to justify the act of writing and publishing itself.[28] (The practice of *explaining* literary activity remained common, however, and women often cited financial difficulties and male mentorial advice as their reasons for engaging in authorship.) There was need, however, to justify subject matter, and ill-chosen or politically unacceptable topics drew vicious attack, as in the case of Wollstonecraft's posthumous *Maria* and Hays's *Emma Courtney*. The link between character, credibility, reputation, and authority—particularly in the wake of the scandal surrounding Godwin's *Memoirs* of Wollstonecraft—was a vital one to be managed by women who professed moral and narrative authority.

Some reputations were established solely by literary means, and the convention of mentioning previous publications on the title page ("By the Author of . . .") helped to establish a literary history in which each text built on the success of the previous one. Susan Sniader Lanser notes that this practice permitted "the woman properly shy of publicity to be 'named' through a chain of book titles collectively carrying what Pierre Bourdieu describes as the 'symbolic capital' in which reputation exists." Jane West's early novels, for example, were published anonymously, and her later novels referred back to them, helping to establish her as a major voice in moral fiction. Prior to writing fiction, West had achieved modest success as a poet, yet her previous poetic publications do not appear on the title pages of her fiction. This is possibly due to marketing considerations, or a sense of generic endogamy. It may represent an attempt to preserve anonymity, since West's name appears on the title page of her volumes of poems. Another possible reason is that the poetry from the beginning of West's career presents a significantly different authorial figure from the authoritative mentor invoked in the novels. West's *Miscellaneous Poetry* (1786) and *Miscellaneous Poems and a Tragedy* (1791) were marketed under the category of simple poetry by a rural muse, an impression the poems themselves promote, by describing the writer's "natural" inclination for poetry, and by positioning the poet/speaker among the "swains" and maids of a pastoral. "Ease and simplicity are the distinguishing characteristics of the first production of this rustic muse," comments the *Monthly Review* in 1786. In reference to the same book, Horace Walpole wrote nastily to Lady Ossory: "For Mrs. West's verses, I do not think I shall tap them. The milkwoman at Bristol has made me sick of mendicant poetesses. If deep distresses and poverty cannot sow gratitude in the human heart, nor balance vanity and jealousy, these slip-shod Muses must sing better than they do, before I will lend an ear to them."[29]

Ann Yearsley, the "milkwoman" poet of Bristol, was a protégée of Hannah More. In 1784, More was shown verses written by Yearsley, a self-educated woman who lived in comparative obscurity as a farm laborer. Impressed, she appealed actively for subscriptions for Yearsley's first book of poems, taught her "the common rules of composition," and edited her poems. They disagreed over the allocation of the resulting profits. More established a trust for the sum of £360 to "ensure a permanent income for Mrs Yearsley," while Yearsley expected to receive the full amount of her earnings. The resulting conflict infantilized Yearsley and aggravated More, who withdrew from the committee of trustees, and refused any contact with her former protégée. Most members of "society" who expressed an opinion sided with More in the dispute.

The conflict foregounded the problems of patronage, as well as the delicate negotiations of gratitude and submission, which allowed "rustic muses" access to public voice. Walpole, who, predictably, given his class position, sided with Hannah More in her conflict with the "milkwoman" Yearsley, aligns West with her rural poet predecessor, and condemns her unread. His automatic categorization of her suggests something of the public figure attached to the literary text. The *Monthly Review* corroborates this public image, when it aligns West with other "rustic" women poets: "Prompted by nature only, with little advantage from books, she expresses her genuine feelings and sentiments, in numbers which, for neatness and harmony, will entitle her to rank with Mrs. Leapor, Mrs. Mary Jones, and Mrs. Cockburn." Jane West's subsequent transformation into a middle-class moral mentor necessitated the erasure of this problematic public persona. As the *Monthly Review* notes in its review of *Miscellaneous Poetry,* West was also "a person of a truly respectable character."[30] This "truly respectable" figure is the one that was developed for the later marketing of her conduct books and fiction.

West's shift in public character was possible, in part, due to her liminal class position. Her lengthy obituary in the *Gentleman's Magazine* notes: "She had married Mr. Thomas West, a yeoman farmer at Little Bowden, a relative of Admiral West, distinguished by his share in the relief of Minorca in 1756, and also of Gilbert West, author of the treatise on the Resurrection; and whose maternal ancestors constituted an unbroken chain of Rectors of Little Bowden for above 150 years." The obituary foregrounds West's "distinguished" connections over her undistinguished roots, and suggests how West as a writer could occupy the position both of a "rustic muse" and an "amiable and elegant writer," as she was described by the editor of *The British Poets,* Dr. Anderson, in 1800. Indeed, her precise social position became a subject of debate in the *Gentleman's Magazine* in 1802. In January an admirer wrote that she "pays the greatest care and attention to her farm, manages her dairy, and even carries her butter to market," while a letter published in February argues that West was socially above carrying her produce to market, and instead supervised the workings of the dairy. (As Pamela Lloyd notes, neither of these accounts allows time for the prolific writing she was engaged in at this period.)[31] Interestingly, this debate occurred at precisely the moment of West's definitive move from simply writing fiction, to becoming a mentor and authoritative didactic voice, with the publication of her first well-received conduct book, *Letters Addressed to a Young Man,* in 1801. Her early novels, all of which were reviewed positively by the conservative press, created the basis for this shift. The public interest paid to her social position at this time marks the importance of class, and of a particular form of gendered and class-based respectability, in the production of moral and didactic authority.

A similar negotiation of the issue of public presentation appears in the career of Laetitia Matilda Hawkins. The first clearly attributed work by Hawkins is her conduct book, *Letters on the Female Mind*, published in 1793, and written in response to Helen Maria Williams's *Letters* from France. Her opposition to Williams places her safely within the antirevolutionary camp, and her professed beliefs about women's place and function are conservative, insofar as she restricts women to carefully defined and subordinate domestic roles. Hawkins is careful to position herself socially within the first pages of her text, arguing that her objectivity is proven by her class position: "being placed nearly in the middle station of life, [I] have nothing to ask, nothing to hope, and little to fear, from all its vicissitudes."[32] Her actual social location was higher than West's, since she grew up with wealth and access to education, literature, and music, though with no connection to "good" families. Her education is emphasized in the *Letters*, and her exemplarity in relation to Williams is produced as a proof of its excellence.

Hawkins's early novels were published secretively and anonymously and have never been accounted for; it is therefore unlikely that she capitalized on prior performances as West did.[33] Instead, she relies upon prefaces and internal commentary (including footnotes) to establish moral and literary authority. Epigraphs to *The Countess and Gertrude* (1811) in French, English, and Latin, underscore her learning, while prefatorial references to "the almost momentary interruptions of our pen by calls to alleviate the various sufferings of others" establish her moral exemplarity. The *Anti-Jacobin Review* preferred the latter to the former characteristic, commenting: "That the writer possesses a great variety of knowledge will not be denied by her readers; but the major part, whom her remote and scientific allusions will very frequently puzzle, will have reason to wish it less ambitiously, and less resolutely displayed." A "display" of learning was one of the qualities that, according to conduct books and many magazines, exceeded the bounds of the ideally feminine. The *Anti-Jacobin*'s chastisement, however, acknowledges the "purest principles of morality" in this same text.[34] Coupled with the author's self-portrait as a domestic woman, her didactic motives outweigh any transgression in learning. Her education becomes instead the source of an intellectual authority framed by domestic conventionality. Both of these writers achieve the moral authority necessary to their didactic task by balancing elements in their public personae: West balances middle-class industry with elegance, and Hawkins's careful domestication of her public persona balances her excessive learning.

If these two portraits show different ways of "authorizing" didactic texts, they also give a sense of the various conservative positions women adopted. Because of these different positions, talking about "the antirevolutionary novel," as I have done to this point, is potentially problematic, in that this terminology emphasizes the similarities rather than the differences between the texts. This is of course an analytical necessity, as well as a fact: there *are* similarities between these novels that make possible an analysis of the kind I have carried out in this chapter. Yet it is the differences between these novels that make an in-depth study of them interesting and relevant. They vary at the important level of message, differing on the subject of appropriate behavior for women, and on religious practice; their literary practices differ, in their choices of genre and technique, and their negotiations of narratorial "voice." The genre of the didactic novel itself discourages this type of reading for difference, in its straining for monologism, and its concomitant attempt to exclude extraneous information. Yet, as Suleiman argues: "despite its yearning for a repressive readability, the *roman à thèse* gets caught up in the play of writing and finally designates the arbitrariness of its own authority."[35] How this happens is one of the central concerns of the following chapters: how, in particular, the demands of fiction work to destabilize the monologism of the authoritarian message—in short, how the *roman* comes into conflict with the *thèse*. More immediately, I turn to the issue of gender, focusing specifically on the ways in which the assignation of narratorial gender affects narrative authority in an authoritarian text, and on how, in their negotiations of authority and ideology, antirevolutionary women writers attempted to construct a feminine authority that simultaneously legitimized their texts and upheld conservative models of gender, rank, and literary form.

4

Narrative Authority: Antirevolutionary Women Writers and Literary "Voice"

> The Author entreats, that, in this and the following Stanzas, she may rather be considered as a Female judging from Sentiments of Moral Right, than as a presuming Politician. Warmly attached to the Cause of lawful Government, Subordination, and Property, she equally laments and reprobates the narrow Motives which induced Sovereign Princes to swell the Triumphs of Anarchy, and to undermine the Principles by which their own Thrones are supported by the forcible Dismemberment of Poland, an independent Kingdom, and by converting a War professedly undertaken on the broad Basis of Universal Security, into a selfish System of partial Emolument.—She confesses her Ideas may be too theoretical for Practice; and she is convinced, that her recluse Habits, and limited Information, will not allow her to judge, whether Political Necessity may not in some Degree diminish the Turpitude of Actions, which, in the private Intercourse between Man and Man, would be accounted Crimes.
>
> Jane West, *Elegy on the Death of the Right Honourable Edmund Burke*

I HAVE QUOTED THIS LENGTHY PASSAGE BY JANE WEST IN FULL BEcause it aptly illustrates the problem that is the critical focus for this chapter. It appears in West's elegy on Edmund Burke, and is drawn from a footnote to a passage that deals with the political state of Europe after the French Revolution. The footnote is framed by statements that set femininity and "Moral Right" in opposition to (implied) masculinity and political knowledge; this frame works ostensibly as an apology for political presumption and potential ignorance, the latter of which is linked to the habits and retirement of the proper Englishwoman. Yet the body of the paragraph draws on the authority inherent in "Moral Right" to chastise European monarchs for greed, and to uncover the hypocrisy in the war effort. The modest assertion that "her Ideas may be too theoretical for practice" carries a tone of disingenuousness following her bold critique, as does her deferral to "Political Necessity." The strong concluding clauses of the paragraph, under the guise of deferring to greater political knowledge, emphasize her alignment of this war with crime, and reassert the moral ascendancy of the domestic over the public and political. The placement of this passage as a footnote also works to subordinate the apology to the critique in the body of the elegy.

That this footnote exists at all is evidence of the carefully circumscribed position of the woman writer during this period. West understands clearly where the boundaries of appropriate feminine knowledge are, and carefully contains her political critique, foregrounding her "feminine" response to the situation, which is both moral and emotional (she is "[w]armly attached" to the existing order, and "laments" the actions of monarchs). The paragraph itself, in its fluctuating levels of authority, represents how difficult it is for an antirevolutionary woman to speak authoritatively. According to West's political theory, "lawful Government, Subordination, and Property" must continue to survive, since the destruction of order would lead to a breakdown of society and nation, and perhaps even the female subject herself, who is interpellated by a specific conservative ideology. To speak out is, then, a potentially radical and destructive act, if it transgresses the boundaries of gender and destabilizes the order of the social formation. Speech in novels, or narration, is an equally complicated balancing act, requiring a woman writer to negotiate the demands both of fiction and ideology.

It has become a methodological commonplace in feminist literary history of the Romantic period to chart the effects of ideology—generally a dominant, conservative ideology—on both female subjects and their texts. Mary Poovey, for example, has studied the effects of the ideology of the "proper lady" on the form of women's writing, while Marilyn Butler has focused on conduct book ideology in relation to Jane Austen in particular. Eleanor Ty and Claudia Johnson, more recently, have foregrounded female radical and moderate oppositional stances toward conservative gender ideology. Ty's recent book, *Empowering the Feminine*, explores the ways in which women writers from across the political spectrum responded to a dominant patriarchal ideology.[1] A problem on the margins of these critics' purview, however, is of particular concern to my subject here: how do we understand the relationship between a woman writer, the form of her texts, and a reactionary class and gender ideology, when the writer is actively implicated in textually constructing, rather than reacting against, or responding to, that ideology?

In antirevolutionary novels female morality and appropriate gendered behavior become the cornerstone of a stable nation, and ideal femininity stands against revolutionary threats from without and within Britain. Antirevolutionary writers are very careful, therefore, to detail the characteristics of this ideal, and to outline appropriate behaviors and functions for women. For West, a woman's role is to play the "second part in life's concert"; her "soft notes" should never "overpower the bold full tones of manly harmony, instead of agreeably filling up its pauses." Oppression, she argues, occurs only when a woman attempts to leave her "proper sphere." Hannah More, to whom West hopes to be compared, argues that "[i]t is of the last importance to their [girls'] happiness, even in this life, that they should early acquire a submissive temper and a forbearing spirit." Furthermore, a woman of good understanding "will discern that there can be no happiness in any society where there is a perpetual struggle for power; and the more her judgment is rectified, the more accurate views will she take of the station she was born to fill, and the more readily will she accommodate herself to it."[2] Her accommodation becomes the basis for a peaceful, hierarchical—"patriarchal" in the biblical sense—domestic sphere, which in turn provides the basis for a stable social structure. For both writers, women hold a distinct and subordinate social position, while in terms of spirituality their position is equal or greater. "[I]n Christ Jesus," writes More, "as there is neither 'rich nor poor,' 'bond nor free,' so there is neither 'male nor female.'" This list of striking binary opposites from St. Paul's epistle to the Galatians provides little consolation for the present; More's invocation of it is intended to defuse female discontent and to focus upper-class women's attention in the appropriate areas of charity and family.[3] Like many women writers of their period, both radical and conservative, More and West were interested in dignifying middle and upper-class women's social role, and their conduct writings show a correspondent emphasis on women's "usefulness" in the areas of household management and charity. Yet, in conjunction with this increased dignity, both endorse a hierarchical structuring of the domestic sphere and rigid prescriptive limitations on what constitutes the feminine character; modesty, retirement, acquiescence, and selflessness become naturalized components of femininity.

Given this model of femininity, a particular textual problem faces the female novelist who advocates it: the adoption of the narrative authority necessary to the construction of a fictional text entails a subversion of the acquiescent ideal. Further, in order to be didactically effective, an antirevolutionary text must be authoritarian: the narrator must maintain strict control, as far as that is possible, over the reader's production of meaning by adopting a position of moral and exegetical authority. Susan Sniader Lanser's concept of "authorial voice" is relevant here: "I want to suggest as a major element of authorial status a distinction between narrators who engage exclusively in acts of representation—that is, who simply predicate the words and actions of fictional characters—and those who undertake 'extrarepresentational' acts: reflections, judgments, generalizations about the world 'beyond' the fiction, direct addresses to the narratee, comments on the narrative process, allusions to other writers and texts." This narratorial mode, which emphasizes "'extrarepresentational' acts" over representation, works to "expand the sphere of fictional authority to 'non-fictional' referents and allow the writer to engage, from 'within' the fiction, in a culture's literary, social, and intellectual debates." This aspect of authorial voice—intervening in cultural debate in the hope of effecting change—constitutes the essential component of antirevolutionary fiction. In order to be effectual, then, the antirevolutionary text by women must be authorial, thereby necessarily transgressing its own ideological limits of the feminine. Alison Case figures this problem in terms of "preaching" and "plotting," both of which were problematic acts for women in eighteenth-century culture, and which became the main obstacles to female narration. If, she argues, "[w]omen's virtue in the period was more concerned with *being* than *doing*," then "assuming the control over events necessary to shape them into a 'story'" becomes morally suspect.[4] Antirevolutionary women writers, who "plotted" in order to "preach," engaged in a series of literary negotiations intended to reconcile their narrative acts with conservative models of feminine virtue.

Women like West and More, who were overtly implicated in the production of antirevolutionary ideology, confronted the urgent demand that their fictional efforts align ideologically with their more polemical texts, or at least with a clearly defined network of ideals that existed "beyond" the narrative. This chapter charts the differing ways that women writers attempted to address this technical and ideological challenge. The narrative voice of their novels is the site of intersecting ideologies of gender, class, and genre; focusing on this conflictual intersection illuminates the relationship between the three categories. How gender and class ideologies affect narrative strategies, and how, in turn, these ideologies become textual through "ideologically charged technical practices" is my interest in this chapter.[5]

MASCULINITY AND NARRATIVE AUTHORITY IN *COELEBS IN SEARCH OF A WIFE*

"[P]robably the best-selling novel by a woman was then Hannah More's *Coelebs in Search of a Wife*," writes Lanser of the early 1800s, "in which, if I may put it crassly, a male narrator tells women how to please men." This assessment of Hannah More's narratorial practice in her single novel, *Coelebs in Search of a Wife*, is fundamentally correct, if "crass": in this text, a young Evangelical man is both narrative authority and judge of womanhood, the conveyer and legitimizer of the authoritarian messages of the text. What is intriguing and unusual in this novel, however, if it is read in context with More's other works, is precisely this particular masculinized form of narration. As Kathy Mezei argues, "[m]arking or unmarking the sex and gender of the heterodiegetic, autodiegetic, or homodiegetic narrator matters and has always mattered," and More's use of gendered voice here is an essential and strategic component in her negotiation of issues of class and gender.[6] In her didactic nonfictional works More uses an authoritative, mentorial, female voice, through which she engages in overt extrarepresentational acts: she comments not only on the education and role of women, but on religion, politics, and war. The discrepancy between her authority and agency, and the retirement she prescribes for her readers, has prompted some critics to read her as an "enigma" or a "paradox."[7] An early feminist identification of this anomaly configures the problem in this way: "In her printed works . . . she consistently rejects the idea of equality of the sexes and of public careers for women—though apparently she means *other* women." Even sympathetic contemporaries, like Laetitia Matilda Hawkins, questioned More's propriety in advocating narrative and verbal restraint, while engaging in public expression across literary genres. "Does she hold out instructions to others that she does not chuse to submit to?" asks Hawkins. "She is then a very improper teacher."[8] The potential conflict between conservative gender ideology and female authority is ignored or overlooked by More in her educational texts: she speaks in an authoritarian mode to readers of all classes, as well as to the monarchy (in *Hints Towards the Education of a Young Princess*, published in 1805 and written for the young Princess Charlotte).

More's early attempts at didactic fiction, the Cheap Repository Tracts for the poor (1795–98), are closer in narrative tone to More's nonfictional didactic texts than to *Coelebs in Search of a Wife*. Here, the narrative voice is heterodiegetic and ungendered, though it has been read as female: Mitzi Myers, for example, terms More's narrative voice a "compassionate yet corrective *maternal* instructor." In Lanser's sense, the narrator of the tracts is truly "authorial": authoritative and heterodiegetic, but with close implied links to the female author herself. The Cheap Repository project was an attempt, in Susan Pederson's terms, to make "an explicit bid for upper-class leadership in the moral reform of the poor."[9] As such, the tracts spoke to the poor from a mentorial position, teaching them the necessity of patriotism, piety, industry, and, perhaps most importantly, an acceptance of a rigid social hierarchy in which mobility was restricted.

In all of her writing, More carefully aligns religious with class and political concerns, so that Christianity both endorses a naturalized social hierarchy, and becomes the means for controlling a restless population: "there is something so safe and tranquillizing in Christian piety," she writes in *Hints Towards Forming the Character of a Young Princess*, that "it can hardly fail to promote, in the people, the ends of true policy."[10] In the wake of the French Revolution, "tranquillizing" the proletariat became, in More's view, essential to the maintenance of the social order. The Cheap Repository Tracts teach the implied working-class reader that Christianity demands acceptance of the social order, and that discontent is an offense against God. Positive exemplary characters are those like Patient Joe, the Newcastle collier, who accept their lot, however difficult, without complaint—indeed, with gratitude. Each of More's texts promotes a hierarchical social order and insists upon the individual's submission to his or her position within it. In *Strictures on the Modern System of Female Education*, she teaches young ladies "of rank and fortune" their proper place: subordinate to fathers and husbands in the home, yet in a position of moral authority over the working people and the poor of their communities. More's novel, *Coelebs*, inculcates this lesson of acceptance, not only through direct narratorial comment and the example of positive characters, but also through the atypical strategy she utilizes in the narration of the text.

Although she registers her discomfort with it as a vehicle for the communication of moral lessons, More clearly recognizes the more stringent formal restraints of novelistic fiction. Despite the still relatively low cultural position of the novel as genre, it seems apparent that More was aware she was shifting genres, from the working-class forms of tract and broadsheet that she used for the Cheap Repository Tracts, to fictional prose with a more "respectable" literary tradition. For the new form, More uses a masculine voice, one that allows her to access male social and literary authority, and, as Claudia Johnson has intimated, makes it possible to display her learning without transgressing the boundaries of female modesty. Gary Kelly points out that "the sex of the author played a fundamental role in determining the import of a particular text for readers: women venturing into topics and genres gendered masculine were uniformly condemned; men venturing into topics and genres gendered feminine were usually seen as conferring new dignity and seriousness on them." By invoking Milton at the opening of her text, and Johnson, Shakespeare, and Dryden, among others, throughout, More positions her narrative within a canonized, masculine literary tradition. More's allusions to and engagement with Milton, argues Edith Snook, "signal and reinforce a hierarchy of authority between herself and male writers."[11] A male narrator obscures the relationship between More's novel and the domestic and sentimental novel by women, a category in which this text clearly belongs. She thereby avoids a gendered blending of voice with more subversive writers like Mary Wollstonecraft and Mary Hays, as well as with her many respectable but less respected "sister novelists."

The difference between the two strategies of narration—the feminine and the masculine voice—indicates, first, what may seem obvious, that narrative authority changes according to the social and cultural context of the narrator—what position she or he speaks from—and importantly, the position of the implied narratee. The gender of the narrator is a central criterion in establishing narrative authority, and the choice of gender by an author determines, at least in part, the way in which the story may be told and the lesson may be taught. Thus, when More addresses young women in her nonfictional prose, or the poor in the Cheap Repository Tracts, the necessity of conveying her message, as well as her social position above her readers, justifies her adoption of an authoritarian female voice. She assumes a strict conception of rank and hierarchy that encompasses both gender and class: her narrative authority is predicated upon this construct, while her narratorial strategies do the ideological work of reinforcing it. Therefore, when she shifts to a "literary" genre with a potentially wider reading audience, she adopts a voice that carries a greater share of social and cultural authority due to its gender and class: in short, a gentleman's voice.

Coelebs has been described as a novel "in which a male narrator so self-authorizing that he is his own introducer and editor is presented . . . as the ultimate expert on Christian womanhood." Eleanor Ty frames her discussion of *Coelebs* in psychoanalytic terms, but also emphasizes the sense of many readers that the narrator, Charles, is (almost offensively) autonomous in his authority: "More adopts not only a masculine point of view in terms of narrative technique, but also what Irigaray calls the specularizing tendency of the 'male imaginary,' which focuses on itself as the centre or 'sun.'" It is indeed true that the autodiegetic narrator is authoritative, judgmental, and, ultimately, the teacher and conveyer of the text's didactic message. In this sense he acts, to use Suleiman's term, as the text's narratorial "ideological 'supersystem.'" The primary narrative of *Coelebs* makes this role possible: Charles, the protagonist and narrator, who is "a young man, not quite four and twenty, of an ancient and respectable family, and considerable estate in one of the northern counties," engages in a quest to find an acceptable wife.[12] Much of the didactic narrative is comprised of interpolated tales and descriptions of positive or negative exemplary women and marriages. Charles encounters stock negative figures such as the hoyden (1:333), the "Amazon" (2:82), the learned lady (1:47), the accomplished miss (1:66), and the religious hypocrite (1:118), among others, on visits that he considers to be "lessons" (1:129), and his response to each acts as a guide to the reader, indicating the correct interpretation of exemplary passages. The novel concludes with an outline of the ideal woman (Lucilla Stanley) and her family (who, as a unit, are also exemplary) and Charles's appropriate response is (rationally) to fall in love with her. The narrative closes with the approaching nuptials. More's primary message, which promotes the ideal of a femininity that is elegant, sensible, prudent, well-informed, well-bred, consistent, and pious (1:23), is thus conveyed through Charles's function as judge and discriminator of women. His final choice of Lucilla reinforces these ideals: she is "from nature—a woman, gentle, feeling, animated, modest.—She is, by education, elegant, informed, enlightened.—She is, from religion, pious, humble, candid, charitable" (1:239). More's didactic strategy here is simple: appropriate Evangelical femininity is rewarded by the interest of the authoritative narrator, and consequently with marriage. The teleological courtship plot lends weight to the didactic message.

Despite the considerable moral, political, and narrative authority assumed by More's narrator, the argument that he is entirely self-authorizing is not complete. By the term "self-authorization," Lanser means to suggest that, unlike many female narrators, the male narrator of *Coelebs* does not limit his "personal authority by appealing to (masculine) authorities outside the self."[13] In fact, Charles's authority is partly constituted through two acts of deference: to his deceased father, and to his father's best friend and the father of Lucilla, Mr. Stanley. This deference to parental authority determines the shape of the plot, and, to a certain extent, the form of the narrative, as Charles's voice is supplemented by the older mentorial voice of Mr. Stanley. The female narrator of the Cheap Repository Tracts gains authority by her social and class location; yet, when More speaks in a masculine voice, she is equally careful to place her narrator within a set of hierarchical social relations. Her adoption of a masculine narrative voice is thus not a simple appropriation of a position of unequivocal authority.

The catalyst for the plot of *Coelebs* is Charles's father's desire that he seek an appropriate wife, one comprising the virtues of More's ideal woman. It is not until the conclusion of the narrative, however, that the full extent of paternal influence is revealed. Through a posthumous letter, Charles's father informs him that he has been raised and nurtured to become the husband of the woman he has in fact chosen to marry: Lucilla Stanley, who has herself been programmed to become Charles's wife. Mr. Stanley corroborates the paternal assertion: "Without too much indulging the illusions of hope, we agreed that there could be no harm in educating our children for each other; in inspiring them with corresponding tastes, similar inclinations, and especially an exact conformity in their religious views" (2:304). Although Charles is the narrator, the "authors" of the narrative are his father and Stanley, who are the instigators and designers of narrative events, as well as of the text's marital conclusion.

More's use of dialogue is also significant when we attempt to understand Charles's narrative authority. Like the female narrators described by Lanser who appeal to "(masculine) authorities outside the self," Charles invokes masculine authorities, often deferring entirely to Mr. Stanley, whose lengthy explanations of points of moral and theological importance constitute notable breaks in narrative continuity. In arguments and discussions in the earlier part of the text, before his arrival at Stanley Grove, Charles "constantly adduced the paternal authority for opinions, which might favour too much of arrogance without such a sanction" (1:57). After the introduction of Mr. Stanley in chapter 13, More shifts the moral authority to his voice, and he speaks most of the lessons of the text: on women's education (1:195; 1:340; 1:386–93; 2:420; 2:229–49); religion (1:267–78; 2:208–27); the female "character" and role (2:96–98; 2:183); and literature (2:155–57). With the exception of a single sentence from Charles, the narrative concludes with a letter from Mr. Stanley on the importance of a religious, rational education for girls. While Charles's discrimination helps to impart More's didactic message by separating good women from the bad, Mr. Stanley's voice provides the text's coherent and comprehensive statements on the education of women, and on female character; he thereby becomes the text's privileged speaker of moral truths, and shares the function of "ideological 'supersystem'" with the narrator.

By locating the narrators of each of her texts within a network of social relations in which youth defers to age, female to male, wife to husband, children to parents, and the working classes to the middle class, More's narratorial practice itself provides a concrete example of the social order she approves and wishes to impose on British society. Her choice of narrator allows her to defend emphatically those distinctions that are central to her social philosophy: gender and class. This careful solidification of hierarchy is intended to prevent the actualization of More's greatest fears, "leveling" and democracy, yet it also may function as an antidote to the destabilizing effects of the novel form itself. The phenomenal success of *Coelebs* ensured that More's didactic message reached a large reading public, and it is unlikely that it would have been as effective in any other form. Indeed, Sam Pickering Jr. argues that this novel made the genre acceptable to a large segment of the "respectable" middle class who previously rejected it.[14] More's narratorial strategy works to counteract the potential corruption she and others perceived in the generic form. By locating the source of the narrative of courtship, and the power for shaping narrative events, in mentorial father figures, More submits her novel, in theory, to the surveillance and guidance of patriarchs; she also neatly divorces the domestic novel form from its feminine context, separating her text from its potentially subversive analogues. Her narrative is controlled and guided, and ultimately legitimized, by the narrator's submission to the voices and influence of fathers.

Gender and Authoritative Voice: The Ambivalence of Elizabeth Hamilton

Like *Coelebs in Search of a Wife*, Elizabeth Hamilton's satiric *Memoirs of Modern Philosophers* uses a masculine narrator, but the two texts provide an instructive contrast to one another in their strategies for achieving narrative authority. It is important to note at the outset that Hamilton's antirevolutionary philosophy differs from More and West's in quality, to the extent that she has been termed a "liberal" by one critic, while another argues that her ostensible conservatism masks radical ideas: "Hamilton, then, may be speaking for both sides of the argument even though on the surface, her case is a conservative, Christian one."[15] Unquestionably, Hamilton is an anti-Jacobin, and the lessons of her novel inculcate ideals of hierarchy, rank, and order, yet several exemplary characters in the *Memoirs* argue for the validity of some passages of the "*New Philosophy*."[16] A "gentleman of great worth and knowledge" calls Godwin's *Political Justice* an "ingenious, and in many parts admirable, performance" (1:xiv); and the exemplary Henry Sydney defends Wollstonecraft's *Vindication of the Rights of Woman* for its critique of Rousseau. The problem with the text, he argues, is that "the very sensible authoress has sometimes permitted her zeal to hurry her into expressions which have raised a prejudice against the whole" (1:196). Henry's commentary concludes, as Eleanor Ty has pointed out, with a direct refutation of the wild criticisms of Wollstonecraft in Richard Polwhele's *Unsex'd Females* (1798), and an attack on Polwhele himself[17]: "To superficial readers it appears to be her intention to unsex women entirely" (1:196). Ultimately, Hamilton offers an anti-Jacobin critique of the new philosophy, which advocates a thoughtful (but nevertheless oppositional) rather than reactionary response to radical thought.

The narrator of the *Memoirs* is heterodiegetic, compared to More's autodiegetic voice. The narrator, when he refers to himself, uses the editorial "we," engages in occasional metafictional commentary, and often addresses the reader directly; he thus fits Lanser's category of the "authorial" voice. Like other antirevolutionary novelists, Hamilton has a lesson to teach, and her narrator therefore engages in the authoritarian practice of drawing moral conclusions from events in the narrative. As clearly as Coelebs, but more subtly, the narrator acts as a supersystem, attempting to control the didactic impact of his text through direct commentary ("Alas, poor Julia! how deplorably ignorant was she" [1:263]), or by the use of embedded statements: "she very quickly perceived the fatal consequences of yielding to the suggestions of a distempered fancy" (2:95). The narrator is also clearly, though subtly, gendered: at one point in the three-volume novel, the narrator refers to "us lords of the creation," locating himself— perhaps ironically— among men (2:142). Elsewhere, an imaginary interlocutor includes the narrator (and the implied author) under the rubric "men authors" (1:108). Hamilton further distances her narrator from her own gender through the use of prefatory material. In an address to the bookseller, the "editor" of the text, Geoffry Jarvis, a man of "old notions" (and thus a voice for conservatism) (1:viii), describes the circumstances under which he "found" the manuscript: it was the ultimate production of a dying man who lived in a garret in London. Jarvis rescued it from the landlady's thoughtless destruction, and though the "first fifty pages having been torn off to kindle the morning fires, made a mighty chasm in the work . . . the remaining fragment appeared to me so worthy of being laid before the public, that I quickly conceived the design of becoming its editor" (1:xii). The subsequent approval of a "gentleman of great worth and knowledge" (1:xii), who noted the manuscript's "design" of "supporting the cause of religion and virtue" (1:xiii), encouraged him to publish the work. The preface carefully locates literary, philosophical, and moral judgment with men: the author, the editor, and the advising friend, not to mention "Mr. Robinson, Bookseller," who, with great foresight, published the manuscript. Conversely, the landlady sees only the practical value of the manuscript—as kindling—and is ignorant of its more esoteric, ideological value. The preface constructs a moral authority for men, which legitimizes the text of the narrator, who is identifiably masculine.

Hamilton's text is "masculine" in more ways than this, however, and differs on a generic level from the typical female antirevolutionary novel. She uses basic and broad satiric techniques (caricature, ironic allusion, inversion) clearly directed at readers educated in the interpretation of satire. Satire in the tradition of Fielding and Smollett is typical of male anti-Jacobin novels. Hamilton's use of the satiric philosophical dialogue has the effect of aligning her text with those of male anti-Jacobins, in apparent opposition to "female philosophers" like Mary Hays and Mary Wollstonecraft. Hamilton is thus able to adopt the authority of a "masculine" text by using several different strategies, and to solidify her moral lesson with an authoritative voice; gender, authority, and meaning are intimately entwined in her text.

The body of Hamilton's narrative provides a context for the problem of female narration, and suggests why a masculine narrative voice, and a masculinized discourse, fulfills her didactic purposes more completely. Like many of the conduct manuals and novels of Hamilton's contemporaries across the political spectrum, the narrative of *Memoirs* both supports women's education and expression, and restricts it within specific, marked boundaries. These boundaries are illustrated, as in *Coelebs*, by reference to characters constructed as exemplary figures of conformity or transgression. The novel opens *in medias res*, due to the landlady's assaults on the text, during a conversation involving the novel's ostensible "heroine," Bridgetina Botherim. Bridgetina, a "female philosopher" (1:57), is a parody of the radical writer Mary Hays (with debts to Mary Wollstonecraft). Hamilton's footnotes make frequent reference to Hays's *Memoirs of Emma Courtney*, the title of which appears in parodic form in Hamilton's title. Bridgetina is indebted to Hays "for some of her finest thoughts" informs one note (2:83), while elsewhere she quotes full passages from *Emma Courtney* (2:398–99). Another obvious echo in the title is Godwin's *Memoirs of the Author of "The Rights of Woman"*, the scandal of which would have been at its height at the time Hamilton was composing her satire. Wollstonecraft's *Vindication of the Rights of Woman* appears throughout Bridgetina's discourse in a simplified and exaggerated form, and is made to advocate women's dereliction of domestic duty, or "bondage" as Bridgetina describes it: "Ah, miserable and deplorable state of being, in which these [women's] powers are debased by the meanness of household cares! Ah, wretched woman, restrained by the cruel fetters of decorum! Vile and ignoble bondage! the offspring of an unjust and odious tyranny, a tyranny whose remorseless cruelty assigns to woman the care of her family!" (1:196). Bridgetina's beliefs are made absurd through her unthinking adherence to and self-serving exploitation of them, as well as through her ridiculous and outlandish appearance: "'Beauty, madam . . . is a consideration beneath the notice of a philosopher' . . . continued she [Bridgetina], drawing up her long craggy neck so as to put the shrivelled parchment-like skin which covered it upon the full stretch" (1:195).[18]

Bridgetina's doting mother indicates early in the novel where her daughter belongs on the scale of domestic utility: "she is far too larned [sic] to trouble herself about doing anything useful" (1:3). Her primary flaw, as well as her primary narrative characteristic, is her propensity to talk too much on philosophical topics, at inappropriate times, ignoring the social signals of others. She rejects both the domestic role of women and antirevolutionary ideals of femininity, and the discrepancy between the conservative ideal and Bridgetina's textual "reality" provides the basis for her satirization. The implications for a narrative that deals extensively and authoritatively with philosophy are clear: an adoption of a feminine narrative voice would bring the narrator into alignment with Bridgetina, who dominates discourse, and would thereby transgress the feminine ideals established elsewhere in the text.

Harriet Orwell is the positive exemplary figure in this novel, and she is contrasted with Bridgetina through explicit juxtaposition in the narrative. Harriet is the actual love object of the man Bridgetina desires, and the two women are portrayed in similar activities, such as nursing the sick, at which Harriet excels and Bridgetina, predictably, fails miserably (2: chaps. 2, 3). Harriet is "lovely" (1:21), "amiable," and "considerate" (2:12), and her actions prove her to be well-bred, well-educated, charitable, and modest. Further, she "had too much delicacy and good-sense officiously to obtrude her opinions, even upon her most intimate friends" (2:42). This positive attribute is the site of a problem within Hamilton's novelistic feminine ideal, and helps to illuminate the problem of female narration. The issue on which Harriet is delicately silent turns out to be tragic: the badly educated Julia Delmond is subsequently ruined, and dies, pregnant and penitent, at the end of the final volume. Certainly, Harriet's "good-sense" promotes the instructive lesson of Julia's death (though, as Nicola Watson points out, bearing the name "Julia" is in itself almost invariably a death-sentence in the anti-Jacobin novel); yet Harriet's exemplary character is drawn into question by its demonstrated inability to effect real moral change. Her ineffectuality supports Ty's contention that Hamilton critiques as well as supports prevalent conservative ideals. The text's female ideal is patently flawed and unable to impose moral order; her exemplarity is drawn into question, as is the validity of those ideal females she resembles, from Hannah More and Jane West's conduct books, and from antirevolutionary didactic novels.

In terms of narration, which in a didactic, authoritarian novel, consists of obtruding opinions on the reader, adhering to a feminine narrative voice would necessarily place that voice beyond the limits of the appropriately feminine. The benefit of a male narrator, therefore, is that the device enables an unproblematic display of learning, as Claudia Johnson has noted in the case of More's *Coelebs*. It also makes less problematic the authoritarian narratorial function of moral exegesis; Hamilton's narrator easily and authoritatively addresses questions of morality, philosophy, and literature. As Gary Kelly has noted, in her wide-ranging critique, and her utilization of masculine discourses and genres, Hamilton is herself "something like the kind of 'female philosopher' she deplores"; therefore, the anonymously published first edition allowed her to elide the problems of gender and transgressive narrative authority.[19] When the second edition of the very successful *Memoirs* came out in late 1800, Hamilton's name appeared on the title page, and a prefatory "Advertisement" explained her former authorial anonymity: she was "sensible that . . . prejudice against the known opinions, or even the *sex*, of a writer may unwittingly bias the reader's mind" (1:iii). A conventional feminine excuse for writing—"To divert the languor of sickness in the seclusion of a country retirement" (1:iv)—follows, and this stereotypical explanation of female literary generation contrasts noticeably with the "masculine" discourse of the original text.[20] The necessity for this apology is further evidence of the usefulness of Hamilton's narratorial strategy, and the preface itself works to destabilize the careful gendering of her narrative. The narrative authority achieved in the first edition is compromised by the addition of Hamilton's name on the title page, and provides a cogent reminder of the role of context and gender in the construction and maintenance of narrative authority.

Jane West and the Paradoxical Authority of the Gossip

Jane West differs from both Hannah More and Elizabeth Hamilton by utilizing an overtly female narrative voice in her novels. Novels by revolutionary women writers of the period commonly use a female narrator, a textual decision that becomes a radical act. Mary Wollstonecraft uses female narrators to explore female subjectivity and to illustrate the "wrongs of woman" in *Mary* and *Maria*. Mary Hays's *Memoirs of Emma Courtney* is likewise narrated by a woman, and the first-person narration allows an intimate representation of female thought and desire. West's texts represent an attempt to access narrative authority without disguising or obscuring the author's gender, while at the same time avoiding the radical implications of foregrounding a female voice. For this reason her novels are vital to a study of narrative authority in the fiction of conservative women, and are as instructive for the ways in which they fail as for their narrative successes.

Mrs. Prudentia Homespun is the narrator of West's five novels published between 1793 and 1810. Prudentia's advanced age gives her the authority to speak as a mentor; and West carefully constructs her implied audience as female, and, in most cases, as young, allowing her to take advantage of the unequal relations of power between younger and older women, which justify the adoption of an authoritative voice. Her first novel, *The Advantages of Education* (1793), for example, is subtitled "A Tale for Misses and Their Mamas," foregrounding the mentorial role of the narrator and her authoritative position in relation to her readers. West is also careful to situate her narrator on the margins of the social structure: Mrs. Prudentia lives, as she tells us in *A Gossip's Story*, in "a small market-town called Danbury, in the north of England"[21]—which makes her geographically marginal, at least in relation to London and the south—and she is a self-described "old maid," who lives at the edges of a social formation predicated on the nuclear family as a basic unit. As More does in *Coelebs*, West presents her narrator as autonomous and authoritative due to her position in relation to a hierarchical social structure. West's narrator, however, finds her authority on the boundaries of the hierarchy rather than within it.

Unmarried women hold a privileged position both in West's fiction and in her educational writing. In her conduct book for girls, *Letters to a Young Lady*, West writes wistfully of the possibilities available to women without husbands, but concludes regretfully that women are created by God to be wives. Of "old maids" she writes: "Destitute of nearer ties, and unfettered by primary obligations, the whole world of benevolence affords a sphere for their actions, and the whole circle of science offers to adorn their minds. It seems, indeed, difficult to pourtray [sic] a more enviable being, than a single woman possessed of affluence, who has passed through the tempest of youthful passions with untainted character, unvitiated temper, and unfettered heart."[22] This paean to broader spheres is necessarily limited by the carefully defined boundaries of the unmarried woman's life, which demand an Evangelical vigilance over female desire and character. The expanded sphere itself is contained within the appropriately feminine field of "benevolence"—though "science" seems to offer an undefined area for development—and is dependent upon the material condition of affluence. It is in the repetition of the adjective "unfettered," however, that West's understanding of the "old maid" becomes clear. Situated within a lengthy discourse on the responsibilities and duties of marriage—which bring a sense of usefulness rather than enjoyment—this portrait of the role of the single woman promises unusual freedom. Her primary role is as a friend or a benefactor, and she is rarely, except within an extended family, subordinate. She therefore holds an anomalous social position, on the margins of—though as a woman still subject to—the system of power relations that underwrite domestic hierarchy.

This unfettered woman was, for the most part, a construct, perhaps the product of wishful thinking by the busy, married, mother and writer. Even given the fortunate circumstance of independent means, women were often bound in relations of subordination to family members, and their actions were limited by the ideological imperatives of class and gender. We return, then, to the boundaries that circumscribe the "old maid." Yet it is the unfettered construct West draws on in her utilization of Prudentia Homespun as narrator; she is a woman of modest but independent means, who lives in a town that seems to prefigure Elizabeth Gaskell's *Cranford*, in that it is "in possession of the Amazons." It is her distance from the nuclear family, and the resulting freedom that distance implies, that allows her to write. "As my annuity is regularly paid," she comments, "and my family consists of only myself, a female servant, and an old tabby-cat, I have but little domestick care to engage my attention and anxiety." In *A Tale of the Times*, her freedom from domestic constraints allows her to travel, and thus to access the source of the tragic story she relates in the body of the novel. Prudentia's liminal social status becomes the source of her narrative authority, and the condition that enables and impels the narrative itself. The irony of this authority is, as Susan Allen Ford notes, that Prudentia is "a giver of domestic advice without domestic ties of her own" who "speaks from a position that subjects her to no other—and, significantly, to no male—voice even as she recommends to women an acceptance of their subjection."[23]

West's second novel, *A Gossip's Story,* was published in 1796, and, even in its title, it foregrounds the issues that form the focus of this chapter: narration, in the generic designation "story"; and a female voice in "gossip," a word that itself contains in microcosm conservative anxiety about women's speech. The "story" of *A Gossip's Story* is of less interest to me here than the method of narration; it is a simply-structured didactic narrative that opposes two contrasting sisters, one prudent and the other "romantick." The exemplary tale predictably valorizes and rewards the former, while the latter's dysphoric plot culminates in misery, teaching the reader the lessons of self-discipline and prudence. In order to produce and to solidify the narrative authority required to support the novel's didactic purpose, the narrator of *A Gossip's Story* engages in a series of extrarepresentational acts. West's preface, for example, carefully frames Prudentia as a mentor and instructor, and draws endorsements from "ladies . . . of maternal character . . . [who] may be presumed to be judges of what is best adapted for the perusal of youth" (1:xiii). At the opening of an early didactic passage, Prudentia notes, "I have looked on life with deep attention," thereby establishing her capacity for judgment, and the basis for her pedagogical expertise (1:47). Her name foregrounds the qualities she claims make her a suitable mentor: prudence (in "Prudentia") and middle-class common sense ("Homespun").[24] From the opening pages, therefore, Prudentia is established as a moral authority, capable of guiding the reader to the appropriate interpretation of the events narrated.

Throughout the narrative, Prudentia supplies exegetical guidance, proving that specific causes, such as sensibility, lead inevitably to certain effects, such as unhappy marriages or familial disruption. Direct narratorial statements mark ideologically positive and negative behaviors or characteristics: "I do not hold forth this conduct as prudent" (1:81), Prudentia remarks of one character's snobbery, while another's usefulness is judged "superior excellence" (2:59). In Prudentia's "intrusively expressed views," as Claudia Johnson describes them, West achieves a significant level of moral and narrative authority.[25] In her authoritative voice, Prudentia becomes, like the narrator of *Coelebs*, an "ideological 'supersystem,'" and promotes a correct interpretation of the narrative as a whole. West's narratorial strategy is often effective, especially when narrative digression leads to authoritative commentary, yet her success elsewhere is questionable. No narrative, of course, achieves total closure, yet West's texts are marked by persistent subversions of the narrator's authority, which act to complicate and disrupt the narrative's overarching ideological purpose.

In her statement of moral intent at the opening of her text, West explains that her didactic object is "to expose to ridicule, CAPRICE, AFFECTED SENSIBILITY, and an IDLE CENSORIOUS HUMOUR" (1:ix). Problematically, in order to combat the latter, West positions her narrator in the negative exemplary position. Prudentia is introduced in chapter 1 as a member of a "*scandalous* club" that "meets three times a week, to communicate the observations which the levity of youth, the vanity of ostentation, or the meanness of avarice have suggested" (1:3, 1:2). As a gossip, Prudentia becomes aligned with what West in *Letters to a Young Lady* characterizes as "a species of detraction known by the name of gossiping, which is the general pest of all rural associations" (3:50). This portrait is qualified: Prudentia is more "good humoured and tender hearted" than her "lady associates," and is consequently less quick to judge harshly or thoughtlessly (1:3). Her membership in the "sisterhood" is, however, clear in her practice of circulating unverified information: "I have often," she reports, "though encumbered with my umbrella and pattens, carried a piece of intelligence round the town in the morning, which in the evening, I was forced to step out and contradict" (1:35). It is significant that this practice leads eventually to Prudentia's demise; the preface to *The Refusal* (1810), the last novel in which Prudentia appears, reports that she "never recovered from the illness occasioned by her plunging through the snow to tell Betsey Boldface, that Mr. Stanza had made a madrigal on her purple elbows."[26] These passages function exemplarily to mark the gossip's behavior as negative, and to devalorize her voice. The fact that Betsey Boldface ultimately becomes Mrs. Stanza, on the very day of Prudentia's untimely death, further undermines Prudentia's credibility as a conveyer of information, and as a narrator.

In terms of frequency, these subversive moments are rare: in the two-volume *A Gossip's Story* Prudentia shifts into a self-ironic "gossip" voice five times, maintaining for the greatest part of the narrative an "authorial" stance that is omniscient and morally authoritative. These few moments, however, are disproportionately influential in their disruption of narrative stability; even the mildest ambiguity may be subversive in an authoritarian novel, which requires reductive closure. What West effectively demands is that her narrator be read as two voices, one authoritative and exemplary, the other negatively-valorized or dysphoric. What makes the text so intriguingly complex in terms of its narratorial mode, is that both the negative exemplary figure—the gossip—and the authoritative voice whose "supersystem" determines the moral interpretation of the meaning of the gossip, are contained within a single identity. As April London notes, she is "at once a member of the gossips' circle and an ironic observer of the shifting grounds from which its judgements issue."[27] The narrative voice is thus dialogic and radically unstable, as its two facets compete with and modify each other, and persistently defy coherence and continuity.

The interplay between Prudentia's two opposing identities foregrounds the problem of women's voices in conservatism, and of women's voices in a dominant patriarchal culture; as Kathy Mezei has noted, "ambiguity, indeterminacy, and transgression" are in many ways essential to women's narratives. It also suggests a larger issue: the uncomfortable relationship among women, conservatism, and fiction during the post-French Revolutionary period. As Patricia Meyer Spacks has noted, in this novel "a gossip functions explicitly as the originator of compelling fictions."[28] The qualities that Prudentia characterizes as peculiarly suited to the exercise of gossip, are also ideal qualifications for a producer of narratives: "I have," she remarks, "a retentive memory, a quick imagination, strong curiosity, and keen perception. These faculties enable me not only to retain what I hear, but to connect the day-dreams of my own mind; to draw conclusions from small premises; in short, to tell what other people think, as well as what they do" (1:2). As Spacks notes, "the gossip thus typifies the novelist."[29] West's unusual narrative strategy serves to question not only the narrative authority of a female voice, but also the place of women in the production of fiction itself; by aligning the novelist with the narrator-gossip, she situates the potential for ideological instability—and therefore the disruption of the authoritarian text—in the feminine voice. If West accepted the novel form for its potential marketability, her anxiety around her exploitation of the genre is reproduced in the voice of the gossip.

The narration of *A Gossip's Story* suggests the instability of the position of a woman novelist within a conservative culture that places the authorial voice on the boundaries of the acceptably feminine. Hannah More circumvented this problem by adopting a masculine narrative voice in her novel, a strategy that allowed her to disguise her own "paradoxical" authority even as she portrayed an ideal of feminine submission and retirement in the almost voiceless Lucilla Stanley. Hamilton uses a similar strategy in *Memoirs of Modern Philosophers* by creating a masculine, heterodiegetic narrator, and the narrative distance produced this way allows her to elide potential conflict between femininity and authority. West's interest in "gossip" foregrounds the conflict between conservative ideology and the possibility for an authoritative female voice; and her failure, through the instability of her narratorial mode, to achieve fully the authoritarian demands of ideological fiction, marks the difficulty, for prominent conservative women, of achieving an authoritative voice in fiction. Ultimately, in *A Gossip's Story*, an authoritative female voice is imaginable but only partially representable, and the instabilities in West's narrative voice are a consistent reminder of her tenuous position at the intersection of gender, politics, and literary practice.

An attention to the intricacies of narration in novels by conservative women can help us to a broader understanding of the position of women writers in relation to conservative power structures during the Romantic period. Women were authorized by the conservative press to adopt an authoritative voice in print, as long as their didactic purpose recognizably aligned with the antirevolutionary effort. Conservative ideology, therefore, enabled a form of feminine agency in print. This authoritative voice, however, was carefully circumscribed, and women writers undertook a delicate negotiation of authority as they attempted to balance the demands of both genre and ideology. Narrative voice, as a site where ideologies of gender, class, and genre intersect, is a particularly fruitful area for analyzing the effects of ideology on narrative form. The next chapter examines developments in the use of narrative voice over a period of generic change, 1810–14, as the search for an effective vehicle for antirevolutionary didacticism led women writers to explore alternative forms of narration.

5

Antirevolutionary Didacticism, Formal Change, and Narration, 1810–14

"MRS. PRUDENTIA HOMESPUN, YOUR LORDSHIP KNOWS, IS DEAD AND buried," wrote Jane West to Bishop Percy in 1811. "I knew how to manage her calash and cane, but what to do with the ruff and farthingale I scarce know: however I will attempt it, and will hide my ignorance under the prudent caution of avoiding *minutiae*." The novel West is contemplating in this passage became *The Loyalists*, which was published in 1812 to mixed reviews, and which fulfills its didactic function by using historical analogy—the novel is set during the British civil war and interregnum period of the seventeenth century—to "recommend loyal and constitutional principles." This historical novel, like West's earlier domestic novels, is openly didactic. Its aim, according to its "Introductory Chapter," is to draw women into the battle against democracy by presenting the "domestic hearth" as its antidote ("the exercise of the milder virtues is imperiously called for in seasons of national alarm").[1] Despite her familiarity and long successful history with Mrs. Prudentia, West chose to shift narrative mode and genre for *The Loyalists* after seventeen years of publishing novels. The death of Prudentia deserves further examination, particularly since her disappearance occurs in a text marked by epistemological and narratological uncertainty. West's concerns about the fitness of the novel as a vehicle for sound doctrine are enacted here at the narratorial level, and provide the motivation for her shifts across novelistic genres that occur over the years between 1810 and 1814.

Prudentia's voice is clearly identifiable only in the introductory pages of *The Refusal* (1810), the last novel in which she appears. As a character, she is absent from the events of the story. The body of the narrative is related almost entirely in the third-person, with a minimum of didactic exegesis, and the text of the novel resists narratorial "intrusion" (with very minor exceptions). Yet Prudentia's presence is strongly marked in the "Introduction by the Editor" in this text, as a character rather than a narrator. The introduction itself is a multilayered text, in which levels of irony are, sometimes confusingly, intertwined. The "Editor," Eleanor Singleton, claims a close and lengthy relationship with Prudentia (a claim that seems to be borne out by Prudentia having left her five trunks and two "scrutoires" full of unpublished manuscripts as a legacy): "I was the depository of her secrets, the patient and wakeful hearer of all her manuscripts, the nurse of her geraniums and the protectress of her cat during her summer excursions."[2] Like Prudentia in *A Gossip's Story,* however, Eleanor quickly becomes an unreliable narrator; she reveals her vanity in her comparison of her own "face and nymph-like figure" to Prudentia's "beauties of the mind" (1:20), contradicting the (now obviously satiric) chapter heading, which reads: "Introduction by the Editor. A tribute from partial friendship to departed excellence, without any base admixture of envy or vanity, containing the life and opinions of the late Mrs. Prudentia Homespun" (1:1).

Prior to this, Eleanor has openly contradicted what loyal readers will know are the very basic tenets of Prudentia's social philosophy and moral aesthetic. Prudentia's novels, Eleanor insists, are *romans-à-clef,* based on Prudentia's appetite for prurient gossip: "In these delectable tales, truth and falsehood, calumny and flattery, are blended with such enchanting confusion, that all the world is at once enjoying the exquisite delight of finding out secrets, and hearing scandal, without undergoing the fatigue of morning visits, or evening dissipation. The equivocation of ambiguous delineation is so charmingly preserved in these compositions, that not only are reputations murdered with impunity, but all parties, though looking at the same magic lanthorn, see the caricature of their neighbours, without any one of them perceiving his own" (1:10). The echo of Swift here, in the updated "magic lanthorn" metaphor, marks the serious content of this passage: the fear that "improving" literature may miss its intended mark.[3] The rest serves both to emphasize Prudentia's project by stressing what it is not, and to undermine the teller. The discourse is dialogized, as is Prudentia's in *A Gossip's Story,* and remains unstable throughout the introduction, as the object of satire shifts from Eleanor Singleton (the vain old maid), to irresponsible aristocrats who undermine the basis of their power, to the "fashionable" set, and to reviewers. Eleanor's voice is by turns authoritative and suspect, sometimes conveying the satiric, didactic message, and alternately becoming the object of satire. This extraordinary introduction ends with a threat and an intimation of blackmail: "I now commend this compendium of secret history to the world with all its imperfections, and I assure the public, that unless some people whom I will not name, make it worth my while to be silent, I shall next time be less careful about personality" (1:44–45). Eleanor reveals her avarice by threatening to expose the "true" narrative, which the reader knows to be false, and titillates the reader with the suggestion that the generic boundaries between history, biography, and fiction are permeable and far from absolute.

It is not a complete surprise, then, that the next piece of prefatory material is concerned with precisely the question of truth in narrative. The "Introduction by Mrs. Prudentia" is described as "A Fragment" in the chapter heading, a circumstance that itself foregrounds the problems of truth and coherence in narrative. The epigraph, from Pope, describes the mingling of fact with untruth in speech:

> There, at one passage oft you might survey,
> A lie and truth contending for the way;
> And long 'twas doubtful, both so closely pent,
> Which first should issue through the narrow vent.
> At last agreed, together out they fly
> Inseparable now, the truth and lie.
>
> (1:46)

As an epigraph, this is problematic. Is it the choice of Mrs. Prudentia? Or is it, like the description of the "editor's" introduction, the product of an unidentified extrafictional voice?[4] More important is the question of what it refers to: there are at least two possible interpretations of the epigraph's relation to the introduction that follows. First, and simplest, is that the epigraph provides a summary of the introduction's contents: the body of the introduction is a reported conversation between Mr. Stanza, the poet, and the local doctor, who discuss the generic similarities between novelistic fiction and historical writing. Stanza's argument that history is unknowable and that the personal biases of the writer determine the form of the historical narrative are illustrated with reference to the obituaries in the *Gentleman's Magazine*, which are demonstrated to be distorted (1:54–57). Stanza's argument shares premises with postmodern historiography, but differs from it in his emphasis on "truth" as an essential category that is the ideal end of historical discourse. As Stanza comments: "When one acknowledged bias to any particular party, or system, is considered as laudable in an historian, you, my good friend, are I know too candid to look into his labours with an expectation of finding them to be the well in which you may discover truth" (1:50). His exercise of refuting points in the obituaries serves to illustrate the role of personal bias in reportage, especially when the considerable influence of class comes to bear on its production. The obituaries also provide the source for the novel's primary narrative, and Prudentia subsequently races Stanza to press with the life story of the deceased Lady Selina Delamore.

The story of Selina Delamore similarly foregrounds questions of truth in narration, and the dangers of hasty interpretation based on tenuous facts. Selina refuses to marry the Earl of Avondel because (as the reader discovers at the end of the novel) she is his half-sister due to a "guilty assignation" on the part of their father (3:238). In the absence of this information the Earl of Avondel speculates on the reason for Selina's refusal (the event foregrounded by the title of the novel), and concludes that she must be "polluted" (1:255). His bitterness over this conclusion leads to an unhappy marriage (coincidentally to Selina's niece), adultery, and, ultimately, his death in a duel. Selina is proved, by the novel's end, to be exemplary in her piety and virtue. The Earl's plot trajectory provides a harsh lesson in the dangers of misprision.

A second, broader interpretation of the epigraph is that it provides a commentary on the likelihood of unadulterated "truth" in Prudentia's introduction, in the text as a whole, or even in literature (in its broadest eighteenth-century signification) in general. As a narrative frame, the epigraph draws attention to the constructedness of the narrative that follows, and even of the prefatory material itself. The prefaces in this novel enact an extended meditation on the possibility of truth in fiction, on personal bias in narration, and on the reader's perception of narratorial veracity. The question posed by West's complex narrative strategies is: how does a novel convey an authoritarian, monologic message when it is unable to control the reader's production of meaning, including his or her interpretation of what constitutes the "truth"? Mr. Stanza in Prudentia's introduction reproduces the reader's role in the interpretation of fiction: his relatively sophisticated analysis of the writer's personal or party biases results in his acceptance or rejection of the text on the grounds of its "truth" or "falsehood."[5] Stanza's authority is supported by the number of pages his commentary occupies, and his ideological alignment with West's stance in previous texts. He states the primary problems of narration with the weight of didactic authority: "shall they pass for faithful narrators who, without any authentic document to support their assertions, invent motives which very likely never entered into the minds of the personages to whom they ascribe them, or who, on a few detached circumstances, founded on loose testimony, erect a magnificent system of ideal speculations?" (1:51). Stanza's rhetorical question, though it refers overtly to historical writing, accurately describes the process of writing a novel as described by Prudentia in *A Gossip's Story* ("[t]hese faculties enable me not only to retain what I hear, but to connect the daydreams of my own mind; to draw conclusions from small premises; in short, to tell what other people think, as well as what they do" [1:2]) and therefore serves to question the entire subsequent narrative.

Prudentia, in contrast, makes overt statements of the "truth" of her narrative. Her novel, she claims, draws on "copious and correct information" from an unnamed source, "as will enable me to fill three volumes (allowing for proper margins and amplifications) with the circumstances connected with this extraordinary lady" (1:60–61). It is hardly necessary to point out the potential for distortion inherent in "amplifications," and when she continues in the next sentence to deny any similarity to the "historians so severely treated by Stanza," the connection is made and her veracity undermined. Her subsequent statement that "when I am barren of materials I *dare not invent*" (1:61, West's emphasis) becomes ironic through contextualization. Prudentia's self-ironizing discourse also suggests personal bias in her narration of the novel, in the concluding sentence of the introduction: "And though I own it is undertaken with a determination of establishing the honour of our sisterhood ['spinsters'], I do not despair of occupying a high place among impartial historians" (1:62). Further, for the first time in any of West's novels, Prudentia refers directly to the financial and remunerative aspects of literary production, when she remarks the "vast advantage in being first at market" (1:61).

This web of authority and subversion, satire and self-irony, is further complicated by the narrator's assertion, in a rare moment of self-reflexivity well into the body of the narrative, that "one part of the moral I mean to enforce is, the folly and danger of drawing hasty conclusions" (1:82). One example of this "folly" is Stanza, who thoughtlessly condemns Lady Selina on hearsay, and the narrator's statement of moral and didactic intent forces a reconsideration of Stanza's authority in questions of historical truth. The many-layered problems of narrative authority that are unwound and explored in this prefatory text preclude the possibility of a reliable voice, and the authoritative certainty that a didactic text relies upon for its efficacy. A homodiegetic voice in particular is, the text implies, necessarily flawed, lacking in veracity and authority, an unstable and uncontrollable form of narrative discourse. A narrator's personal involvement in events, Eleanor Singleton shows, precludes her objectivity and therefore her narrative "truth," even if, as Stanza argues, narrative truth is a tenuous and barely attainable achievement at best.[6]

After the complexity of the introductions, the primary narrative comes as a relief. Despite the very rare occurrence of self-reflexivity, and the explicit suggestion in the introduction that the narrator be aligned with the voice of Prudentia Homespun, at no point do narrative levels intertwine. The novel takes place entirely on one narrative level (that of the events of the story), and the narrator is heterodiegetic. At no point do the destabilizing questions and narrative mode of the introductions contaminate the authoritative assurance of the prose. When the narrator states her moral intent it is unironic, and when, at various moments throughout the text, she comments on the progress of the plot, or on the morality of the characters, her voice carries unquestionable authority.

Why, then, are the introductions constructed apparently to cast doubt on the narrative act? First, the instability of the narration and reception of stories—especially "lives"—forms a key element in West's didactic message in this novel. Her text is presented as a corrective to inaccurate narratives that rely upon gossip and hearsay rather than thorough investigation of the "truth" (a truth that, in the case of the story of Lady Selina Delamore, serves to support a lesson in piety, loyalty, virtue, and patriotism). The introductions in this novel provide negative exemplary models of narration and interpretation, which are "corrected" by Prudentia's subsequent truthful version. Secondly, the unstable discourse of the prefatory material functions to undermine the possibility of truth in narration—most specifically in homodiegetic narration. Prudentia does not take part in the events of the narrative in this novel, and it is her absence from events that ostensibly gives her the objectivity to present the correct version, which carries a didactic message. The narrative that follows teaches another lesson, then: that a particular model of heterodiegesis, which moves toward a transparent narrator, equals objectivity, and that authority is achievable only through narratorial distance from the events narrated.

Resisting Narrative Distance: West and Hawkins

The problem with the Prudentia of *A Gossip's Story*, in terms of her authoritarian function, is in the homodiegetic content of her texts, in the moments in which she is present in the narrative. Her character in the novel carries the lessons of satire, while her heterodiegetic voice, which narrates the primary story line, carries didactic authority. Introducing an entirely heterodiegetic narrator would seem, then, to be an ideal solution to the problems of narrative authority posed by the homodiegetic mode. The erasure of Prudentia is, in this sense, a corrective to her earlier texts, and a bid to achieve greater narrative authority. The authority of the heterodiegetic over the homodiegetic mode is taken for granted by most readers of the novel, for the simple reason that while the homodiegetic mode may achieve a greater level of emotional and psychological realism, the events narrated are compromised by the narrator's perceived proximity to them. As Susan Sniader Lanser puts it in reference to "authorial" narration, "paradoxically, authorial narrative is understood as fictive and yet its voice is accorded a superior reliability, while personal narrative may pass for autobiography but the authority of its voice is always qualified." Susan Rubin Suleiman notes that in an "omniscient narrator who 'speaks with the voice of Truth' and makes explicit judgements . . . we have the clearest, least ambiguous manifestation of monologism." For this reason it is the most effective narratorial strategy in producing an "authoritarian" text that efficiently conveys a didactic message. A heterodiegetic voice is effective for women writers in particular, because it can obscure the gender of the narrating voice.[7] By using this narrative strategy, then, West solved a specific textual and didactic problem: the instability of Prudentia Homespun's narrative and moral authority.

In many cases, the heterodiegetic voice of the turn of the century is an "authorial" voice that comments authoritatively on events and ideas both fictional and actual, referring "outside" the narrative to make moral or political points. For women writers in particular, this shift can be seen as something of a triumph, because the authorial voice allowed them to engage actively with the political and public events of their historical moment. As Lanser has noted, women "worked 'up'" to this authoritative voice. Yet this is also a voice that required tact on the part of its female speaker. Lanser argues that Jane Austen, whose authorial *Northanger Abbey* was initially rejected, retreated from overt authoriality toward a more transparent and "indirect" form of narration in her subsequent novels, in which "covert" authoriality avoids occasions for readerly dissent. Austen's adoption of a new narrative style prefigures a similar, broader, development in narration during the first half of the nineteenth century. Novelists turned increasingly to a seemingly "objective" mode of narration in which the narrator is "transparent." The object of transparent narration is to create the illusion that the events of the narrative reach the reader without mediation; this is what Gerard Genette calls narrative "distance." A "distanced" narrator conveys the maximum of narrative information with a minimum of narratorial presence. It is therefore more mimetic than a narrative in which the narrator is obviously present (Genette calls a narrative in which little information is conveyed by a narrator who is present in the text "diegetic" as opposed to "mimetic," the emphasis being on the act of narration rather than on representation). The famous late-nineteenth-century differentiation between "telling" and "showing" exemplified by Henry James and Gustave Flaubert valorizes the transparency of the narrator; as Genette comments, "pretending to show is pretending to be silent."[8] James's ideal novel, the form of which was developing near the beginning of the century in the writing of Austen, was, therefore, a narrative that presented itself as almost unnarrated.

This is not to suggest that the novel lost its didactic purpose, however. In *The Novel and the Police,* D. A. Miller has argued that the novel became "conservative" during the nineteenth century. Miller's Foucauldian argument reads the nineteenth-century novel as a mechanism of social control; in his interpretation, the mainstream Victorian novel functioned in a "policing" role, asserting and defending conservative social norms, and is therefore deeply didactic. Yet the didacticism of the Victorian novel differs from the form of didacticism I explore in this study. The "serious" Victorian novel avoids the overtly didactic and authoritarian voice of the antirevolutionary novels of West and More, which appear naive in relation to the more highly developed forms of the later nineteenth century. Victorian novels sophisticate and obscure their own authoritarian intentions; the critically sanctioned form of the mid to late nineteenth century excludes the naive didacticism prevalent in novels of the turn of the century. In the Victorian novel, Wolfgang Iser notes, "the author had to use a variety of cunning strategems to nudge the reader unknowingly into making the 'right' discoveries." The period of Lanser's "authorial" novels, therefore, was succeeded over the following decades by novels in which artistic and narrative authority was often achieved through an erasure of the authorial narrator.[9] This is not, of course, to say that the homodiegetic voice disappeared entirely from the mainstream novel. Some of the most canonical Victorian novels, such as *Great Expectations, Jane Eyre,* parts of *Bleak House,* and (with a little more complexity) *Wuthering Heights,* are narrated in the first person. And, arguably, the feminine didactic novel can be traced to novels like Charlotte Brontë's *Jane Eyre,* Gaskell's *Mary Barton,* and the less canonical *Helen Fleetwood,* by Charlotte Elizabeth Tonna. Yet the type of authoritative and didactically referential female voice I describe here rarely appears in mainstream novels after the mid-1810s. What was lost in this process toward narratorial transparency was a sense of the immediacy of a narratorial entity; a connection between the world outside the novel and that inside; and, as I will argue here, a relationship between narrator and reader that was explicitly didactic, and unique to women's novels.

Several recent critics read this shift in the dominant narrative mode as a political process. For Nicola Watson, the change in narration to heterodiegesis is reflective of a social and literary "project of disciplining revolutionary energy"; she suggests that the new mode of narration worked to produce a sense of authority and order in the wake of the French Revolution, local and national economic crises, and social unrest. The heterodiegetic narrator in an antirevolutionary novel thus provides the voice of community and "objective" authority, in contrast to the personal, and potentially subversive, voices of homodiegetic and epistolary narratives. Gary Kelly, similarly, argues that anti-Jacobins utilized third-person narration to counter the radical subjectivity of Jacobin novels: "anti-Jacobin novelists use authoritative, often satirical third-person narration to formalize their ideal of a hierarchical but not autocratic society." According to Janet Todd, the authoritative "third-person method" allows "moral novelists" to "avoid the self-centeredness of sensibility."[10] With the authoritative and ideologically compatible discourse of heterodiegesis available to them, however, some conservative women writers persisted in retaining elements of homodiegesis in their novels. Examples of the retention of the absolute homodiegetic voice in addition to Hannah More's *Coelebs in Search of a Wife* include Elizabeth Le Noir's epistolary journal, *Village Anecdotes*, and Mary Brunton's 1814 conversion narrative, *Discipline*, both of which are highly successful didactic narratives. Between this mode and the purely heterodiegetic are transitional texts: novels in which the heterodiegetic mode is adopted for strategic reasons, yet in which the presence of the narrator remains—sometimes literally—in the margins, as in Laetitia Matilda Hawkins's novel, *The Countess and Gertrude* (1811). The movement toward heterodiegesis was, therefore, a complex one, even for conservative writers who were interested in "policing," to use Watson's term, the revolutionary nature of personal narratives. Watson's reading of West in particular suggests a simplicity of narrative and political intent, which, upon closer examination becomes extremely and interestingly complicated.[11] My interest here is in the ways in which the narratorial "distance" from the narrative offered by heterodiegesis is subtly subverted by writers who would seem most to benefit from its adoption. Unlike literary historians who interpret the replacement of homodiegesis by heterodiegesis as a replacement of the personal and subversive with the communal and conservative, I argue that elements of homodiegesis serve an important conservative didactic purpose within the novels of antirevolutionary women writers.

My contention here is that heterodiegesis, especially the "transparent" form exemplified by Austen, which seems to provide direct, unmediated access to characters and narrative events, is not necessarily the most effective form of narration for didactic writers. In part because of the critical position of Jane Austen as the exemplary novelist for this period (according to the conventional canon of the novel), it is difficult for modern readers to see the drawbacks of her subtle omniscient narrative style for writers who, unlike Austen, intend to teach a lesson. Austen has been a focus for modern feminist readings of women's prose of the Romantic period, in part because her position within the literary canon provides a critical rationale for examining women's novels. Her canonical status is partly due to her nondidactic narrative voice (which highlights the "unliterary" didacticism of her female contemporaries), as well as her apparently apolitical stance, and it is precisely these qualities that make Austen difficult to interpret, particularly by critics who attempt to place her writing in its social, cultural, and political contexts. The range of readings of her political location suggests exactly how problematic this narrative voice, based on free indirect discourse and narratorial "indirection," could be for a writer with a didactic agenda. Austen has been read as essentially anti-Jacobin by Marilyn Butler, and as deeply conservative by Anne Crippen Ruderman. Claudia Johnson reads Austen's writing as "depolemicized" rather than "depoliticized," and explores how Austen "smuggle[s] in" social criticism through indirection.[12] Austen's lack of overt "extrarepresentational acts," to use Lanser's term, necessitates a reading of subtler and less explicit narrative elements, such as characterization and indirect discourse. These readings constitute valuable contributions to a politics of form, yet the uncertainty around Austen's potential "message" demonstrates how her narratorial technique could be ineffective for writers whose primary aim is to teach a lesson. Unlike Austen, writers like Jane West and Laetitia Matilda Hawkins explore a more didactic model of narration, by attempting to bridge two narrative modes.

Prudentia Homespun provides one example of the persistent narratorial presence in nominally heterodiegetic texts. The problematic conflation of omniscient authority and homodiegetic voice, which I examined at length in the previous chapter, can also be read in terms of the broader shift in narration that is evident in the novel during the Romantic period. In her early novels, West accesses the authority of third-person narration in her relation of the primary events of the narrative; it is on the margins that Prudentia acts, in peripheral events in the village that do not impinge on the actions or plots of the main characters. During the early years of the nineteenth century, Prudentia's presence within the novels became less pronounced, and her voice became more strictly heterodiegetic; she remains a notable presence in West's novels, however, until her demise in 1810. West's transition to heterodiegesis was, therefore, hesitant. Prior to Prudentia's "death," the homodiegetic and heterodiegetic modes competed within her narratives, to the detriment of narrative coherence and the didactic message. Yet even after her final transition to heterodiegetic narration with the death of Prudentia, West retained textual space for a more personal voice. To use her own metaphor, her prefaces and afterwords "seem to be infected with the disease of the enchanted helmet of Otranto," and grow far beyond comparable pages in earlier novels.[13] West was clearly reluctant to present her novels to the reader without the benefit of mentorial mediation. The prefaces, advertisements, and afterwords in later novels such as *The Loyalists* and *Alicia de Lacy* provide authoritarian stability to her texts, by suggesting the correct way in which the narrative is to be interpreted.

Hawkins's novel, *The Countess and Gertrude*, is clearly a heterodiegetic narrative, through which the unnamed narrator—who refers to herself as "we" (she calls this "wegotism")—is a careful and excessive exegetical guide.[14] The novel itself is subtitled *Modes of Discipline*, a description that aptly indicates the narrative's didactic focus. The plot deals with the education of a young girl from a state of wildness to one of civilized propriety and internalized self-discipline, a trajectory that describes the purpose of most antirevolutionary novels for girls, in which self-discipline is represented as the basis for social stability. This text is what could be termed a "footnote-novel," in that much of the important information regarding the lessons to be taught by the narrative are located in copious footnotes. Many of these notes refer to stories from "real-life," which either corroborate the realism of a passage in the fictional text, or repeat a moral lesson to be drawn from the narrative. As the *Anti-Jacobin Review* commented in its review of the book, the figures in the notes take on the characteristics of "inferior characters."[15] In a sense, however, it is the narrator (or "implied author") herself who becomes an inferior character through the notes, in that she develops a presence beyond her narratorial function in the primary narrative. The heterodiegetic narration of the body of the novel is bounded by, and intimately linked to, the narratorial presence of the footnotes, which observes and judges, experiences and relates. The novel's discourse is effectively dialogized; the text is characterized by a continued conversation between the "reality" of the footnotes and the "fiction" of the narrative, and between the distanced narrator of the story, and the almost gossipy observer of "real life."

That women would continue to insert a narratorial "self" characterized by a certain degree of presence suggests that they intended to produce a particular narrative effect. One of the reasons for the persistence of a narratorial presence in the novels of West and Hawkins may be the pedagogical necessity of replicating an instructional situation in the didactic relationship between narrator and reader. These writers wrote in a tradition of women's didactic writing that assumed the preeminence of relationship in the successful transmission of moral lessons. It has often been noted that the moral novel of the Romantic period is a fictionalized conduct book; I would add that both genres—conduct book and didactic novel—depend upon an understanding between reader and narrator in which each adopts her appropriate position within a didactic relationship that refers outside the narrative. Both West and Hawkins were also authors of conduct books: Hawkins wrote her *Letters on the Female Mind* in 1793, in response to Helen Maria Williams's *Letters* from France; West wrote two critically approved and differently gendered conduct manuals, *Letters Addressed to a Young Man* in 1801, and its counterpart, *Letters to a Young Lady*, in 1806. These texts are characterized by an intimate relationship between the speaker and the reader—one that is exemplified in the form of the personal letter. The conduct manual refers outside the body of the text, to a particular configuration of the writer/narratee relationship, which is figured as an "actual" relationship existing in the real world. In West's case, she writes to a son and to the daughter of a friend, locating her texts within the network of local and familial relationships. The reader is invited (or commanded) to position herself with the narratee, as subject of an instructional relationship.

According to West's conduct book for girls, the ideal friendship for a young woman was an "unequal" one, in which the elder could give the younger valuable "reproof and advice." The mother/daughter relationship is an exemplary one for West, though, interestingly, mothers appear rarely in her novels.[16] West reproduces this relationship when she creates Prudentia Homespun as a type of "maternal instructor," to use

Mitzi Myers's term, or "monitor," to use her own.[17] Prudentia's presence within the texts she narrates mimics the narrative presence of the speaker in the conduct manuals, and invokes a similar extratextual relationship. The ultimate end of these novels is to produce a self-monitoring woman, who has been wholly and successfully subjected to a specific political and gender ideology. To achieve this end, West perpetuates the fictive relationship between teacher and pupil, between monitor and subject, reproducing the instructional moment in her narrative structure. This same relationship is implied in Hawkins's *Countess and Gertrude*, where the explanatory footnotes are a form of teaching through exempla. They function didactically in two separate ways: first, by enforcing the moral meaning of the narrative through repetition; and secondly, by foregrounding the implied author's experience, wisdom, and understanding, which legitimize the moral judgments made by the more distant narrator of the story. Hawkins's persistent reference to the "real" in these notes reminds the reader that morality has a social context, and that it is learned not merely within the pedagogical arena of the didactic novel, but also within the confines of the personal mentorial relationship.

During the final years of West's writing career in the 1810s and 1820s, the novel became increasingly professionalized, and the end of the Revolutionary Wars in 1815 decreased the immediate and obvious need for political tales. As a new model of realism developed that excluded the openly didactic and valued a more transparent form of narration, writers like West and Hawkins may have recognized the potential loss of didactic control inherent in the change. In an attempt to control the didactic effect of their novels, both invoked the narrative mode of their more monological conduct books. In the face of an increasing depersonalization of the narrative voice in novels, they adopted strategies that allowed them to straddle two forms of narration. In producing this form of "double-voiced" discourse, West and Hawkins attempted to access simultaneously two disparate sources of narrative authority. In their texts, authoritative third-person discourse is in conflict with the authority of the conduct book, which is gendered female, and which depends upon a carefully configured relationship between narrator and narratee. The latter voice, along with much that was overtly didactic, nearly disappeared from mainstream literature during the first half of the nineteenth century, while the distanced heterodiegetic voice, with its model of the relationship between speaker and reader that is less insistently referential, became the privileged mode of discourse. Tracing the disappearance of the didactic voice in the nineteenth-century novel may help to complete the story of the shifting basis of female literary authority during a period in which the novel became increasingly professionalized, legitimized, and masculinized. Within this context of change West and Hawkins, in similar ways, negotiated the problem of achieving literary authority without compromising a feminine didactic voice. They could not, however, negotiate the changing demands of the novel genre, as their particular form of didacticism lost credibility as a criterion of "serious" fiction. That both writers rapidly fell out of print is a measure of their lack of success in this venture, and evidence of the devaluation not only of didacticism, but of didactic feminine narrative authority.

6

Domesticity and the Feminine "Circle": Reading the Evangelical Novel, 1808–14

PREVIOUS CHAPTERS HAVE DEALT ALMOST EXCLUSIVELY WITH THE antirevolutionary didactic potential of a specific novelistic subgenre: the domestic novel. The domestic novel form, with its emphasis on women as subject and subjects, and on the "female" plot of courtship and marriage, provided an ideal vehicle for antirevolutionary writers' intervention in the political discourses of the period. The action of these novels occurs within domestic space, and therefore the models of domestic femininity they propose could easily be absorbed and imitated by female readers, most of whom also occupied the domestic sphere. Antirevolutionary novels politicize domestic femininity, drawing explicit links between female subjectivity and activity and the antirevolutionary project, drawing women (and especially young women, who are the novels' intended audience) into the battle against revolutionary theory and practice. This process of politicizing the domestic reconceptualizes the arena of political conflict, expanding it to include feminine spaces and players, while containing female activity within a redefined domestic sphere. The domestic novel form seems ideally suited, therefore, to the promulgation of a didactic message.

But what form does the antirevolutionary project take in a period when novelistic genres are shifting? The early nineteenth century was a period of generic change within the novel. The first two decades of the century saw the increasing centrality of the historical novel, popularized by Walter Scott, but already a developing form prior to the publication of *Waverley* in 1814. Maria Edgeworth pioneered the regional tale with *Castle Rackrent,* set in Ireland, and was followed by Jane Porter (*The Scottish Chiefs*) and Elizabeth Hamilton (*The Cottagers of Glenburnie*) in Scotland. The Evangelical novel, which Hannah More has been credited with inventing and popularizing with her publication of *Coelebs in Search of a Wife,* was another of these developing genres.

More's innovation was to use the domestic novel form to promote a specifically Evangelical didactic lesson. "*Coelebs* is fascinating," writes Christine Krueger, "as the first major effort to combine the forces of two media so volatile as the evangelical idiom and the novel."[1] Mary Brunton built on this model in her development of what has been termed the "Evangelical romance," which incorporates elements of romance while maintaining the central didactic purpose of More's more strictly domestic novel. Due to the proliferation of style and form, the search for the "vehicle" of "sound doctrine" became more complex after 1800, as antirevolutionary women writers continued to give political and social concerns fictional form. My interest in this chapter is in the implications of one of these generic changes, the development of Evangelical fiction, for a politicized antirevolutionary model of femininity and domesticity. Taking as my point of departure contemporary metaphors of the feminine domestic "circle," I explore the ways in which a heroine's move away from the domestic sphere, and the domestic plot, affects the structure of the "authoritarian" novel.

Domesticity and the Feminine "Circle"

> Women . . . in their course of action describe a smaller circle than men; but the perfection of a circle consists not in its dimensions, but in its correctness.
>
> Hannah More, *Coelebs in Search of a Wife*

> Why do we suffer ourselve[s] to be confined within a magic circle, without daring, by a magnanimous effort, to dissolve the barbarous spell?
>
> Mary Hays, *Memoirs of Emma Courtney*

These two passages, from opposite sides of the feminism debate of the Romantic period, demonstrate the divergent usage of the metaphor of a gendered "circle" (or, alternatively, "sphere") in discussions of women's "place." Hannah More's comment of 1808 has a note of consolation; it replaces the range and scope of male activity with "correctness" for women. While the metaphor of a "correct" circle implies restraint and control, it is important to bear in mind More's understanding of domesticity. For More, who helped to expand women's "circle" into the community through activities of philanthropy and education, the feminine, domestic circle was one in which some of the most valuable work in religion and national preservation was being done. Women's work at the local level, according to her philosophy, provided the basis for social stability and peace. For More, then, the feminine "circle" is restrictive, demanding "correct" behavior, but is also dignified by its very "correctness." Mary Hays, writing *The Memoirs of Emma Courtney* during the turbulent 1790s, uses the "circle" metaphor to emphasize the restrictiveness of separate gendered spheres, which bar women not only from male activities in the public sphere, but from education, discussion of many subjects (including politics), and affective responses such as desire or passion. While More, throughout her work, frames her discussion of separate "circles" within a theological context, arguing that this social model was decreed by God, Hays conceives of the "circle" in terms of "magic." This combined metaphor—of sorcery and circles—is structured to foreground the arbitrary and unnatural basis of gendered spheres. Hays's radical vision of domesticity breaks down the boundaries between sexes, obscuring gender differences and allowing women access to the broader circle of masculine activity and thought. That the eponymous Emma Courtney in the novel encounters tragic difficulty is a sign of the inadequacy of a society that denies women's equality, rather than a negative comment on the heroine's feminism.

The metaphor of the gendered "circle" was also in use at this time in postrevolutionary France. The context, however, was different. After the revolutionary government in France outlawed women's societies in 1793 because they were openly political, a contemporary French journal commented: "Each sex is called to the kind of occupation which is fitting for it; its action is circumscribed within this circle which it cannot break through, because nature, which has imposed these limits on man, commands imperiously and receives no law."[2] This use of the metaphor of the gendered "circle" is similar to More's, with the difference that it is grounded in an ideology of "nature" rather than in Christian theology. As British feminists were beginning to realize by the early 1790s, French revolutionary philosophy was primarily concerned with the rights of "man," rather than of humanity. The "natural" limits placed on man, however, affected both men and women. The rhetoric of "circles" was utilized equally by revolutionary writers in France and counterrevolutionary writers in England to justify the limitation of female activity.

What, then, does it mean for a woman of the Romantic period to move outside the female "circle" of domesticity? Is it necessarily a radical act? Mary Hays's Emma Courtney became an instantaneous model of all that is "unfeminine" in radical philosophy, when she moved outside the "magic circle" that confines female behavior and "affections."

Hays's literary transgression of this boundary made her a target of satire in the conservative press, as well as in novels such as Hamilton's *Memoirs of Modern Philosophers*. Even as late as 1811, Mary Brunton clearly drew on the sexualized metaphor of the "magic circle" that developed after Hays published *Emma Courtney*, when she warned: "Let the fair enchantress tremble who approaches even in thought the utmost verge of discretion. If she advance but one jot beyond that magic circle, the evil spirit is ready to seize her, which, before, feared even to rise in her presence."[3] For women who promoted an antirevolutionary agenda, transgression of the boundaries of gender was counterproductive and undermined their authoritarian purpose. Most, then, worked from within antirevolutionary conceptions of gender and gender roles, accepting women's domesticity as "natural," while reforming prevalent models of the domestic sphere. Thus, for Hannah More, the domestic "circle" became the site of philanthropy and community service, while for Jane West it was politicized as the site of ideological reproduction (through child-rearing) and the counterrevolutionary model of British femininity.

Yet domesticity was the site of some concern for conservative women writers. In her work on Hannah More, Mitzi Myers notes what she terms the "More enigma": the disjunction between the feminine ideal of More's conduct manuals, and her own life of agency, which ensures that she cannot be read as simply either a "feminist heroine" or a "compliant patriarchal victim." During her lifetime More was an authoritative figure whose influence reached all levels of British society; her conduct and moral literature addresses most social ranks, and her intimacy with Queen Charlotte, as well as with the Duchess of Gloucester, the King's sister-in-law, is well documented. With her sister Martha ("Patty"), she managed a network of rural Sunday Schools. At her death she left £30,000 to some seventy charities, a significant achievement, especially considering that the legacy represented the profits of her literary career. Yet throughout her career More was able to negotiate the difficulties of being a prominent woman, managing to submit "to propriety's curbs," as Myers argues, even as she "plies them to advantage."[4] By these means, she retained a spectacularly unobjectionable reputation throughout her lifetime (with the temporary exception of the Blagdon Controversy). More's success lies in her redefinition of what constitutes an appropriate arena for female activity. By expanding the concept of domesticity to include charity, More was able to justify her more widely political activities, such as the publication of the Cheap

Repository Tracts or the establishment and management of a string of Sunday Schools.

There is also a disparity between Jane West's conduct book ideals and her actions, especially in her engagement in a literary career. She is eager to emphasize the accuracy of her domestic appearance: "You noticed my pile of stockings," West writes to Bishop Percy after he visited her; "they were not affectedly introduced." Yet despite her insistence that "[m]y needle always claims the pre-eminence of my pen," and her careful ideological and spatial location of herself within an acceptable domestic environment, her adoption of a textual position of authority places her on the boundary between the public and the private, between the ideally feminine and the transgressive. Further, in conjunction with West's engagement in what she calls "the duties of active life," she was also committed to a literary life, devoting, by her own account, six hundred hours to each of her novels (and longer to her conduct books).[5] She publicly idealized the possibilities for "old maids" to excel in benevolence and "the whole circle of science," and she privately expressed her sense of the conflict between her artistic and domestic lives: "Shall I say," she wrote to Bishop Percy in 1811, "you kindly consider me, not as what I am, but as what I might have been, had my situation permitted me to devote myself entirely to the Muses, instead of having my mind occupied with cares, and my hands with the needle?"[6] The development of new novelistic genres during the early years of the nineteenth century provided the site for playing out this type of ambivalence around domesticity. While novels by conservative women like West continued to advocate domesticity as the cornerstone of a strong British nation, new novelistic genres enabled changes in the plot of the heroine over the period. One of the effects of Brunton's incorporation of the romance genre with Evangelical fiction is that domesticity is decentered; in her novels the female protagonist's religion is tested through conflict with the world outside the already evangelized feminine world of the home. In contrast to Brunton's plot of departure, Hannah More's novel, *Coelebs in Search of a Wife*, focuses on containment. Brunton and More share an antirevolutionary motivation, yet the textual form of this motivation differs; in terms of domesticity, the differences are profound. While More's novel reiterates the centrality of domesticity in the construction of antirevolutionary femininity, Brunton's novels provide a site for rethinking the shape of domesticity, as well as the roles of both men and women in relation to it.

Hannah More and Mary Brunton shared, with all of the writers I address in this study, a loyalty to established institutions, and especially to the established church. Both also attempted to promulgate their religious and moral lessons through the literary form of the novel (Brunton published two full novels, *Self-Control* in 1811 and *Discipline* in 1814, and a fragment of a novel, *Emmeline*, in 1819). Lynne Vallone points out that Evangelical fiction by writers like More and Brunton "attempts to organize experience from a consistent, coherent vantage point— . . . combining the soteriological imperative with political and social conservatism." Both writers, as Nicola Watson has noted, produced antirevolutionary novels intended to "police" female desire and the revolutionary narratives associated with it.[7] Both also provide models of domesticity which, by analogy, figure the potential for a regenerate British nation based on hierarchy and the established institutions, but informed by the revitalizing qualities of Evangelicalism and middle-class virtue. There are significant differences, however, in the shape of their novelistic productions, at the root of which are diverging conceptions of the relationship between religion and domesticity. For More, Evangelical Christianity is proven (for the female subject) in a consistent submission to an ideology of religious domesticity. Domesticity and femininity are, in More's formulation, ideally intertwined and mutually constitutive. Brunton's heroines, on the other hand, prove their piety through conflict and combat with the world outside the home before they are rewarded with an ideal form of domesticity. In More's novel, then, the domestic "circle" is the site of religious action, while Brunton's narratives explore the challenges that beset both heroines and heroes in their progress toward domesticity. The heroine's triumph outside the home produces the domestic circumstances for national regeneration in Brunton's novels; for More, the feminine triumph of domestic "correctness" produces the same patriotic effect.

Gender and Domesticity in *Coelebs in Search of a Wife*

Initially, the structure of *Coelebs in Search of a Wife* resembles the more "masculine" form of the antirevolutionary novel; the protagonist's "search" for an ideal woman among the satiric stereotypes of London echoes the structure of Isaac D'Israeli's anti-Jacobin novel, *Vaurien*. The narrative's shift to a rural setting in chapter 13 signals a new type of plot, a domestic one interwoven with lessons on female education. The lessons all tend toward the same end: fitting a young woman to fulfill her ultimate domestic role as wife and mother. The exemplary heroine, Lucilla Stanley, provides an object lesson in ideal Evangelical womanhood: she is pious, submissive, retiring, companionable, modest, and charitable, and she lives a highly orderly life, in which each hour is accounted for, and that incorporates time for charitable activity. Like More herself, she regularly visits the poor, and helps to run a school for working-class girls based on More's own Sunday Schools. Domesticity thus comprises activity within the local community.

Education also plays a role in the production of the Evangelical domestic woman. Lucilla is educated in Latin and the classics, primarily so that she may be a pleasant companion to a husband. The hero Charles comments that he appreciates "reading ladies," "if they bear their faculties meekly," and as long as they do not become "scientific."[8] His reasons for this preference are domestic: "I should greatly prefer a fair companion, who could modestly discriminate between the beauties of Virgil and Milton, to one who was always dabbling in chemistry, and who came to dinner with dirty hands from the lab. . . . [A]rts, which are of immense value in manufactures, won't make my wife's conversation entertaining to me. Discoveries which may greatly improve dyeing and bleaching, will add little to the delights of our summer evening's walk, or winter fire-side" (2:149–50). This short but rich passage situates female education within the domestic circle; its justification is in its utility in producing a companionate marriage, rather than in any scholarly or scientific contribution it may make more broadly. Charles also carefully differentiates between the public and private spheres, which he implicitly genders; a woman who contributes to the capitalistic world of "manufactures" will of necessity fail domestically. Not only will she fall short of her moral "duty" to be companionable (1:347), but she is characterized as slovenly. Her research is similarly denigrated as "dabbling." This distinction is sustained throughout the narrative; whenever Charles meets a woman whose learning is not subordinated to her domestic role, she is demonstrated to be inadequate if not absurd. As Lucilla's father comments, "the true science of a lady" is "domestic knowledge" (2:232). Earlier, in *Strictures on the Modern System of Female Education*, More had argued a similar point: "The great uses of study [to a woman] are to enable her to regulate her own mind, and to be useful to others."[9]

The passage also demonstrates why More's writing is subject to various differing readings in terms of its "feminism." Female learning is subordinated here to a domestic ideal that demands that individual inclination be repressed, supporting Watson's contention that the narrative is a conservative one that polices female desire. Lucilla's education, according to her father, carefully contravened her personal desires:

"The turn of the mind, the tendency of the employment, the force of the practice, the bent of the conversation, the spirit of the amusement, have all leaned to the contrary direction, till the habits are gradually worked into a kind of nature" (2:420). This education, based primarily on opposing desires rather than on inculcating specific information, echoes More's advice in *Strictures on the Modern System of Female Education* that girls must learn early to be thwarted in their desires; she argues that "[a] judicious, unrelaxing, but steady curb on their [girls'] tempers and passions can alone ensure their peace and establish their principles" (1:154–55).

How then to account for Christine Krueger's contention in *The Reader's Repentance* that this novel provides examples of More's "Christian feminism"? First, the emphasis on thwarting female desire must be placed within an Evangelical context. A basic doctrine of Evangelicalism was (and continues to be) original sin, in which all souls, male and female, were assumed to be corrupt. Evangelical educational philosophy focused on combating evidence of corruption in children rather than on protecting their innocence. "Is it not a fundamental error," asks More, "to consider children as innocent beings, whose little weaknesses may perhaps want some correction, rather than as beings who bring into the world a corrupt nature and evil dispositions, which it should be the great end of education to rectify?" As Robin Reed Davis puts it, for Evangelicals children were "little repositories of natural corruption who desperately need correction and instruction." Lucilla Stanley's education in restraint is therefore understandable within the contexts of Evangelical theology, and not necessarily evidence of More's antifeminist goals. The fact that Charles, in his descant on learned ladies, approves an intellectually rigorous education for women is also grounds for Krueger's claim. More reconfigures domesticity, in Krueger's argument, to accommodate female intellect, and More's great achievement is that she used evangelicalism, "even in a highly reactionary period, to encourage the intellectual and verbal empowerment of women."[10]

Krueger's argument is compelling, and acknowledges the subtle contradictions within More's "Christian feminism." Yet it is difficult to read More's Lucilla as verbally empowered, despite the fact that "the moral authority of her voice is never undermined." As Claudia Johnson has noted, Lucilla is virtually voiceless: "silence so unbroken cannot be distinguished from insipidness or imbecility," she comments. The novel focuses on Lucilla's actions, and on Charles's interpretations of those actions, rather than on her voice. Neither is her subjectivity an object of concern. Krueger's evidence for Lucilla's "hidden, inner life" (121), which is represented through an interest in botany, is undermined several pages later, when Mrs. Stanley informs Charles that Lucilla restricts her gardening time: "By this limitation a treble end is answered. Her time is saved, self-denial is exercised, and the interest which would languish by protracting the work is kept in fresh vigour" (2:113).[11] A good Evangelical heroine, Lucilla has internalized her discipline, and continues the project of self-limitation her father began. Her presence in the text is exemplary; she teaches an ongoing lesson about what constitutes Evangelical, domestic femininity. For More, the production of the domestic woman equals the production of domesticity; femininity constitutes domesticity. The novel as a whole provides a model for Evangelical domesticity, as well as for the woman who inhabits it (ideologically and literally). The goals of Evangelicalism—conversion, good works, and Christian submission—are played out here in a domestic setting. More's novel is thus a manual for maximizing the religious and antirevolutionary potential of the domestic "circle." Because of the link between domesticity and femininity, Lucilla's plot—as slight as it is—must be played out within the domestic setting. Moving outside the domestic sphere would negate both her femininity, and the domestic space whose center she is designed to be.

Elizabeth Langland has argued rightly that our attention to the celebrated domesticity of women obscures the increased domesticity of men during the nineteenth century. If More's central purpose in this novel is to teach appropriately gendered behavior to girls, her implicit agenda trains female desire toward the Evangelical domestic masculine ideal represented by the narrator. The sentimental domestic novel, as Nancy Armstrong has shown, is ideologically effective in great part because of the role it plays in constituting desire.[12] Who is loved in novels, and why, is important: the desire of characters provides a template for the desire of readers. Sentimental novels of the late eighteenth and early nineteenth centuries worked openly to teach women whom to desire, and how to recognize masculine exemplarity. The plot of Austen's *Pride and Prejudice*, for example, engages in this didactic process, warning about the dangers of "first impressions" and advocating prudence in the process of choosing a husband. The sober Darcy can therefore become a more attractive marital choice than the dashing and handsome Wickham.

Yet Austen was not promoting an Evangelical domestic hero (though she later produced one in the religious Edmund in *Mansfield Park*), and More was faced with a particular challenge in her construction of Charles. Evangelicalism valorized Christian attributes—such as meekness, sexual restraint, piety, and humility—which, particularly in conjunction with domesticity, were conventionally considered feminine. Thus, when More has Charles approve for everyone "meek and passive virtues which we all agreed were peculiarly Christian, and peculiarly feminine" (2:184), the premise is exemplified by the speaker, who virtuously abstains from gambling and alcohol, meekly obeys his father, and prefers the companionship of the domestic circle—what he calls his "fireside"—to the more public arenas of politics, business, and "society." "I had naturally a keen relish for domestic happiness," comments Charles early in the novel. "Home was the scene in which my imagination had pictured the only delights worthy of a rational, feeling, intellectual, immortal man" (1:18). As a young man of "considerable estate" (1:11), who is not "of any profession, or likely to be engaged in public life" (1:19), he is able to explore and indulge his "natural" appreciation for domesticity, and the narrative positions him almost exclusively in a series of domestic settings. The novel opens with a report of Charles's attendance at the sickbed of his father: "I attended him with an assiduity which was richly rewarded by the lessons of wisdom, and the example of piety, which I daily received from him." After his father's death, the "grief of my mother was so poignant, and so lasting, that I could never prevail on myself to leave her, even for the sake of attaining those advantages and enjoying those pleasures, which may be reaped by a wider range of observation, by a more extended survey of the multifarious tastes, habits, pursuits, and characters of general society" (1:11–12). With the important exception of his degree from the University of Edinburgh (completed shortly before his father's illness), More places Charles in the position of an upper-middle-class domestic woman, one of whose "natural" roles—as represented in novels and conduct literature of the period—was to nurse ailing parents and relatives. The retirement resulting from his decision to stay with his mother is another prescribed component of middle-class femininity in this period, and is opposed to the "life in the gay and busy world" characteristic of masculinity (1:12).

With his "natural" domesticity and self-imposed retirement, Charles represents an Evangelical form of domestic masculinity that is set in opposition to men who are characterized by secular and urban pursuits. As More demonstrates the exemplarity of Lucilla Stanley through comparison to a range of inadequate feminine stereotypes, so she foregrounds the domestic masculinity she advocates by setting it against representations of the "worldly" man. Two of the mentorial figures in the novel, Sir John Belfield and Mr. Stanley, report narrow escapes from the trivialities and vice of the "world" of London before their salutary retreat into domesticity. Mr. Carlton, an acquaintance of the Stanleys, lives as a "worldly" man, staying out all night and engaging in expensive "irregularities" (1:250), until the religious example of his forbearing wife convinces him that religion is not a "visionary system of words and phrases" (1:255), but a model for practice for both men and women. There is a problem in the representation of domestic masculinity, however: in order to represent in her protagonist Evangelical "meek and passive virtues," More must contradict conventional representations of masculinity as necessarily worldly. Her novel foregrounds the domestic role of men, marginalizing to the point of invisibility men's roles in other areas, such as government, justice, and commerce. In so doing she "feminizes" her male protagonist, and, more importantly, fails to provide a model for male Evangelical behavior outside of the domestic sphere. Pressure from her chosen genre also contributes to the difficulty of representing a masculinity that is both Evangelical and worldly. The domestic novel conventionally uses domestic settings, and focuses on domestic issues. The actions of male characters are only significant insofar as they affect action within the domestic setting. More's unusual narrative choice of a male protagonist in her domestic novel effectively demands his domestication. Can a man represent an Evangelical ideal and not remain at home? Can a man be domestic and still take part in the business of middle-class masculinity? More's novel evades these questions by locating her hero purely within domestic space.

More also evades another implicit problem in her feminization of Charles: that the feminine qualities she represents as central to the Evangelical doctrine of equality of souls could be interpreted as effeminacy. As Michèle Cohen has argued, it is effeminacy, rather than femininity, that is most often set in opposition to masculinity in British texts of the late eighteenth and early nineteenth centuries. Effeminacy was linked to characteristics that were considered French, or at least continental: vanity, frivolity, sociability, possibly homosexuality, and, in Cohen's analysis, a facility with language. In contemporary slang, an effeminate man was a "jessamy," a term used by both More and West to describe inappropriately effeminate behavior. By the last decade of the eighteenth century, of course, anything French or francophile was suspect, thus this model of effeminacy carried subversive political meanings. More's novel carefully avoids any suggestion of effeminacy in her exemplary man. He exhibits patriotic British "common sense" and "masculine" simplicity in his behavior and tastes. The title of the novel indicates from the outset his conformity with a heterosexual model of masculinity. In fact, Charles's desirability as a mate provides the basis for the novel's lesson: by conforming to the ideal of femininity privileged by More's text, the exemplary Lucilla Stanley ultimately wins Charles's affection. In constructing the Evangelical domestic man as an object of desire, More challenges dominant constructions of masculinity. Her silence around questions of effeminacy and worldliness erases the disjunctions between her new model and conventional concepts of masculinity, and allows her to present the Evangelical ideal as already culturally accepted.

In spite of the challenge to gender orthodoxy that Charles's character presents, it is around Lucilla's subjectivity—or lack thereof—that contemporary comment cohered, and reviews of the novel raise key questions about genre, characterization, and didacticism. A reviewer in the *Scots Magazine* found the character of Lucilla to be "inanimate." The *Christian Observer* countered this criticism by generalizing on the nature of Christian femininity: "Religion is such a neutralizer of the character, that, unless pious women are loved for their piety, they must often be content to be passed by altogether."[13] The characteristics that crystallize around this Evangelical form of femininity, however, are ones that in many ways contradict the conventional qualities of a novelistic heroine. More's insistence on the silence, retirement, and relational qualities of ideal womanhood limit the plot to a sequence of examples of Lucilla's domestic exemplarity, and her focalization of the narrative through the male observer precludes the heroine's consciousness as an object of investigation. As one of the characters in *Coelebs* remarks, the narrative of Charles's search for a wife makes "a sad, dull novel" since there are no difficulties in it (1:286); in the same way, Lucilla makes a sad, dull heroine, since she is morally and emotionally fully developed at the opening of the text.

Romancing the Didactic: Mary Brunton's Evangelical Fiction

In her first novel Brunton attempted a similar didactic project to More's and placed an exemplary heroine at the center of her narrative, yet much of the narrative interest resides in an exploration of the character's responses to morally difficult situations of the kind that never occur in *Coelebs*. Brunton obliquely confronts the problem inherent in More's style of didactic fiction when she writes into *Self-Control* a discussion of Fielding's *Tom Jones*. Predictably, the exemplary heroine,

Laura Montreville, resists the novel's morality, while the badly educated Julia (another misled namesake of Rousseau's Julie in antirevolutionary fiction) approves Jones's "noble" character.[14] The debate prompts Laura's father to comment on the central problem of didactic fiction: "Even the excellent Mr. Alworthy excites but feeble interest; and it is not by the character which we respect, but by that in which we are interested, that the moral effect on our minds is produced" (72). The *Scots Magazine*'s criticism of Lucilla as "inanimate" describes a similar problem: Lucilla does not engage our interest because she does not develop, and, in fact, recedes as a character. Brunton's novel suggests that More's didactic effect is therefore weakened, despite the good example Lucilla may set.

Brunton's central motive in writing, she claims, is that her work may be "useful"—that it may teach a lesson in religion and virtue—and she stresses this point repeatedly in her correspondence. In describing *Self-Control* to Joanna Baillie after its publication, Brunton comments: "I merely intended to show the power of the religious principle in bestowing self-command; and to bear testimony against a maxim as immoral as indelicate, that a reformed rake makes the best husband."[15] It is vital for Brunton that her didactic message be effectively conveyed. When she creates her exemplary heroine in *Self-Control*, therefore, Brunton makes her more "novelistic" than More's. Laura Montreville is well-educated and pious, and epitomizes the moral and psychological characteristic foregrounded in the title. As such, she is exemplary. Yet she uses bad judgment when she falls in love with a rake, and is naïve when she expects him to reform. This error not only illustrates the book's lesson, but also contributes to a psychological realism that is absent in More's depiction of Lucilla Stanley. While More was concerned, through much of her writing, with the social manifestations of Evangelicalism in action, Brunton's focus was on the importance of self-reflection, and the continuous monitoring of the "passions" according to an Evangelical ideal. Laura is, therefore, a "vigilant observer of her own actions" (234). The result in Brunton's novels is the foregrounding of a young woman's consciousness; the heroine's moral concerns and spiritual development provide the major interest of the plot.[16] In *Self-Control* Brunton places this self-reflecting heroine in the context of a more typical romance plot (as opposed to More's domestic plot) that teaches the value of "self-control" even as it provides incidents to "interest" a more secular reader.

The plot of *Self-Control* prompted Jane Austen to write to her sister Cassandra: "I am looking over Self Control again, and my opinion is confirmed of its being an excellently-meant, elegantly-written work, without anything of Nature or Probability in it." Brunton herself wrote to a friend that "I do not see the outrageous improbability with which it has been charged."[17] The novel opens with an encounter between Laura Montreville, the virtuous and well-connected (though poor) seventeen-year-old Scottish heroine, and her admirer, the aristocratic Colonel Hargrave. "His person was symmetry itself," explains the narrator, "his manners had all the fascination that vivacity and intelligence, joined to the highest polish, could bestow" (6). When Hargrave proposes that Laura become his mistress, she, in response, faints, with "blood gushing from her mouth and nostrils" (11). Laura sets the remorseful Hargrave a penance: he is to live virtuously away from her for two years, after which time she will welcome him as a "friend." Hargrave is, predictably given the novel's didactic purpose, unable to comply: his personality is too "passionate"—a blanket term describing his "impetuosity" (6), his lack of sexual restraint, and his inability to control his emotions (35–38). Juxtaposed against Hargrave is the novel's exemplary man, Montague de Courcy, who is virtuous, pious, and an old family friend. After the death of Laura's father, Hargrave continues to persecute Laura, and gradually further evidence of his debauchery comes to her attention. Her affection for de Courcy grows, and they plan to marry. Hargrave's minions abduct her at this point, carrying her to "America" where he has been posted. Laura travels up the St. Lawrence River accompanied by native guides and is imprisoned in a cabin in the wilderness. Hours before Hargrave's arrival to "ruin" her, she escapes in a canoe, traveling over Niagara Falls (the event that prompted the most incredulity in her readers) before reaching safety near Quebec City. A confessional suicide note from Hargrave restores her reputation; she is married to de Courcy and happily enters the non-narratable: "the tranquil current of domestic happiness affords no material for narrative" (500).

What is non-narratable in Brunton's novel forms the central subject of More's. For Brunton, the "domestic happiness" of Laura's marital home comes only after she has proven her religious worth through conflict with temptation and poverty. Laura loses her family home early in the novel, when her father is "ruined," and subsequently moves between inadequate establishments. Her marriage represents the ultimate achievement of a quest for domesticity that dominates the entire narrative. While Laura spends most of the novel in virtual exile from domestic space, de Courcy's country home, Norwood, provides a model for domestic behavior and happiness. The house strikes a balance between "humble simplicity" and affluent "splendour," "grandeur holding the second place to usefulness" (274–75). The dinner is "plain, neat, and substantial" (275), family prayers are conducted daily, and the estate houses a small population of happy, neat, and industrious laborers (281). In short, "[c]omfort, neatness, and peace reigned every where, and Norwood seemed a fit retreat for literary leisure and easy hospitality" (275). The construction of Norwood as a site in which middle-class Evangelical virtues exist within a gentry country-house setting replicates the values Nancy Armstrong reads in contemporary conduct books. "[F]emale conduct books," argues Armstrong, "changed the ideal of what English life ought to be when they replaced the lavish displays of aristocratic life with the frugal and private practices of the modern gentleman."[18] Norwood epitomizes for Laura ideal domesticity, especially when contrasted to the nearby "fashionable" home in which she lives with an aristocratic relative. Lady Pelham's tastes restrict Laura's visits to Norwood; she argues that "your good sort of people were always intolerably tiresome; that clock-work regularity was the dullest thing in nature" (287). Laura's sense of duty to a close and elderly relative prevents her from contradicting Lady Pelham; the domesticity that formed the subject of *Coelebs in Search of a Wife* thus takes a peripheral position in relation to the main narrative. It functions rather as an instructive contrast to the less ideal circumstances in which Laura finds herself. Laura's appreciation of Norwood signals her alliance with the middle-class values of the conduct books; yet the repeated deferral of the culmination of her domestic desires suggests that this form of domesticity is not, as female conduct books suggest, "natural," but rather a product of class and opportunity in conjunction with carefully nurtured personal domestic qualities.

Significantly, domesticity in this novel is not necessarily associated with femininity. Here, the male de Courcy, rather than the female protagonist, is the character figured as "naturally" domestic; he inhabits the idealized domestic sphere throughout the narrative, while Laura is markedly marginalized from this setting until the very end. One of the earliest indications of de Courcy's suitability as a husband is his affection for domestic values. "You know I have no ambition," he says to his mother, "all my joys must be domestic. It is as a husband and a father that all my wishes must be fulfilled" (264). In addition to his simple appreciation of domesticity, de Courcy represents his subjectivity as relational: located within domestic space, and dependent upon domestic relationships. Fittingly, he adopts a nurturing domestic role in the narrative. He is, as Laura's sick father claims, "a better nurse" than she is (122): "He soothed," the narrator confirms, "the little impatiences of disease; contrived means to mitigate the oppressiveness of debility; knew how to exhilarate the hour of ease; and watched the moment, well known to the sickly, when amusement becomes fatigue" (121). Laura herself represents these qualities as "feminine": "if sickness or sorrow ever be your portion," she exclaims to de Courcy, "may your kindness here be repaid by some spirit of peace in woman's form—some gentleness yet more feminine than de Courcy's!" (137). De Courcy accurately reads this comment as proof of Laura's sexual indifference to him; at this point in the text she has yet to recognize his masculinity, and thus his potential as a sexual partner.

Laura's appreciation for domesticity is established from the opening of the text. Her acknowledgment of the value of masculine domesticity is less clear. Her passion for Hargrave is based on his physical attractiveness, his polished manners, and his impetuosity, to which Laura dangerously adds imaginary qualities of honor and self-control (7); her "natural" attraction, therefore, is to a man who represents a more conventional aristocratic model of masculinity. The closure of the plot is made possible when she learns to value the "calm, dispassionate affection" of "a man of respectable abilities, of amiable dispositions, of sound principles, and engaging manners" over the "extravagant passion" of Hargrave (378). This lesson is a common one in novels of the period (including *Pride and Prejudice*). More significantly, Laura reconfigures her assumptions about masculinity to include domestic qualities she formerly considered feminine. The "domestic happiness" of Laura's marital home comes only after she acknowledges the value of domestic masculinity—indeed, after she accepts it as "manly." Brunton's novel not only teaches a lesson about exemplary femininity, therefore, but offers a model of masculinity that incorporates Evangelical values—nurturing, piety, and domesticity—which were most often figured as feminine. Unlike More, however, she acknowledges the departure this model makes from conventional ideas about masculinity, by representing her heroine's shifting desire, and her slow realization of the desirability of the domestic man.

As Nicola Watson has noted, Evangelical romances like Brunton's novels often end with a fantasy of national regeneration, in which the nation is figured as whole, united, and unthreatened by internal or external conflicts. Here, this euphoric closure is enabled by the heroine's acceptance of domestic masculinity, and her ultimate union with the English de Courcy in the idealized domestic setting of Norwood. The final portion of the narrative, in which Laura travels to Canada, solidifies de Courcy's association with domesticity. As the heroine travels to the periphery of Empire, which is represented as dark and excessive, de Courcy comes to figure "home"—the center against which the chaos of the periphery is measured. Unlike the military Hargrave, who is associated with public action in imperial space, de Courcy's value is linked to domestic activity in British space. Laura's marriage represents, then, the union of Scotland and England, as well as the valorization of British domesticity over the masculine adventure of Empire.

After her acceptance of the domestic de Courcy, and before her marriage, Laura undergoes her improbable American journey. This passage, in structural terms, is what Brunton calls a "patch," since "the joining [to the rest of the narrative] is clumsily visible": "We have all heard of a 'peacock with a fiery tail;' but my American jaunt is this same monstrous appendage tacked to a poor little grey linnet."[19] If we assume that the point of Brunton's plot is that Laura must learn to appreciate the correct lover, then this criticism makes sense. If we read beyond the domestic plot, however, and focus on Brunton's religious concerns, the episode achieves a measure of coherence. The novel is as much—or more—concerned with Laura's spiritual development as it is with her worldly success in marriage. Thus, even after she learns the secular lesson of the courtship plot, Laura undergoes events of romance that allow her to exercise her characteristic virtue, even as she develops deeper religious faith. The wilderness of Canada becomes a metaphor for Laura's "darkened soul" (483), against which she struggles in her progress toward a submissive acceptance of God's will. The abduction teaches Laura "that the rugged and slippery ways of this dark wilderness shall, at the dawn of everlasting day, be owned as the fittest for conducting us to the house of our Father" (466). Laura's actual escape (through her own initiative) is prefigured by her spiritual reawakening: "The raptures of faith beamed on her soul. By degrees they triumphed over every fear" (482).

That the American trip functions as a climax suggests that—as her correspondence confirms—Brunton privileges Laura's individual religious development over the courtship plot. Brunton's use of genre separates the two concerns of the narrative: the worldly marriage plot and the spiritual narrative of religious trial and faith. It is the romance elements in the plot—the evil seducer, the abduction, the improbable adventures—that foreground religious concerns. By introducing this generic combination to the Evangelical novel, Brunton is able to engage the reader's "interest" (necessary, as she claims, for a didactic text) and to illustrate exemplary religious conduct in extraordinary circumstances. In the process she creates in Laura an example of what Nicola

Watson calls Evangelical "covert revolutionaries, albeit in the service of God." Laura's spiritual development requires moral autonomy, which occasionally sets her at odds with secular authorities, such as her father, who urges her marriage to Hargrave in spite of "the follies usual to men of his rank" (199). Setting scriptural above parental or spousal authority is common in evangelical women's writing and biographies, according to Christine Krueger, who characterizes this behavior as "rebellious."[20] Citing scriptural authority as the grounds for resistant behavior provided a means for justifying actions that challenged traditional class and gender hierarchies. In this sense, Brunton's novels can be read as progressive, in that her heroines base their actions upon individualistic religious interpretation, rather than on the customs of community and the "world." When, early in the narrative, the narrator cites as Laura's "leading principle" the belief that "I am here as a soldier, who strives in an enemy's land; as one who must run—must wrestle—must strain every nerve—exert every power, nor once shrink from the struggle till the prize is my own," she establishes an active model of Christianity that supersedes any socially prescribed laws (14). Sarah W. R. Smith argues that Brunton's Evangelicalism is at the root of her reevaluation of women's work outside the home. Laura is not ashamed of her efforts to support her father in London by painting; and de Courcy, the novel's exemplary male, "approved of the spirit which led a young woman of family to dare, in spite of custom, to be useful" (152). Usefulness, as Brunton's correspondence makes clear, is at the center of her theology; women's work outside the home is therefore valued as highly as men's. Smith argues that this valorization of female work constitutes "feminism."[21]

Yet Brunton's religion, in general, supports the same social structures that are privileged by other antirevolutionary writers. When Laura returns from America with a sullied reputation, she refuses marriage to de Courcy until Hargrave's confession clears her name, on the grounds that de Courcy's "best affections" would be turned to "poison by domestic shame" (491). Significantly, "[t]he world's neglect was trivial in her estimation" (491); yet the effects of the "world's" opinion and customs on her behavior and on the plot are the same as if she valued social custom over religious doctrine. Women's work outside the home is also clearly delimited by ideals of "delicacy"; Laura "wished not indeed to intrude on the world's notice" (152). The boundaries between public and private, domestic and extra-domestic, remain essentially intact in this novel, despite Laura's "useful" engagement in the ladylike and semiprivate activity of painting. When at the close of *Self-Control* the plot drifts into the non-narratable, the domestic harmony that rewards the heroine reinforces class and gender hierarchies, even as it solidifies a revisionist model of domesticity that foregrounds female activity and "feminine" Evangelical masculinity. Moving beyond the "magic circle" of conservative domesticity is not a revolutionary act in Brunton's novels; rather, the extra-domestic plot provides a site for rethinking domesticity and gender while supporting an essentially antirevolutionary agenda.

Despite her success at making the exemplary heroine of *Self-Control* "interesting," Brunton expressed reservations about repeating the project: "If I ever undertake another lady," she wrote to a friend as she was finishing *Self-Control,* "I will manage her in a very different manner. Laura is so decently kerchiefed, like our grandmothers, that to dress her is a work of time and pains." The dress of her next heroine, to stretch the metaphor, is not nearly so decent. Ellen Percy is a spoiled heiress who undergoes ruin and suffering before she learns Evangelical values of piety, service, and self-denial. Even as Laura's "characteristic virtue" was self-control (500), Ellen's "ruling frailty," which she must combat in order to reform, is "self-will." In his memoir of Brunton her husband describes the novel's project in this way: "to show the means through which, when Self-Control has been neglected, the mind must be trained by suffering ere it can hope for usefulness or for true enjoyment."[22] *Discipline* is, therefore, a conversion narrative, narrated in the first person, which foregrounds the religious and moral development of its young heroine, and her move toward self-discipline. Despite their differences in plot, *Discipline* and *Self-Control* teach similar lessons. Both valorize "usefulness"—Ellen's financial ruin demands that she support herself as a governess—and domesticity. Both foreground their heroines' subjectivity and moral development. Both reconfigure masculinity to include domestic and Evangelical characteristics that are initially figured as "feminine," including piety, nurturing, and an appreciation for a retired family life. Both also conclude in an Edenic domestic setting, in which social ties and responsibilities are strong, and in which hierarchy is maintained. Both, in short, maintain a balance between social and domestic reformism and fervent support for antirevolutionary principles. Like More's novel, Brunton's teach lessons about gendered behavior and domesticity that ultimately support "things as they are." Yet Brunton's experimentation with form and plot improves on More's didactic project by establishing the means of "interesting" a reader. More radically, her innovative practice enables a fuller exploration of female subjectivity, and a reconceptualization of the relationship of both women and men to the domestic circle. The next chapter explores the ways in which historical fiction provided a similar opportunity to Jane West, who, like Brunton, refigured domesticity and gender, with even more radical implications for domestic femininity.

7

Historicizing the Domestic Subject: Historical Fiction and Antirevolution, 1810–14

DURING THE EARLY YEARS OF THE NINETEENTH CENTURY THE HISTORICAL novel rapidly became a mainstream genre. Walter Scott's *Waverley* is presently the most widely-read text in the new genre, but its publication in 1814 was preceded by a significant number of novels with "historical" plots and settings. Several earlier texts, popular during their own period, are rooted in historical specificity, and integrate their primarily sentimental plots with the broader narrative, and alternative discourse, of history: Jane Porter's *Thaddeus of Warsaw* (1803) and *The Scottish Chiefs* (1810); Robert Bisset's *Douglas; Or, The Highlander* (1800); Charles Lucas's *The Infernal Quixote* (1798); and Jane West's *The Loyalists* (1812). All of these texts are more or less conservative: loyalist, supportive of existing institutions, and overtly or implicitly antirevolutionary. Two—by Bisset and Lucas—are explicitly anti-Jacobin, while the others are both historical and moral tales, utilizing historical narratives to promote a renewed sense of national order and stability. While a small number of historical novels of the period were intended to promote radical theory, the majority were conservative and loyalist in intent. As Nicola Watson has argued, conservative writers habitually utilized historical analogues of the French Revolution in their antiradical projects; thus, the Irish Rebellion of 1798 could function (as it does in Lucas's *Infernal Quixote*) as both the historical background for the narrative, and as the justification for commentary on the revolution in France. The English civil war of the seventeenth century, in the case of West's *Loyalists*, fulfills a didactic function when it is contrasted with, and compared to, the political situation in Europe in the nineteenth century.

Even as they engage in a committed assault on radical and revolutionary social and political theory, these novels function to support conservatism by reformulating the events of history to legitimize a conservative political position, and social formation, in the present. Jane Porter's *The Scottish Chiefs*, published in 1810, provides a useful example of how this works. The novel is set in thirteenth-century Scotland and charts the life of the Scottish national hero William Wallace, who led Scotland to victory over the English after the murder of his wife. Characters in the novel fill recognizable didactic roles, and conform to models established in the didactic domestic novels of the 1790s. Exemplary femininity finds its form in Wallace's wife, Marion, who, early in the novel, is murdered by the English while protecting her husband. Her death provides the impetus for Wallace's heroic project to free Scotland from English rule. Porter's "enlightened" Wallace is similarly an exemplary man who epitomizes Evangelical and middle-class values of the period in which the novel was written.[1] He has clearly nineteenth-century plans for his country: a voice of antirevolutionary morality, he advocates "virtuous independence" over "licentious unrestraint," and hopes his victory will result in Christianity, industry, and temperance for the people of Scotland (2:8). For the working classes he foresees discipline, and advocates moderation and justice in the aristocracy (2:9). The result of the mingling of the genres of history and domestic fiction in this novel is "a naturalization (an historic inevitability) of the type of subjectivity that produced a national symbol like Wallace (and, by implication, a nation that must eventually 'naturally' structure itself according to the domesticated politics he espoused)."[2] It is in the context of this political project, which the form of the historical novel enabled, that I will place the historical novels of Jane West.

In many ways Jane West is the presiding genius of this study, in that her career and her writing epitomize many of the complexities in the relationship among women, conservative politics, and writing during this period. This is particularly true of her use of genre. During the second decade of the nineteenth century, West continued her search for the best vehicle for a conservative didactic message, and like many of her contemporaries, she rejected the domestic novel form to write historical fiction and historical romance. Her writing draws together several strands in the narrative of generic change I am relating here; in an attempt to access a wider audience, she combines historical fiction and Evangelical "militant" Christianity with a loyalist, antirevolutionary message. Through readings of West's two historical novels, *The Loyalists* (1812) and *Alicia de Lacy* (1814), I examine the ways in which the genre of historical fiction enables new types of plots. The historical novel form, with its focus on times of national crisis, enabled the heroine's engagement in "heroic" action, and, often, her departure from the domestic sphere. *The Loyalists* widens the domestic sphere to include any portion of society in which nurturing and care is needed. West's next novel, *Alicia de Lacy*, takes the expansion of femininity further, incorporating "female heroism" and physical bravery into a model of exemplary womanhood. In these two novels the nondomestic plot coincides with a revised model of domesticity that comes into conflict with West's model of femininity from her earlier fiction and conduct books. The new feminine behavior prescribed by West introduces the possibility of agency and independence to an essentially conservative ideology of femininity, producing a new conservative model of exemplary womanhood.

Heroic Domesticity in *The Loyalists*

Like Jane Porter and other writers of historical fiction, West used the form to legitimize the imposition of conservative social policy in the present, by "showing" the source of this policy to be deep in British history and tradition. West's *Loyalists* fulfills this didactic and political function simply: set during the English civil war and interregnum of the seventeenth century, it locates "true" religion and morality on the side of the Royalists and the Church of England. West openly uses history as a tool for teaching in this novel, showing, as the narrator comments in a digressive aside, "an admonitory picture of those times" in order to draw analogies between "modern Reformers" and seventeenth-century Puritans.[3] Widespread agitation for "rights" in the nineteenth century, her narrator argues, is comparable to early-seventeenth-century social unrest, and history thus provides a warning, as well as the possibility of prevention in the present. It is "unpitied poverty" that is at the root of agitation, not the political system (1:336); her narrative thus provides a lesson that supports hierarchy while correcting the behavior of the middle and upper classes, whose compassion and sympathy for the poor may be the key to social stability. Sympathy and benevolence are, of course, functions to which women were widely considered to be well-suited, and it is in this way that the "domestic hearth" becomes the major line of defense in the present against the "wildest theories of democracy" (1:8, 1:7).

Rather than discarding the domestic plot entirely, West adapts it to a historical one. Her novel charts the experiences of one Royalist family—the "Loyalists" of the title—during the years of the Puritan Revolution and Cromwell's rule. The novel's characters and concerns are similar to those of her earlier novels: the characters include a clerical father figure who provides commentary on events as well as moral advice, a young man who is tempted and tested by a corrupt aristocracy, and two female protagonists who remain virtuous despite encounters with temptation and danger. The didactic purpose of the novel is to teach loyalty to England and its national church, as well as an acceptance of the necessity of a hierarchical social structure (a misled servant acknowledges in the final pages of the novel that he needs to be directed "by those who know better" [3:349]). As in domestic novels by West, these lessons of loyalty and patriotism are imparted primarily through her focus on correct female behavior during the period between sexual maturity and marriage. Because of the historical context, this period is considerably extended. West's protagonists do not marry until the Restoration; there is a simultaneous achievement of the domestic courtship plot's goals, and the political goal of the Royalists—as England's king is restored to power, the heroines take the husbands to whom they have been affianced for many years. The characters are thus well into their thirties at the culmination of the courtship plot, and have undergone physical deterioration due to time and hardship (3:309); the integration of the historical with the domestic plot has changed the trajectory of West's earlier domestic novels, and the new plot questions the necessary fictional alliance of youth and beauty with the successful achievement of the marriage plot.

According to West's argument, women's domestic role is crucial in the battle against revolutionism. It is useful, therefore, to look at the roles women play in *The Loyalists*, in order to determine the way in which femininity is conceptualized in this novel. Three central female characters function to establish appropriate feminine behavior. One purely negative character establishes the outer limits of feminine behavior, and ensures that exemplary femininity remains firmly tied to the domestic. Lady Bellingham is an ambitious aristocrat who, like Lady Macbeth, pushes her husband (who made the mistake of marrying for external rather than internal beauty [3:189]) to evil acts in her effort to achieve rank and influence. In coming between her husband and his best friend, who saved his life in childhood, Lady Bellingham undertakes one of the distinguishing acts of a negative female character in West's novels; positive female characters, like Louisa in *A Gossip's Story*, help to cement positive male friendships. Most significantly, Lady Bellingham is resolutely undomestic and lacking in the affective qualities of a mother and wife: she hates her husband and feels no love for her son (3:53, 3:55). A staunch Puritan, she is described by one character as "a domestic and public traitress" (3:84). The ideological link between husband and monarch is suggested by the coincidence of the novel's concluding marriages with the Restoration; this link is made literal through Lady Bellingham's simultaneous rebellion against spousal and monarchical authority. The fact that she defends her behavior on religious grounds warns of the possibility for the subversion of traditional hierarchies in women's involvement in dissenting forms of Christianity. West's novel, when it explores alternative female behaviors, charts a course that avoids the dangers exemplified in the transgressive Lady Bellingham.

The Loyalists juxtaposes two female protagonists. One, Constantia, is a more typical heroine of domestic and sentimental fiction, in her combination of beauty, delicacy, and sympathy, tempered, of course, by piety and virtue (1:162). Constantia's major function in the plot is (as her name indicates) to remain constant to her cousin, Eustace, whom she marries at the conclusion of the narrative. Eustace's sister Isabel is the second female protagonist, and it is in her character that West begins to redefine what constitutes the boundaries and characteristics of femininity. Isabel and Eustace have been brought up in rural retirement, by a "womanish" father, and a mother with "masculine courage" (1:190). Upon the death of their mother, they come to live with their cousin Constantia and her father, the Reverend Beaumont. Isabel is self-sufficient from her first appearance in the novel: she is an herbalist, glazes windows, and helps her brother Eustace to rebuild Dr. Beaumont's library, which has been burned by the rebels (an unfeminine act for which, the narrator explicitly informs us, she goes deliberately unchastised by her punctilious female guardian) (1:183, 1:244, 1:250). Isabel's defining characteristic is her usefulness to others in times of difficulty, whatever the context. She is brave and capable in an escape from capture (1:289), shows resilience in reduced circumstances, in which her happiness is in serving others (2:175), is notable for her charity and "utility" while in prison (3:257), and deals with the report of her brother's death by increased "bodily exertion" (3:40).

Isabel's more physical behavior is justified by her strict confinement to what the narrator figures as a domestic feminine role. More than any other character in the novel, Isabel is committed to nurturing and caring for others; all of her extraordinary activities are a result of her charity toward other characters. The concluding statement of the novel is a comment on Isabel: she is happy, the narrator observes, like all those who "devote their abilities to the call of duty instead of wasting their lives in self-indulgence" (3:352). Here, the call of duty is toward the suffering and ill of Isabel's immediate social circle. Because that circle shifts, due to the historical plot, Isabel's domestic space moves from home to home and even to prison. Her unconventional qualities are enlisted in the service of a conventional—however shifting—model of domesticity, providing space in the novel for imagining a new form of femininity without contravening the conservative boundaries of gender established in West's previous novels.

Isabel's style of active femininity is, in fact, privileged in the novel. Constantia, whose quiet and submissive piety coincides with the imperatives of a domestic novel, undergoes a change of character that brings her, by the end of the novel, closer to the standard set by Isabel. This involves her adoption of what she terms "female heroism," when she asks to stand beside her father at his trial for subversion. Her refusal to be cowed in public, evidenced in her not lowering her gaze (3:199), foreshadows the behavior of Alicia de Lacy in a similar circumstance in West's next novel. According to these novels, circumstance redefines gender. That the novels provide, in their plots, circumstances for female development suggests that West's conceptions of gender were undergoing change at this period, though her antirevolutionary purpose remained the same.

"Female heroism" is a key concept in West's novels of the 1810s. Tracking changes in her definition of the term is one way of marking the change in gender ideology that coincided with her shift in genres. One of the main didactic purposes of West's early novels was to convince girls that: "it is but seldom that they will be called forth to perform high acts of heroic excellence, but that they will be daily required to exert those humble duties and social virtues, wherein the chief part of our merit and our happiness consists." Like Hannah More, who in *Coelebs in Search of a Wife* reconfigures heroism for women to include quiet submission to illness and pain, and dying with dignity, West here positions heroism for women within the traditional domestic sphere.[4] In a chapter in *Letters to a Young Lady* on women's "natural" role and abilities, she outlines the companionate nature of female existence: "to be the helpmate of man, to partake of his labours, to alleviate his distresses, to regulate his domestic concerns, to rear and instruct the subsequent generation." West's argument ties women's domestic role to national security, and insists that "the presence of a woman in her own family is so salutary, that she is not justified in withdrawing her attention from home, except in some call of plain positive duty." Examples of "female heroism" are thus, according to the *Letters*, necessarily rare: "It is possible, I allow, to produce many illustrious examples of female heroism and capacity; but *singular* occurrences do not overthrow the general conclusions of experience."[5] The plot of *The Loyalists* provides an opportunity for the exercise of this rare quality; in fact, it becomes central to the form of ideal femininity presented to the reader as exemplary. Yet the quality is also carefully circumscribed: in the cases of Isabel and Constantia it is exercised within an expanded conception of the domestic sphere. In the next novel she wrote, West developed the concept of "female heroism" in conjunction with a new type of feminine ideal. In *Alicia de Lacy* the plots of history provide the motivation for a narrative of female action that moves outside the domestic sphere, and a model of femininity that incorporates agency. West's antirevolutionary message remains the same here as in her earlier domestic novels, and she makes, in her preface, the standard connection between female behavior and the stability of the social order. Yet *Alicia de Lacy*, West's "historical romance," rethinks the type of femininity necessary to the support of a stable social order and nation.

Alicia de Lacy and the Lessons of Romance

One of the central lessons of West's early novels is both a moral and a narrative one: in a concerted and sustained attack on "romance," West demonizes both the literary form, and its related affective manifestation, sensibility. The evangelical simplicity of her prose stands as an implicit condemnation of more "romantic" texts. The early novels narrated by Prudentia Homespun avoid the distinctive elements of romance discourse, characterized by West as "extravagance of character," "variety of incident," and "pretty language," which have the dangerous effect of "dazzling the imagination and inflaming the passions."[6] Continuing the antiromantic argument several years later in *Letters to a Young Lady*, she asks the bleak rhetorical question: "Shall we inquire what impressions romantic adventures, high-wrought scenes of passion, and all the turmoil of intrigue, incident, extravagant attachment, and improbable vicissitudes of fortune, must make upon a vacant mind, whose judgement has not been exercised either by real information, or the conclusions of experience and observation?" The answer is repetitively played out in the plots of her novels: a young woman's adherence to a "romantick standard" destroys her own possibilities for contentment, especially in marriage, and, more significantly, infects the social formation as a whole.[7] Marianne Dudley in *A Gossip's Story* and Charlotte Raby in *The Advantages of Education* both suffer unhappy marriages, and Marianne is virtually ostracized by her rural community. More insidiously, the romantic Geraldine Powerscourt of *A Tale of the Times* is seduced by a Jacobin philosopher-villain and dies, her narrative an epidemiology of the moral infection of the "times." In these texts, romance is a potential catalyst for moral, social, and national disorder. This link is made explicit in the anti-Jacobin use, during the 1790s, of "romance" to designate "the various narrative forms through which radical principles are expressed." In this sense the term was used to denigrate texts as generically different as Godwin's *Political Justice* and Holcroft's *Anna St. Ives*.[8] Heroines who are corrupted by "romance" in antirevolutionary texts represent the corruption of unwary readers by radical and revolutionary discourses.

For West, who adhered to a philosophy of linguistic simplicity, the language of romance was the object of considerable disapproval. In many of her novels simplicity of language is the moral indicator of a simple heart, and, conversely, complex language is linked to deceit and moral subversion. The connection between language and morality was of particular concern to her two years before she wrote *Alicia de Lacy*, when she was occupied with *The Loyalists*. Excessive language, or, as the narrator puts it, "tautological verbiage" (2:191), marks negative characters in *The Loyalists*. Cromwell, the villain of the piece, is particularly prone to the use of metaphor and analogy in his speech, while a Calvinist cleric's sermons are made "obscure by bold metaphors and strained allusions" (2:190). One positive male character is notable for his "fearless candour" (1:42), and he counsels his son to avoid perverting language by using qualifiers and diminutives (2:92). The plot reaches its climax in the trial of the virtuous Dr. Beaumont for "evasions and subtleties of expression" (3:204). The narrative vindicates Dr. Beaumont, who provides a voice of paternal authority throughout the novel, and "subtleties of expression" are demonstrated to be the province and weapon of the negatively valorized Puritan rebels. The moral meaning of style is a concern throughout this text, and provides a background for West's risky venture into the linguistically excessive genre of romance two years later.

Alicia de Lacy: An Historical Romance was published in 1814, the same year as Scott's *Waverley*. West clearly indicates the generic shift this novel represents in her subtitle. If we read the historical novel, with its typical heterodiegetic narratorial mode, in the politicized sense that critics like Nicola Watson suggest, West's engagement with the genre of historical fiction becomes explicable. In order to promulgate her authoritarian novelistic "message," she adopted an authoritative form of narration, and a narrative form that readily accommodated conservative lessons. A historical novel, however, differs from a historical romance, in that the latter diverges from conventionally acknowledged historical "fact," is set in a more distant period, and foregrounds the customs and ceremony of "remote times."[9] It also, as West claimed earlier, privileges "variety of incident," and "splendour" of language and content, elements that West strove diligently, by her own account, to excise from her didactic texts.[10] The preface to *Alicia de Lacy* acknowledges the incongruity, and attempts to justify it; West is careful to acknowledge as forerunners in this genre of literature only those writers who were solidly legitimized by the processes of canonization: Shakespeare, Virgil, Homer, and Scott (1:vii). West's patron and friend, Bishop Percy, whose *Reliques of Ancient English Poetry* (1763) helped to establish the Romantic interest in things medieval, is another member of the group, and is acknowledged at the conclusion of the text (4:309). Female romance writers, and the French, are scrupulously excluded from her list of influences. Despite her canny negotiation of literary legitimacy, however, West's generic decision remains a notable divergence from her earlier moral and literary position.

West's choice of the romance form is less obscure, however, if we consider that she had earlier stated her belief in utilizing the tools of corruption to combat corruption, or, to use her own metaphor, "poison." In the search for a "vehicle" for "sound doctrine," the popularity of a genre played an important role. According to West's argument, conveying an "antidote" to revolutionary "poison," and thereby fulfilling the function of an antirevolutionary text, becomes the justification for the utilization of an unfamiliar and formerly devalued narrative form. In *Alicia de Lacy*, therefore, West takes considerable care to ensure that the narrative form and her conservative didactic message are in alignment. In order to contain the subversiveness of the romance form, and to produce a morally satisfactory narrative, West mixes genres, an act she claims makes her "an adventurer in an unknown department of literature" (1:xii). History and romance are, of course, the initial components of the historical romance genre; to these West adds the didactic domestic plot, and the evangelical conversion narrative.

It has been argued, however, that "[w]e generally regard the mixture of genres as a threat to endogamous, hegemonic order," and an anonymous contemporary reviewer of *Alicia de Lacy* isolated exactly this point: "we . . . must enter our protest against blending and confounding together historical truth and romantic fiction, each of which ought to be rigidly restrained within its own peculiar province." The *Gentleman's Magazine*'s review of *Alicia de Lacy* comments that "we think the confounding of History and Romance should generally be avoided, for reasons we need not point out to our Readers." The assumption that the danger of mingling genres is common knowledge signals the prevalence of this view. In taking this position, these reviewers are articulating a conservative, antirevolutionary understanding of the relationship between romance and history. April London has argued that, for anti-Jacobins of the 1790s, romance became the negative antithesis of "history," which was presented as "the most appropriate guide to private and public conduct."[11] Separating the two, then, was part of a project of controlling revolutionary discourse. West's own discomfort with her generic experimentation is evident in the twenty-seven-page "Historical Notices" appended to the final volume, which are intended "[t]o prevent any possibility of misleading those who travel to the end of this maze of history and fiction" (4:309).[12] More importantly in didactic terms, the "Historical Notices" provide a preventative to the kind of generic solecisms practiced by Arabella in Charlotte Lennox's *The Female Quixote* (1752). For West, Lennox's heroine's misreading provides a model of the dangers of using the romance form for didactic purposes, and the factual "Notices" attempt to forestall the potentially anarchic effects of generic misinterpretation: "They are designed to save the enlightened reader the trouble of reference, and to prevent the juvenile one from so confounding the Lancaster of romance and the Lancaster of history, as to become as warm as advocate for the purity of his motives, as was the female Quixote for the decorum of the Empress Julia" (1:xiv).

The "Historical Notices" strategy was not effective, according to at least one critic. The review of *Alicia de Lacy* in the *British Critic* notes that, "seemingly conscious of the impropriety of mixing [fiction] with truth, she has added to her work a chapter, for the purpose of minutely pointing out her wanderings from history. This disenchanting chapter, into which probably not one reader in a hundred will ever look, is an aukward [sic] contrivance. It reminds us too strongly of the wise precautions of Bottom, in the Midsummer Night's Dream. 'If you think I come hither as a lion, it were pity of my life: No, I am no such thing; I am a man as other men are.'"[13] The *British Critic*'s reviewer argues that West's attempt to combine history and romance in the service of antirevolutionary didacticism is unsuccessful. In the case of *Alicia de Lacy*, the mixture of genres has a non-transgressive aim: it is intended explicitly to maintain textual and social order, and to control the radical instability of "pure" romance. In spite of her efforts at narrative control, however, the monologism necessary to a clear didactic message is not achieved in this text.

The first half of *Alicia de Lacy* follows a conventional didactic and domestic plot of moral improvement. In her preface to the novel, West outlines her ethical motivation for constructing the narrative in this way: "It is hoped that a delineation of the different effects of prosperity and adversity on a well-intentioned but infirm mind, may produce some moral impression, especially on those whom parental indulgence or the flattery of inferiors has induced to rank themselves too high in the scale of intellectual being" (1:xiv–xv). The eponymous, negative exemplary heroine is an erring wife with an unruly desire for freedom: she disobeys her husband, squanders her money, neglects her domestic and charitable duties, and holds a masquerade. Most egregiously, she allows a male admirer to act as her "*cicisbeo*" in her husband's absence, which gives her the social appearance of adultery, despite her relative innocence. The events of her misbehavior—particularly the masquerade, which, as Terry Castle has pointed out, was a characteristic topos of the eighteenth-century novel—locate this narrative in the eighteenth or early nineteenth century, and highlight its affinities with the didactic novel of the 1790s. The setting of the narrative in fourteenth-century England functions primarily, in the first half of the text, as historical embellishment, with an emphasis on costume and architecture, as well as on the alien practices of an English Catholic national church. The plot of moral improvement reaches its climax with Alicia's mock death: she is drugged and abducted by her unscrupulous *cicisbeo*, leading her friends and family to presume her dead. It is at this point in the narrative that Alicia undergoes repentance and a complete spiritual and moral transformation, a rebirth that forms the resolution of the didactic plot. She learns piety, social propriety, and submission to masculine authority: both to her husband and to God. Hidden in a rural convent, she becomes a "militant" Christian, completing her conversion to a proto-evangelical religious ideal (3:300).

Alicia's conversion could conceivably form the conclusion of the didactic narrative, yet, significantly, it does not. The transformation occurs only slightly more than halfway through the novel, and it is at this point that the romance narrative enters the text, in a more complete form than the superficial embellishments of historical setting. It is only after her participation in the plot of the didactic novel that Alicia takes part in the events of romance. Her conversion, in effect, inoculates her against the potential immorality of the romance genre, and the "infection" of "romantic adventures."[14] The events of the narrative change in quality from those previous to Alicia's conversion, from situations involving moral choice in a domestic setting, to physical action outside the limits of the domestic sphere. After a daring and imaginative escape from the fortified castle of her abductor, Alicia sets out on a quest "to detect an impostor, recover her child, preserve the reputation of her husband, and rescue him from the machinations of a cabal" (3:352–53). This undertaking demands that she travel almost alone through war-torn England, infiltrate the court of Edward II in disguise, and risk her life to prove her identity. As in West's earlier didactic fiction, in which good behavior leads to a companionate marriage, the result of moral exemplarity is greater freedom for the heroine, but here of an unconventional and extensive variety. Circumstances demand that Alicia move beyond the conventions and constraints of her domestic role, both physically, as she travels freely through England, and metaphorically, as she adopts responsibilities formerly outside her jurisdiction as a domestic woman. In her experience of the events of romance, Alicia explores what Laurie Langbauer conceives as a romantic "realm of freedom for women outside the constraints of male power."[15] It is in the tension between history and romance, between the attempt to control and the desire to captivate readers, that a more active model of femininity is generated, in conjunction with an expanded conception of women's domestic freedom.

With the beginning of the romance plot, the protagonist develops the quality of "female heroism" first introduced in *The Loyalists* (3:353). West continues to preach the necessity of domestic heroism in *Alicia de Lacy*, yet she also places her central character in situations in which she is compelled to perform "high acts of heroic excellence." In fact, the positive events at the text's conclusion are a direct result of Alicia's exercise of this characteristic. According to the logic of a didactic text, the value of female heroism is proven by its euphoric effects. The newly valorized attribute is incorporated, in this text, into West's construction of ideal femininity. Submission to authority, though the precipitating factor of the female exemplar's expanded freedom, is no longer her predominant quality: her character now comprises greater authority and agency. This authority is echoed in the portrayal of a peripheral character, the Queen of Navarre, who is lauded for defending her castle, Kenilworth, in spite of a debilitating illness (2:222). Her "masculine" mind is used to prove the narrator's contention that there is a danger in the division between active masculinity and passive femininity; passivity allows women too much time to think, while activity produces virtue and heroism (2:243).

In this novel, "female heroism" is firmly linked to what West terms "militant" Christianity, which was a key concept in early nineteenth-century British Evangelicalism. West literalizes the common theological metaphor of the "church militant," meaning the church struggling against sin on earth as opposed to the "church triumphant" in heaven.[16] Through her fortuitous meeting with a member of the "militant church" (3:234), Alicia becomes a "militant combatant" against the passions (3:300), and ultimately a "militant christian" (4:280). This metaphor for religious practice is similar to Brunton's description of a Christian as a "soldier." It is Alicia's conversion to "militant" Christianity, and her consequent disavowal of selfish considerations, that produces her "female heroism." In *Letters to a Young Lady* West had argued the rarity of this quality ("It is possible, I allow, to produce many illustrious examples of female heroism and capacity; but *singular* occurrences do not overthrow the general conclusions of experience"). West's invocation of female heroism in *Alicia de Lacy* does not necessarily undermine this rule; Alicia's behavior may constitute a "singular" occurrence, and the novel's setting in the distant past reinforces the uniqueness of her situation and diminishes its applicability to modern women. Yet the didactic novel's demand to be read analogically of necessity positions the reader in the place of the heroine, drawing connections between the historical past and the present, and creating in "female heroism" a potential course of behavior for the novel's readers. That this behavior involves moving outside the "magic circle" of domesticity creates an opening for a challenge to purely domestic models of femininity.

It is instructive to read West's novel in relation to Porter's earlier *The Scottish Chiefs*, particularly in terms of the issue of female agency. As I have noted, Porter's novel, like West's, engages in the conservative project of historical fiction, which reconstructs a fictional past to support counterrevolutionary social theory in the present. Her hero, William Wallace, embodies the morality of an early nineteenth-century conservative Evangelical, advocating values of domesticity, patriotism, and piety, all embedded in a philosophy of sentimental Christianity. As Rhonda Batchelor has argued, Porter's novel valorizes silent and domestic femininity while demonizing agency through the character of the politically and sexually manipulative Lady Mar: "Porter portrays agency in woman as an immoral and socially destabilizing effort to increase her social power and to gratify her sexual desires."[17] Unlike West's heroine, positive female characters like Wallace's murdered wife Marion are remarkable for their silence and their quiet support of the male characters who engage in political and military action (in Marion's case it is the ultimate silence of death that makes possible her mobilization as a symbol for national defense).

West's novel seems a response to Porter's on a number of levels. First, setting the novel during approximately the same historical period allows her to respond to Porter's Scottish attack on an English monarch. Hardly the tyrant of Porter's account (primarily in chapter 17), West's Edward I is a leader characterized by "chastity, magnanimity, and temperance" (1:124), who helped to strengthen the "middle class of society" (1:291), a positive social development according to the text. Like Porter, West situates the health of the nation within the domestic sphere; England's sufferings under Edward II are due to "domestic discord" (2:90), just as the heroine's personal trials are a result of her rejection of correct domesticity. Yet, as I have argued, West's novel leaves room for female agency, in a way that Porter's novel does not. Through the common romance strategy of doubling characters, West draws a line of distinction between appropriate and inappropriate agency. Where Porter distinguishes between silent domesticity and sexual and political agency, West allows for the possibility of virtuous extra-domestic feminine agency, by marking carefully the limits of the sphere of feminine activity.

Alicia's doppelgänger is Agatha, the descendant of Alicia's great-grandfather and a "Moorish" lover, who was brought to England by a pilgrim. Agatha's foreign background provides some justification for her transgressive behavior, even as it distances her more effectively from the exemplary Englishwoman Alicia becomes. The two women are, coincidentally, almost identical in appearance; their differences, as the narrative makes clear, are internal. As a teenager, Agatha has an affair and undergoes a terrible punishment—live burial in a cave—at the hands of Alicia's father, the Earl of Lincoln. She does not play a major role in the narrative until after Alicia's mock death and abduction, after which she reappears to take Alicia's place in courtly and aristocratic society. Her close resemblance to Alicia allows her to appropriate her lands and titles, carrying out her revenge on Alicia's family. At the climax of the novel Alicia, penniless and improbable (after all, the vivacious Agatha behaves much more like the former Alicia than the newly pious Alicia does), must confront Agatha to regain her property and her son. Her final test occurs when Alicia's young son Edmund is asked to identify his mother. He wavers until Alicia sings a song she sang to him before her abduction, then immediately recognizes his mother (4:184). Agatha leaps (or is pushed) from a rooftop to a grisly death, after which, the narrator informs us, she goes to the "dolourous regions" (4:60). Alicia triumphs due to the maternal and domestic virtues she possessed in embryo prior to her conversion; her success valorizes these qualities. Conversely, these qualities justify Alicia's actions, which are rooted in an agency unprecedented in West's domestic novels. Agatha's agency, unconnected to the text's privileged virtues of piety and maternity, is demonized as vicious and self-centered, a sin in Evangelical terms, as well as in terms of a conservative gender ideology in which femininity is defined as nurturing and relational. *Alicia de Lacy* proposes a model of female agency that is positive only insofar as it is rooted in feminine and domestic virtues. Agatha demonstrates the negative form of agency; her transgression enables West's depiction of a feminine agency that is positive.

In West's earlier *A Gossip's Story*, the heroine is ultimately rewarded for her exemplarity with a companionate marriage that offers limited domestic freedom. The didactic conclusion of *Alicia de Lacy* diverges from this exemplary form of closure: married near the beginning of the text to the noble Earl of Lancaster, Alicia is never reunited with her husband, who is ultimately hanged for treason (4:267). Instead, she raises their son alone, exercising sole parental authority, a refiguring of the domestic sphere that erases the male/female hierarchical relationship. When her son reaches maturity, Alicia becomes the abbess of a convent, a "bride of Christ" whose primary purpose in life is to submit to the Christian God, the supreme patriarchal authority within English culture and religious doctrine. Christine Krueger suggests, however, that for the female evangelicals of the period in which West was writing, "submission to the will of God often meant a break with temporal authorities," and therefore "gave women tremendous leverage."[18] West's exemplary heroine in *Alicia de Lacy* draws on this paradoxical source of social power. Her conversion to "militant" Christianity allows her to reject the traditional domestic structure based on marriage, and to adopt a position of authority in a community of women, within but also beyond the limits of a patriarchal hegemony. Alicia's actual social and political power is inscribed in a brief scene near the conclusion of the text, in which the new king, Edward III, brings his family to receive her "blessings and instructions" (4:282). Patriarchal and monarchical power submits, in this moment, to feminine religious authority.

It is significant for the purposes of my reading that the final portion of the text, in which Alicia converts and lives a virtuous life, is West's invention, as she admits in the "Historical Notices" at the conclusion of her text. The historical original of Alicia de Lacy did not repent; in fact, West tells us, "her deportment was such as made her real adventures unfit even for a fabulist, who studiously avoids combining an air of heroical perfection with the manners of a comparatively barbarous period" (4:287). By allowing a socially transgressive woman to live and repent, West not only revises history, but rewrites her own earlier novelistic plots. "As the plan of most of my former novels was to condemn what was wrong," she writes in 1810, "I felt obliged by principle to give a melancholy termination." Rebellious women in the domestic novels therefore follow an inevitable decline into misery and tragedy. Their stories prove what Gary Kelly calls "the sliding scale of sin—the idea that small errors and transgressions . . . lead to major ones." In *Letters to a Young Lady* West describes the process in this way: "A slight indiscretion, which scarcely alarms the most scrupulous conscience, if suffered to pass without observation, prepares the mind for a serious error; error delivers it over to crime; and crime, when often repeated, petrifies the moral feelings into insensible depravity."[19] Moral and social solecisms are ruinous, and locate the transgressive female well beyond the limits of potential moral and social recovery. *Alicia de Lacy* opens a space for resistance to this model, and challenges the necessity of the transgressor's tragic plot. More radically, the novel imagines the possibility, not only of survival for the heroine, but of subsequent contentment, independence, and agency.

My reading of the contradictions in West's novel between conservative social ideology and a progressive ideology of femininity may seem to echo Georg Lukács's conclusions regarding the historical novel, which (in Lukács's literary history) reaches its apotheosis in the fiction of Walter Scott. Lukács contends that "there is a certain contradiction . . . between Scott's directly political views [as a "Scottish petty aristocrat"] and his artistic world picture." Despite Scott's "narrow conservatism," argues Lukács, his attention to historical realism has a number of progressive effects. Most importantly, rather than focusing on the effect of historical crises on the social and political elite, "Scott portrays the great transformations of history as transformations of popular life." Further, Scott's fiction represents the potential for heroism in the conventionally unheroic lower classes: "The important thing for these great writers [Scott and Goethe] is to lay bare those vast, heroic, human potentialities which are always latently present in the people and which, on each big occasion, with every deep disturbance of the social or even the more personal life, emerge 'suddenly,' with colossal force, to the surface." My conclusions here differ, on a number of significant levels, from Lukács's. West would certainly not conform to Lukács's definition of a "great writer"; her emphasis is not on historical realism, and her representations of "the people" relegate them to roles as faithful retainers, misled dupes, or comic relief. Her historical fiction supports social hierarchies; it manipulates the material of history to teach a lesson about the necessity for hierarchy and distinction. Unlike Lukács's "great historical art," which consists in "bringing the past to life as the prehistory of the present" in order to understand modernity, West's novels create a past with the didactic intent of commenting on and changing the present.[20] Yet West does explore the "vast, heroic, human potentialities" that may be present in *women*, through the enabling power of evangelical religion. This is, implicitly, what Lukács argues as well: his two examples of heroism in "the people" are Jeanie Deans in Scott's *Heart of Midlothian*, and Dorothea in Goethe's *Hermann and Dorothea*.

In *Alicia de Lacy*, the mixture of genres enables a revision of conservative, prescriptive ideals of domesticity and femininity. Further, it destabilizes West's own theories of domesticity as they are formulated in her prefaces and conduct manuals. West remained politically conservative throughout her lifetime, and maintained an appreciative conservative reading public. It is a testament to the strength of her moral authority that *The British Critic* could write of *Alicia de Lacy*: "That the morality is uniformly pure we need not say. On that head, the name of the writer is a sufficient security." Despite this endorsement, West did not repeat the experiment of the historical romance. In fact, the publication of *Alicia de Lacy* marks the beginning of a thirteen-year hiatus in her fiction writing; her next novel, *Ringrove: Or, Old Fashioned Notions*, was not published until 1827. Once again, the subtitle signals a generic shift: a return to the values and form of earlier didactic texts, such as *A Gossip's Story*. Formally and structurally it resembles the earlier novels; unlike *Alicia de Lacy*, it is characterized by discursive, generic, and moral simplicity. A woman's appropriate place is once again firmly within the domestic sphere, and under her husband's guidance. "Female heroism" has become "passive courage," and "appears in actions, of which the discriminating characteristic is concealment," especially of suffering and unhappiness. In her preface, West carefully states her abhorrence of "blending truth with falsehood," ostensibly aiming her critique at other, "fashionable" novelists.[21] Yet, the similarities between the "truth" and "falsehood" of "fashionable" novels, and the "maze of history and fiction," which was West's attempt at a "fashionable" genre in *Alicia de Lacy*, suggest that *Ringrove* is a deliberate erasure of her own former literary errors. Ultimately, the effect of the rewriting is this: the disruptive discourse of the romance is rigorously controlled, purified, and left in the past, an unsettling anomaly in a highly regular writing career.

West's experiment with *Alicia de Lacy* indicates the extent to which she was prepared to go in her effort to find a "vehicle" for "sound doctrine" that conformed to public and critical taste. The novel baffled West's critics, however. While conservative reviewers approved its moral, its form and style received criticism. West created a hybrid genre, not only by mixing history and fiction, but by combining her didactic project with a new genre. For critics habituated to the domestic novel as a "vehicle" of "sound doctrine," West's historical romance was difficult to interpret. Mary Brunton's novels more easily combine the elements of domestic fiction and didacticism with a modified form of romance. As Robin Reed Davis notes, Brunton "pioneered a version of feminine romance that would be morally acceptable to conservative religious women," without departing from the literary mainstream. Along with Hannah More, then, she worked to make the novel a respectable form for the "serious" middle classes. As her husband comments in his biography of Brunton, however, her novels "rose very fast into celebrity, and their popularity seems to have as quickly sunk away."[22] West's popularity underwent a similar decline: by the time she returned to the domestic novel in 1827, public and critical taste had moved beyond her form of explicit and authoritative didacticism. Both of these writers took different routes in their search for marketable "vehicles" for moral and religious lessons. Both produced idiosyncratic literary forms—the Evangelical romance and the didactic historical romance—intended to fulfill this didactic and political need. The decline in their novels' popularity, however, is testament to the fact that neither learned the aesthetic lesson that would make their productions palatable to a new generation: not so much that novels could no longer be didactic, but that they could not be considered purely as "vehicles" of morality. The "moral" novel was in the process of displacing the "moralistic" one. The critical terrain was shifting, and West and Brunton, along with the other writers I have examined in this study, were either unable or unwilling to move with it.

Postscript

JANE WEST, WHO SAW HER WORK DISAPPEAR FROM PUBLIC CONSCIOUSNESS well before her death in 1852, wrote querulously but with some justification to a young autograph-seeker in 1834: "How you chance to recollect an old Q in a corner whom the rest of the world has forgotten I know not however the request is too complimentary to be refused." This self-deprecating comment marks not only West's own loss of public attention, but the cultural devaluation of the openly didactic genre at which she excelled. The narrative I sketch here, then, is one of decline: I take the conservative didactic novel from the peak of its popularity in the 1790s to the beginning of its critical and popular decline in the mid-1810s. The "rage for novels" did not decrease, but the rage for this type of novel certainly did. By the second decade of the nineteenth century, literary journals like *Blackwood's Edinburgh Magazine* were attempting to differentiate between the artistic value of novels that attempt to record "the developements [sic] exhibited by the human mind," and the moral value of novels that "are meant to show the causes of success or failure in this life." This valorization of a form of psychological realism of necessity devalues "a didactic purpose." The reviewer stumbles a little in the face of "immoral" novels, such as Goethe's *Sufferings of Young Werther* and Rousseau's *Nouvelle Héloïse*, falling back on a conventional didactic defense of the novel form by claiming that these ones are not "works of art, holding up models of perfection to the imagination." Yet his basic premise, that the purpose of a novel is not to teach but to record, marks a shifting ideology of form that leaves little space for arguments like Hannah More's in *Coelebs in Search of a Wife*: "Knowledge of the world should always be used to mend the world." Certainly when in *Northanger Abbey* Jane Austen describes the novel as a genre "in which the most thorough knowledge of human nature, the happiest delineation of its varieties . . . are conveyed to the world in the best chosen language," she foregrounds precisely the qualities the *Blackwood's* reviewer values.[1] What both of these accounts foretell is the development of the nineteenth-century realist novel, which is essentially mimetic in emphasis, and depends upon the fiction that it merely reflects reality.

Changes in the novel as a genre "edged out" women writers with a primarily didactic, rather than aesthetic, purpose. Yet it would be inaccurate to see this process as one in which these writers were hapless victims of some sort of aesthetic plot. The writers I analyze in this study were agents as well as subjects of this alteration; they were affected by, but also helped to constitute, the changes that occurred within the genre over the next decades. Sam Pickering Jr. has rightly argued that the writing of Hannah More and Walter Scott made the novel an acceptable literary form for the consumption of the "respectable" middle classes during the early decades of the nineteenth century.[2] Yet the process toward respectability began much earlier, and had its roots in the political battles waged through the form of the novel in the turbulent years after the beginning of the French Revolution. Writers like Jane West, who was admired for her "elegant" prose as well as her exemplary morality, and Elizabeth Hamilton, who combined incisive political critique with entertaining fiction, paved the way for the gradual "rise" of the novel into moral and aesthetic respectability. West, in particular, broke into mainstream conservative culture; reviews of her work in the *Gentleman's Magazine* and the *British Critic* emphasize the social and political usefulness of her work, without negating its aesthetic value. The attention of major political and literary journals like these, as opposed to publications aimed explicitly at women, helped to make the novel form acceptable to a wider reading public, and thereby worked to establish its growing moral and aesthetic respectability. The process that West and her peers seem shut out from, then, is one in which they themselves are intimately implicated.

What, then, happened to the antirevolutionary didactic voice I have charted in this study? It did not simply disappear, but rather metamorphosed into different forms with slightly different concerns. With the end of the Revolutionary Wars in 1815 the "antirevolutionary" purpose became slightly outdated (though the equally topical *Anti-Jacobin Review and Magazine* continued to publish for over a decade). At this time conservative women writers began to publish more regularly in the nonfictional fields of moral literature and religious writing. Most of the novelists I have discussed wrote in these genres at the same time as they published fiction; Hannah More, for example, published broadly on religious and moral subjects throughout her writing career, and Jane West garnered more praise for her "monitory letters" than for her novels. As Robin Reed Davis has noted, tract writing and religious journalism became respectable and lucrative professions for women during the first decades of the nineteenth century. Her figures show that between 1801 and 1835, 22.2 percent of all books published in England were religious, a percentage that increased during the second half of the century. Some literary careers began, as Charlotte Elizabeth Tonna's did, with tract writing (she belonged to the Dublin Tract Society). A related move for women was into philanthropic societies, and thereby into publishing on charitable topics. F. K. Prochaska has charted the routes by which middle-class women became involved in a range of philanthropic activities over the course of the nineteenth century, as organizers, promoters, and administrators of a multitude of charitable societies. Tracts, prospectuses, and journalism on philanthropic subjects provided a venue for women's writing. This activity, as Prochaska has argued, opened new avenues in the movement toward female social equality; subsequent philanthropic generations turned their attention towards the "Woman Question" as well as the reform and regulation of the poor and disadvantaged. The Victorian "social problem" novel deals with similar philanthropic subjects, fictionalizing, for example, the plight of factory workers or prostitutes. Charlotte Elizabeth Tonna's *Helen Fleetwood* uses strategies that are recognizable from the antirevolutionary novel. Her descriptions of the "hell-born reptile of socialism" and her attacks on Chartism echo the violent rhetoric of the *Anti-Jacobin Review and Magazine*, and work to set her critique apart from radicalism.[3] Her evangelical solutions to social problems, which involve evangelizing the working classes and encouraging charity in the "great," are echoes of the novels of More and Brunton.

Another form of writing in which women's conservative didacticism flourished was conduct literature, in the plethora of etiquette and conduct manuals published during the Victorian period. Conduct literature and the novels I have discussed in this study share common subjects and didactic intentions, being concerned primarily with the regulation of domesticity. Defining and imposing rules of conduct is an ideological act with concrete social effects, and is therefore well-suited to the promulgation of antirevolutionary "messages." Leonard Tennenhouse and Nancy Armstrong argue that conduct literature played a significant role in the reproduction of "culturally approved forms of desire," which produced and supported dominant ideologies of gender and domesticity during the eighteenth and early nineteenth centuries. Elizabeth Langland has argued that during the nineteenth century the emphasis on conduct shifted from the domestic subject to include domestic space; household management became the site of "an exercise in class management."[4] Producing advice literature on household management and domestic economy thus allowed writing women to engage in a similar form of class control as that attempted by their predecessors in the early 1800s through the form of the novel. The "ephemeral" nature of the writing and publication done by women in these capacities—religious, philanthropic, mentorial—creates a misleading impression that didactic women writers "disappeared" from publishing history. What really changed was the form in which their projects were carried out.

Reading the novels of antirevolutionary women writers broadens our understanding of the relationship between politics, gender, and literature during this period of British history. How women "speak" in fiction has been a subject of many feminist inquiries into literary history. Achieving "voice," in many of these studies, is an oppositional act, pitting feminine agency and verbal empowerment against a conservative establishment. A close analysis of their narrative strategies shows that writers like More, West, Brunton, and Hamilton carefully negotiated their entrance into literature, particularly in the area of narrative voice. They were aware of the difficulties for women of achieving narrative authority in a conservative culture, but supported the structures that made this process difficult. The delicate negotiation around issues of narration and genre we find in novels by antirevolutionary women writers indicates the tensions within their position as women writers and conservatives. In this sense, these writers were what modern feminist theory identifies as the "self-different" female subject, "situated at diverse cultural locations, for whom gender intersects dynamically with numerous other social categories and discourses."[5] These lines of intersection are most obvious when a writer like Jane West uses a female narrative voice in fiction: conservative politics, ideologies of class and gender, and the novel's demand for narratorial authority produce a text that is profoundly "unsettled."

Yet the engagement of these writers with philosophical and political ideas, their experimentation with form, and their positive reception by conservative periodicals of their time shows that their authoritative acts in print were accepted by their culture. By building narrative and moral authority, and achieving literary "voice," while simultaneously and gladly supporting "Order's sacred Laws," their writing demonstrated the possibilities for women to achieve narrative authority without contravening conservative gender boundaries. For these writers, authority and agency were not achieved through opposition, but through conformity with the established power structures and dominant ideologies of their period. Like domestic freedom in Jane West's novels, agency is the result of compliance rather than confrontation. Unlike their revolutionary contemporaries, Mary Hays and Mary Wollstonecraft, who also used the novel form to engage in political debates, writers like West and Hamilton offered models for women writers who did not subscribe to revolutionary politics. However compromised their authority seems through its complicity with patriarchal power structures, it represents a significant strategy for negotiating problems of gender and authority in literature.

Reading the group of antirevolutionary women writers I have brought together in this study in the context of conservative print culture helps to illuminate the ways in which they carved out for themselves a peculiarly feminine form of discourse, which interrogated, accommodated, and adapted the political and social theories presented in more openly political genres. Writers like West, More, and Hawkins were influenced by and contributed to the many passionate political and moral debates, about democracy, women's rights, revolution, education, and art, of the period in which they lived. The conservative culture with which they interacted was not homogeneous, nor was their writing. By reading them in relation to one another, we can see the unique responses of each writer to the perceived need to combat revolutionary thought and action. Their work shows the various ways in which they were in conversation with conservative and radical writers and concepts, and how the search for the vehicle of sound doctrine led them to experiment with a range of styles and forms as they responded to changes in critics' aesthetics, readers' buying patterns, and to the unstable political circumstances of their time. Their writing remains a fertile and rewarding source as we continue to construct the compelling narrative of women's relationships to culture, power, and to literature during this uneasy and turbulent period.

Notes

Chapter 1: Poison or Pudding?

1. West, *Tale of the Times*, 2:80.

2. On the "remasculinization" of British culture, see Kelly's *Women, Writing, and Revolution*, and see D. A. Miller, *The Novel and the Police*, for a discussion of the "ideological" novel of the Victorian period.

3. Kadish, *Politicizing Gender*, 5.

4. I include publication dates for primary texts in the body of the chapter only if it is relevant to my argument. For original publication dates, please see the bibliography.

5. More, *Strictures*, 1:190–91; Hawkins, *Countess and Gertrude*, 1:xiii, 1:xxi, 1:xxviii, 1:xxix, 1:2; *Anti-Jacobin* 45 (September 1813): 263. As J. Paul Hunter has pointed out, credibility was an important component of the novel as it developed during the eighteenth century (*Before Novels*, 23). In the conservative didactic novel of this later period, however, credibility and narrative "truth" carried increased moral weight, as the revolutionary potential of the genre became manifest.

6. *Anti-Jacobin* 15 (May 1803): 41; More, quoted in Davis, "Anglican Evangelicalism," 60; Brunton, *Discipline*, 59. For an intriguing account of the interpenetration of politics and representations of disease in the 1790s, see Tim Fulford and Debbie Lee, "The Jenneration of Disease: Vaccination, Romanticism, and Revolution."

7. Barbauld, "Origin and Progress," 370; West, *Infidel Father*, 1:6; West, *Loyalists*, 1:2; West, letter to Bishop Percy, 18 November 1810, in Nichols, *Illustrations*, 8:425; West, *Letters Addressed to a Young Man*, 1:xxvi.

8. Bishop Percy, letter to West, 7 June 1800, in Nichols, *Illustrations*, 8:328. As it turned out, *Letters Addressed to a Young Man* (1801) sold very well and helped to solidify West's reputation as a moralist.

9. More, *Coelebs*, 2:33; Barbauld, "Origin and Progress," 368, 371; Colby, *Fiction with a Purpose*, 10. The Jacobin novelist Thomas Holcroft concurs with Barbauld: "When we consider the influence that novels have over the manners, sentiments, and passions, of the rising generation,—instead of holding them in the contempt which, as reviewers, we are without exception said to do,—we may esteem them, on the contrary, as forming a very essential branch of literature" (*Monthly Review* 10 [March 1793]: 297, quoted in Kelly, *English Jacobin Novel*, 115).

10. Bakhtin, *Dialogic Imagination*, 316. Bakhtin's bias, in this essay and elsewhere, is in favor of heteroglossia. For him, representing "the living heteroglossia of language" is one of the central "tasks of the novel as a genre" (326, 327). The writers I examine in this study betray Bakhtin's vision of the novel in their striving toward monologism, yet his concepts of dialogism and heteroglossia provide a useful critical framework for examining the ways in which monologism is undermined by social forces, and the instability of language in use.

11. Wilde, *Plays, Prose, and Poems*, 138; Butler, *Jane Austen*, 97; James, "Art of Fiction," 402; Poe, "The Poetic Principle," 75–76. The term "intentional fallacy" was coined by W. K. Wimsatt and Monroe C. Beardsley in their 1946 essay, "The Intentional Fallacy."

12. Selden, *Contemporary Literary Theory*, 20; Suleiman, *Authoritarian Fictions*, 18, 22; Miller, *Novel and the Police*, xi.

13. Wordsworth, preface to *Lyrical Ballads*, 153, 158.

14. Vaughan, *Romanticism and Art*, 9.

15. This model did not gain prominence until the middle of the twentieth century; prior to this period, both the model and the term "Romantic" were contested. Until the 1980s, however, this model remained dominant in scholarship (it is still common in undergraduate English courses), and it is against this construct that much recent revisionist criticism positions itself. The term "Romantic ideology" is Jerome McGann's.

16. Several anthologies of the poetry and prose of this period implicitly or explicitly challenge the narrow definition of "Romantic literature" by presenting a much more heterogeneous literary landscape. See, for example, Roger Lonsdale's *Eighteenth-Century Women Poets*; Jennifer Breen's *Women Romantic Poets, 1785–1832*; and Anne Mellor and Richard Matlak's *British Literature, 1780–1830*. The project of expanding the definition of "Romanticism" continues, as the many periodicals dedicated to the study of the period show with each successive issue.

17. Lukács, *Historical Novel*, 34.

18. Ty, *Unsex'd Revolutionaries*, 15; Pederson, "Hannah More Meets Simple Simon"; Kowaleski-Wallace, *Their Fathers' Daughters*.

19. Kelly, *Women, Writing, and Revolution*; Ty, *Empowering the Feminine*; Krueger, *The Reader's Repentance*, 119; Bannet, *Domestic Revolution*; Gerald Newman, *Rise of English Nationalism*, 234; London, "Charlotte Smith," 98.

20. Jameson, *Political Unconscious*, 291.

21. Sarkar and Butalia, *Women and Right-Wing Movements*, 4; Blee, *Women of the Klan*, 3.

22. Nickson, "Behold, the Bible Belles," D1. For a sociological analysis of Real Women, see Lorna Erwin, "Neoconservatism and the Canadian Pro-Family Movement."

23. Brunton, *Self-Control*, viii, 70, 73. The term "war of ideas" is from Marilyn Butler's *Jane Austen and the War of Ideas*.

24. West, *Letters to a Young Man*, 1:203.

25. Lanser, *Fictions of Authority*, 5, 6.

26. See, as a small sample, Bruce Frohnen, *Virtue and the Promise of Conservatism*, on Burke; Claudia Johnson, *Equivocal Beings* and *Jane Austen*, on "conservative novelists"; and Anne Crippen Ruderman, *The Pleasures of Virtue*, on Jane Austen.

27. *Oxford English Dictionary* on CD-ROM, 2d ed.; Montluzin, *Anti-Jacobins*, 40.

Chapter 2. Women, Late Eighteenth-Century Conservatism

1. West, *Letters to a Young Man*, 1:145; More, *Works*, 4:234; West, *Letters to a Young Lady*, 2:181, 2:497.

2. More, *Works*, 4:404; West, *Elegy*, 19.

3. McKeon, *Origins*, chap. 4; Newman, *Rise of English Nationalism*, passim, but especially chap. 4. For an exploration of the link between anti-French sentiment, gender, language, and English nationalism, see Michèle Cohen, *Fashioning Masculinity*.

4. Newman, *Rise of English Nationalism*, 60; Colley, *Britons*, 154; Andrew, "Reading the Demi-Rep," 21. Interestingly, the fiercely reactionary *Anti-Jacobin Review and Magazine*, established in 1798, marks the year 1788 as the beginning of the influx of French philosophy, or "the poison of Jacobinism" (*Anti-Jacobin* 1 [July 1798]: 4). That the journal itself gained a voice and influence, however, is as much evidence of a shift toward conservatism, as of the rise of revolutionary philosophy. These contradictory readings of history serve to highlight the dialectical nature of the development of political thought, which is peculiarly obvious during the period under scrutiny in this study.

5. Davidoff and Hall, *Family Fortunes*, 111–13; More, *Works*, 2:178; Davidoff and Hall, 25; Colley, *Britons*, 233.

6. Lukács, *The Historical Novel*, 24; West, *Loyalists*, 1:8, 1:7.

7. Todd, *Sign of Angellica*, 233.

8. Davidoff and Hall, *Family Fortunes*, 319.

9. Myers, "Reform or Ruin," 204–5.

10. Austen, *Pride and Prejudice*, 34; West, *Letters to a Young Lady*, 1:127–28; Hamilton, *Memoirs*, 1:196.

11. West, *Letters to a Young Lady*, 1:199.

12. Wilberforce, *Practical View*, 40, 43; More, *Coelebs*, 2:403. I use a capital "E" for establishment Evangelicalism (including the Church of Scotland) to differentiate it from other forms, a strategy that may serve to obscure the variety within nonestablishment evangelicalism, but which is useful for clarity.

13. Bebbington, *Evangelicalism*, 2–3; Wilberforce, *Practical View*, 268. See chapter 1 of Robin Reed Davis's dissertation, "Anglican Evangelicalism and the Feminine Literary Tradition," for a description of the process by which Anglican Evangelicals gained influence within the Church of England.

14. Jones, *Hannah More*, 93–94.

15. Brown, *Fathers of the Victorians*, 91; Hilton, *Age of Atonement*, 7.

16. Hilton, *Age of Atonement*, 8. Many Evangelicals joined the Rev. Dr. Thomas Chalmers when he left the established church to form the Free Church in the 1840s. Chalmers's disagreement with the Church of Scotland was not doctrinal; rather, it was a result of his disapproval of the intervention of the state in matters of religious appointment. See chapter 1 of A. C. Cheyne's *The Transforming of the Kirk: Victorian Scotland's Religious Revolution* for an account of Chalmers's secession.

17. Brunton, *Discipline*, 282; Rice, quoted in Hilton, *Age of Atonement*, 26.

18. More, *Coelebs*, 2:184; Braude, "Women's History," 98; Krueger, *Reader's Repentance*, 32–33.

19. More, *Coelebs*, 2:20; Braude, "Women's History," 99; Davis, "Anglican Evangelicalism," 142–43.

20. Newman, *Rise of English Nationalism*, 234–35, Newman's emphasis.

21. Wilberforce, *Practical View*, 274; More, *Works*, 4:175, 4:181; *Christian Observer* 1 (1802): iii, vii. A. C. Cheyne notes a similar duality in Thomas Chalmers's Presbyterian Evangelicalism, when he describes it as "essentially conservative, if not reactionary," in spite of its interest in religious reformation (*Transforming of the Kirk*, 23).

22. Bebbington, *Evangelicalism*, 5; Davis, "Anglican Evangelicalism," 23; More, *Works*, 1:190; Davis, 8.

23. Kelly, *Women, Writing, and Revolution*, passim; Newman, *Rise of English Nationalism*, 97; Davidoff and Hall, *Family Fortunes*, 23.

24. West, *Elegy*, 10; Montluzin, *Anti-Jacobins*, 40; Plumb, *England*, 193.

25. *Gentleman's Magazine* (September–December 1799): 265.

26. *Anti-Jacobin* 3 (May 1799): 35, 37–39; 45 (September 1813): 264; *British Critic* 14 (September 1799): 279.

27. *Anti-Jacobin* 1 (July 1798): 2, 3.

28. Ibid., 15 (May 1803): 42.

29. More, *Coelebs*, 1:397.

30. The circumstances and purpose of their establishment also affected the later success of these two periodicals. After the political impetus for the *Anti-Jacobin* disappeared—the "pressing" occasion of the revolutionary wars—the journal became less influential; the *Christian Observer*, however, continued to be published until 1874, and, despite losing ground to more extreme evangelical journals in the 1830s, remained one of the more popular religious serials.

31. *Christian Observer* 1 (January 1802): iii, iv, iii; 2 (January 1803): v, iv.

32. Ibid., 5 (January 1806): vii; 2 (January 1803): v; 1 (January 1802): vi; 2 (January 1803): vi; 5 (January 1806): vi.

33. *Anti-Jacobin* 6 (1800): 411.

34. *Christian Observer* 1 (January 1802): iii; 1 (March 1802): 176, 177.

35. Myers, "Peculiar Protection," 231.

36. *Anti-Jacobin* 45 (September 1813): 252.

37. Krueger, *Reader's Repentance*, 60, 62.

38. More, *Coelebs*, 2:237, 1:200, 1:203; West, *Tale of the Times*, 1:11.

39. Easthope, *Poetry as Discourse*, 133, 125; Newman, *Rise of English Nationalism*, 127, 131.

40. *Christian Observer* 1 (March 1802): 176, 180; Butler, *Jane Austen*, 94–95.

41. Butler, *Jane Austen*, 94.

42. Kelly, *English Fiction*, 62.

43. Ibid., 63.

44. D'Israeli, *Vaurien*, 1:xvi, 1:xxi, 1:xv.

45. D'Israeli's novel provides a good example of Michel Beaujour's contention that: "Although in practice the novel can be made to convey the Christian or Communist messages of self-oblivion, deferred gratification, desire for the law, its deeper appeal always lies in the depiction of sin, error, disorder, in all that is transgressive, excessive" ("Exemplary Pornography," 348). Vaurien is much more seductive as a character than either of the positive exemplary protagonists, and thus the nondomestic conclusion of the text, which follows Vaurien's plot rather than that of the lovers, is not truly unsatisfactory in Beaujour's "libidinal" sense. This is a rhetorical and moral problem faced by any writer of didactic fiction. Yet, while in the following chapters I analyze the ways in which exemplary novels may be undermined by their own textual practices even as they attempt strict closure, I do not explore Beaujour's argument that all exemplary narratives engage in this form of "pornography."

46. Lucas, *Infernal Quixote*, 3:308; West, *Loyalists*, 2:38.

47. Kelly, *Women, Writing, and Revolution*, 144.

48. Mellor, *Romanticism and Gender*, 84.

49. Johnson, *Jane Austen*, 2.

50. Ty, *Unsex'd Revolutionaries*, 14; Johnson, *Jane Austen*, 6, 23.

51. Burke, *Reflections*, 19; Conniff, *Useful Cobbler*, 3, 2, 17; Watson, "Burke's Conservative Revolution," 90.

52. There is a third argument about women's relationship to establishment conservatism, which seems to me untenable. Eva Figes's ahistorical argument in *Sex and Subterfuge* that women are "outside the political system" demands that she read women writers as forced "into conservative attitudes both to protect their personal reputations and to ensure them some kind of reading public" (151). This reading denies what I contend here: that women formed a part of a conservative writing community, and were not simply victims of a conservative establishment that forced them to mask their oppositional feminist politics.

53. West, *Elegy*, 14. Subsequent quotations from this work are cited parenthetically in the text.

54. Cohen, "History and Genre," 214.

Chapter 3. Persuasive Fictions

1. Todd, *Sign of Angellica*, 229; Colby, *Fiction with a Purpose*, 15; West, *Infidel Father*, 1:ii; Alexander Brunton, "Memoir,"10; Butler, *Jane Austen*.

2. Foucault, *Discipline and Punish*, 131.

3. West, *Sorrows of Selfishness*, 7, 30–31.

4. The fact that children's literature is less sophisticated and more openly authoritarian makes this link clearer. See Samuel F. Pickering Jr.'s *Moral Instruction and Fiction for Children, 1749–1820* for an examination of didactic children's literature and "school stories" during this period. See also Lynne Vallone's valuable study, *Disciplines of Virtue: Girls' Culture in the Eighteenth and Nineteenth Centuries*, for an exploration of the link between adolescent girls' fiction and the production of an ideology of domestic and virtuous femininity. Sarah Trimmer's fiction for children, with its "genteel" Evangelical morality, provides an excellent example of conservative didactic children's literature of this period.

5. Suleiman, *Authoritarian Fictions*, 73.

6. Miller, *Novel and the Police*, xii. Miller, following Foucault's description of the nineteenth century as the "age of discipline," focuses his attention on the novels of the Victorian period (18). His suggestion in his preface that "perhaps no openly fictional form has ever sought to 'make a difference' in the world more than the Victorian novel" tends to erase the socially engaged novels I examine in this study (x). Joseph Childers effects a similar erasure in *Novel Possibilities*, when, defining "politics" narrowly, he describes Benjamin Disraeli's *Coningsby* as "the first English political novel" (12).

7. Suleiman, *Authoritarian Fictions*, 54; Beaujour, "Exemplary Pornography," 345; Suleiman, 22. In my interpretation, I lean toward a phenomenological rather than a reader-response approach, being most concerned with "what a text can do to a reader, not with what a reader can do to a text," to use Richard Harland's distinction (*Literary Theory*, 207). I follow Wolfgang Iser in my use of the term "implied reader."

8. Mary Brunton, *Discipline*, 6; Hamilton, *Cottagers of Glenburnie*, 229; Hawkins, *Countess and Gertrude*, vol.1, chap. 3.

9. Suleiman, *Authoritarian Fictions*, 70, Suleiman's emphasis; West, *Advantages of Education*, 1:iii.

10. Kelly, *Women, Writing, and Revolution*, 154.

11. Hamilton, *Cottagers of Glenburnie*, 73.

12. Defoe, *Moll Flanders*, 3; West, letter to Bishop Percy, 18 November 1810, in Nichols, *Illustrations*, 8:425; *Anti-Jacobin* 45 (December 1813): 533. A theory of the moral aesthetic of novel writing was not limited to conservatives. Anna Letitia Barbauld, in her "Essay on the Origin and Progress of Novel-Writing," concurs with West's basic premise: "to either sex it must be desirable that the first impressions of fraud, selfishness, profligacy, and perfidy, should be connected, as in good novels they always will be, with infamy and ruin" (369).

13. *Gentleman's Magazine* (October 1808): 883, 884; Spacks, "Sisters." For a critique of the formulaic nature of the novel from the early 1790s, see Mary Wollstonecraft's reviews for Johnson's *Analytical Review*, and see *Blackwood's Edinburgh Magazine* 4 (January 1819): 394–96, for a good example of a later critique of the genre's "sameness."

14. Nicola Watson, *Revolution*, 110.

15. West, *A Gossip's Story*, 2:224 (my emphasis), 2:225; Suleiman, *Authoritarian Fictions*, 73.

16. Stone, *Family, Sex and Marriage*, chap. 8; Staves, *Married Women's Separate Property*, 229.

17. Sheridan, *Memoirs of Sidney Bidulph*, 4, 5, 6; West, *Sorrows of Selfishness*, xvi. In her criticism of *Sidney Bidulph*, Anna Letitia Barbauld shares the opinion of the lady critic of *Douglas*: "the sentiments of this work are pure and virtuous; but the author seems to have taken pleasure in heaping distress upon virtue and innocence, merely to prove, what no one will deny, that the best dispositions are not always sufficient to ward off the evils of life" ("Origin and Progress," 368). Barbauld's interest in the implications of plot fifty years after the publication of Sheridan's novel reflects the continuing debate over the moral and aesthetic merit of particular narrative trajectories.

18. *Blackwood's* 4 (January 1819): 394–96.

19. London, "Novel and History," 77.

20. See Watson, *Revolution*, 85–86, for a discussion of Hamilton's *Memoirs of Modern Philosophers*, and 76–78 for a reading of West's *Gossip's Story*.

21. Kelly, *English Jacobin Novel*, 16. Mary Shelley rewrites this plot a generation later in *Frankenstein* (1818). Her father's philosophy is played out in the early experiences of the creature, whose rejection by society produces his violent behavior: "My heart was fashioned to be susceptible of love and sympathy," he informs the Arctic explorer Walton, "and when wrenched by misery to vice and hatred, it did not endure the violence of the change, without torture such as you cannot even imagine" (*Frankenstein*, 212).

22. For further discussions of Jacobin philosophy and form, see the following critical studies: Gary Kelly's *English Fiction of the Romantic Period, 1789–1830* places Jacobin novels in relation to the broader literary context; Katherine Binhammer's dissertation, "The Sex Wars of the 1790s," places women's Jacobin fiction in relation to the developing figure of the "domestic woman," which worked to delimit feminist discourse; Claudia Johnson, in *Equivocal Beings*, reads Mary Wollstonecraft's fiction in relation to prevalent discourses of sentimentality; and Laurie Finke's work on Wollstonecraft's nonfictional *Vindication of the Rights of Woman* usefully analyses her style as a form of feminist practice (*Feminist Theory, Women's Writing*).

23. London, "Novel and History," 74. See Eleanor Ty's "Female Philosophy Refunctioned: Elizabeth Hamilton's Parodic Novel" for an argument that the parodic element in Hamilton's novel "may also paradoxically create new interest or attract a new audience for the master [i.e., parodied] text" (113).

24. Hamilton, *Memoirs of Modern Philosophers*, 3:296; 3:306.
25. Ibid., 1:41; Binhammer, "Sex Wars,"193.
26. *Lady's Monthly Museum* 4 (April 1808): 197.
27. Austen, *Northanger Abbey*, 61. According to Devendra P. Varma, Parsons published sixty novels and romances over the course of her career, a notable achievement considering she died at the age of 63 (Parsons, *Mysterious Warning*, xv). Her biographical entry in the *Dictionary of British and American Women Writers*, however, mentions only twenty works of fiction.
28. Foucault, "What is an Author?"; Todd, *Sign of Angellica*, 218.
29. Lanser, *Fictions of Authority*, 63; *Monthly Review* 75 (July 1786): 69; Walpole, letter to Lady Ossory, 4 November 1786, *Correspondence*, 33:533.
30. Jones, *Hannah More*, 74; *Monthly Review* 75 (July 1786): 69.
31. *Gentleman's Magazine* 38 (July 1852): 100; Anderson, quoted in *Gentleman's Magazine* 38 (July 1852): 101; *Gentleman's Magazine* 91 (January 1802): 7; *Gentleman's Magazine* 91 (February 1802): 99; Lloyd, "Some New Information," 469.
32. Hawkins, *Letters on the Female Mind*, 1:4.
33. According to the *Dictionary of British and American Women Writers*, Hawkins claimed to have written at least one published novel and "many subsequent volumes" prior to 1793, but none of these has been traced (154).
34. Hawkins, *Countess and Gertrude*, 1:xxx; *Anti-Jacobin* 45 (September 1813): 265, 264.
35. Suleiman, *Authoritarian Fictions*, 237–38.

Chapter 4. Narrative Authority

1. See Poovey, *Proper Lady*; Butler, *Jane Austen*; Ty, *Unsex'd Revolutionaries*; Johnson, *Jane Austen* and *Equivocal Beings*; Ty, *Empowering the Feminine*.
2. West, *Letters to a Young Lady*, 1:102, 1:161; More, *Strictures*, 1:155–56, 2:15.
3. More, *Strictures*, 2:32; Galatians 3:28.
4. Lanser, *Fictions of Authority*, 16, 17; Case, *Gender and Narration*, 15.
5. Ibid., *Fictions of Authority*, 7–8.
6. Ibid., 71; Mezei, "Contextualizing Feminist Narratology," 15. Throughout my discussion of narration I will be using Gerard Genette's critical terms from *Narrative Discourse: An Essay in Method*. "Heterodiegetic" is roughly equivalent to "third-person" narration, in that the narrator is absent from the story that is told. "Homodiegetic" refers to a narrator who is present in the narrative as a character; a subcategory of this is "autodiegetic" narration, in which a narrator tells his or her own story. Thus, Lockwood in *Wuthering Heights* is a homodiegetic narrator, since he plays a "secondary role," while Caleb Williams is an autodiegetic narrator (Genette, *Narrative Discourse*, 245).
7. See Myers, "Peculiar Protection," 230; Johnson, *Jane Austen*, 18.
8. Leranbaum, "Mistresses of Orthodoxy," 295; Hawkins, *Letters on the Female Mind* 1:16.
9. Myers, "Hannah More's Tracts," 268, my emphasis; Pederson, "Hannah More," 87.
10. More, *Works*, 4:175.
11. Johnson, *Jane Austen*, 19; Kelly, *Women, Writing, and Revolution*, 12; Snook, "Eve and More," 132. Snook examines the ways in which More not only alludes to, but "con-

struct[s] Milton as a monument in her own image," by rewriting passages from *Paradise Lost* to support her social agenda (132).

12. Lanser, *Fictions of Authority*, 180; Ty, *Unsex'd Revolutionaries*, 17; Suleiman, *Authoritarian Fictions*, 70; More, *Coelebs*, 1:11. Subsequent quotations from *Coelebs* are cited parenthetically in the text.

13. Lanser, *Fictions of Authority*, 177.

14. Pickering, "Hannah More's *Coelebs*."

15. Todd, *Sign of Angellica*, 209; Ty, "Female Philosophy Refunctioned," 117.

16. Hamilton, *Memoirs of Modern Philosophers*, 1:xiii. Subsequent quotations from this work are cited parenthetically in the text.

17. Ty, "Female Philosophy Refunctioned," 121.

18. The ways in which the concept of "beauty" functions in this and other anti-Jacobin novels is complex, and too large a subject to deal with at length here. The beauty of an antirevolutionary Christian is supposed to come from within—and physical beauty is therefore also, for her, beneath notice—yet inner beauty is almost invariably (by the logic of earthly rewards I described in the previous chapter) translated into external attractiveness in these novels. This attractiveness is generally only perceivable by those viewers with taste and correct principles; beauty thus provides the test of a good education (the negative exemplary woman is flashy or exotically beautiful, in comparison to the understated English prettiness of the positive exemplary heroine), as well as a lesson in patriotism and prudence.

19. Kelly, *Women, Writing, and Revolution*, 144.

20. See Kelly's *Women, Writing, and Revolution*, chapter 4, for an extended discussion of Hamilton's blending of "masculine" and "feminine" discourses in both *Memoirs* and *Letters of a Hindoo Rajah* (1796). Kelly reads Hamilton's use of a masculine narrative voice as her resistance to a limiting feminine discourse, and consequently as part of her "counterrevolutionary feminism."

21. West, *A Gossip's Story*, 1:1. Subsequent quotations from this work are cited parenthetically in the text.

22. West, *Letters to a Young Lady*, 3:96, 3:90–91. Subsequent quotations from this work are cited parenthetically in the text.

23. Gaskell, *Cranford*, 1; West, *A Gossip's Story*, 1:1; Ford, "Tales of the Times," 18.

24. The name "Homespun," as West notes in her preface to *The Advantages of Education*, comes from Henry Mackenzie's journal, *The Mirror*. Three installments (1 [1779]: 89–96; 1 [1779]: 193–202; 2 [1779]: 146–55) track the story of the family of John Homespun, whose daughters have been seduced by the luxuries and vanities of the life of an upper-class ("great") relative. Homespun's central concern is that members of his class (he is a "plain country-gentleman, with a small fortune and a large family" [1:89]) are being "infected" by the expensive habits and fashionable morals of the upper classes (which "I look upon as a sort of pestilential disorder" [1:94]). Mackenzie's critique here is of the aristocracy, and his text fits well within the "middle-class revolution" described by both Gary Kelly (in *Women, Writing, and Revolution*) and Gerald Newman (in *The Rise of English Nationalism*), which worked to reform the ruling classes. West's emphasis is much more on the concept of class contagion; the middle classes must maintain their social place, neither adopting the detrimental habits of the aristocracy, nor usurping power and thereby destabilizing the social order. April London also notes links in Prudentia's "lineage" to Goldsmith's *Vicar of Wakefield* and Samuel Jackson Pratt's *Pupil of Pleasure* ("Jane West," 58). The "homespun" persona West adopts here is also indica-

tive of the division in British thought of this period between patriotic English "common sense" and French and revolutionary "theory." See David Simpson, *Romanticism, Nationalism, and the Revolt Against Theory*, for a detailed examination of this polarization, and its social and political sources and implications.

25. Johnson, *Jane Austen*, 7.
26. West, *The Refusal*, 1:26.
27. London, "Jane West," 62.
28. Mezei, "Contextualizing Feminist Narratology," 2; Spacks, *Gossip*, 181.
29. Spacks, *Gossip*, 182.

Chapter 5. Antirevolutionary Didacticism

1. West, letters to Bishop Percy, 22 August 1811 and 18 November 1810, in Nichols, *Illustrations*, 8:431, 8:425; West, *Loyalists*, 1:8, 1:7.
2. West, *The Refusal*, 1:5, 1:4. Subsequent quotations from this work are cited parenthetically in the text.
3. The narrator of Swift's *Tale of a Tub* describes satire as "a ball bandied to and fro, and every man carries a racket about him to strike it from himself among the rest of the company." The preface to the "Battle of the Books" figures satire as "a sort of *glass*, wherein beholders do generally discover everybody's face but their own." The authoritarian Prudentia of West's *The Sorrows of Selfishness* might also appreciate the metaphor in *Tale of a Tub* of satire as a "lash" that goes unfelt by "the world's posteriors" (*"Gulliver's Travels" and Other Writings*, 269, 358, 267).
4. An "extrafictional voice" exists, in Susan Sniader Lanser's definition, on a narrative level between the historical author and the narrator (*Narrative Act*, 144).
5. Stanza's definition of narrative "truth" is relatively complex. He argues the potential for *psychological* truth in fiction—"the strong enchantment of genius fascinates our judgment, by introducing the aspect of reality" (1:48)—rather than simply opposing historical "truth" to fictional "falsehood."
6. The primary narrative is also concerned with truth in narration: evidence from a variety of sources is interpolated in the narrative, and generally shown to be distorted or false by the narrator. Newspaper reports (1:124–28), and circulating gossip (2:104–14), are forms of evidence that are immediately or eventually devalued. Personal letters are generally valued as evidence, but are carefully corroborated by the heterodiegetic narrative.
7. Lanser, *Fictions of Authority*, 20; Suleiman, *Authoritarian Fictions*, 71. For a discussion of how heterodiegetic voice can obscure gender, thereby creating narrative authority, see Lanser, 18.
8. Ibid., 64, 72; Genette, *Narrative Discourse*, 166.
9. Iser, *Implied Reader*, xiv. Lanser suggests that the next stage in the development of novelistic narration is a "selectively focalized, 'figural' narration in which the narrator's text is formally inseparable from the texts of characters" in the twentieth century (*Fictions of Authority*, 87–88).
10. Watson, *Revolution*, 110; Kelly, *Women, Writing, and Revolution*, 155; Todd, *Sign of Angellica*, 233.
11. Ibid., 75–78.

12. Butler, *Jane Austen and the War of Ideas*; Ruderman, *The Pleasures of Virtue*; Johnson, *Jane Austen*, xxv.

13. West, *Letters to a Young Lady*, 2:436.

14. Hawkins, *Countess and Gertrude*, 1:xiii. Subsequent quotations from this work are cited parenthetically in the text.

15. *Anti-Jacobin* 45 (September 1813): 263.

16. West, *Letters to a Young Lady*, 3:65, 3:80, 3:77. Presumably the presence of a maternal mentor would make the story non-narratable, since the (moral and literary) "problem" of a badly educated daughter could not exist in the presence of a virtuous mother. In *The Advantages of Education* the heroine is separated from her mother for most of her childhood, yet her erring ways are cured within months of her mother's reappearance. In *A Gossip's Story* the negative exemplary daughter is raised by a doting grandmother after her mother's death, while her exemplary sister is raised by her father following maternal principles.

17. Myers, "Reform or Ruin," 268; West, *Letters to a Young Lady*, 2:364.

Chapter 6. Domesticity and the Feminine "Circle"

1. Krueger, *Reader's Repentance*, 119.

2. *Le Moniteur* XVIII, 2 brumaire, quoted in Rendall, *Origins*, 68.

3. Brunton, *Self-Control*, 212–3.

4. Myers, "Peculiar Protection," 230; Jones, *Hannah More*, 113, on More's sphere of influence; Myers, "Peculiar Protection," 244.

5. West, letters to Bishop Percy, 7 June 1800 and 22 August 1811, in Nichols, *Illustrations*, 8:330, 8:430.

6. West, *Letters to a Young Lady*, 3:90–91; West, letter to Bishop Percy, 18 November 1810, in Nichols, *Illustrations*, 8:424.

7. Vallone, *Disciplines of Virtue*, 70; Watson, "Purloined Letters," 171.

8. More, *Coelebs*, 2:149. Subsequent quotations from this work are cited parenthetically in the text.

9. More, *Strictures*, 2:2. Subsequent quotations from this work are cited parenthetically in the text.

10. Krueger, *Reader's Repentance*, 119; More, *Strictures*, 1:64; Davis, "Anglican Evangelicalism," 111; Krueger, *Reader's Repentance*, 123.

11. Krueger, *Reader's Repentance*, 121; Johnson, *Jane Austen*, 18; Krueger, *Reader's Repentance*, 121.

12. Langland, *Nobody's Angels*, 39; Armstrong, *Desire and Domestic Fiction*.

13. *Scots Magazine* 71 (June 1809): 440; *Christian Observer* 8 (February 1809): 113, quoted in Davis, "Anglican Evangelicalism," 86.

14. Brunton, *Self-Control*, 73. Subsequent quotations from this work are cited parenthetically in the text.

15. Alexander Brunton, "Memoir," 22.

16. Ann H. Jones argues that evangelical fiction such as Brunton's helped to develop psychological realism in the nineteenth-century novel (*Ideas and Innovations*, 79). The evangelical focus on "self-reflection" brought the protagonist's moral and psychological development to the foreground. Gary Kelly, conversely, argues that English Jacobin

fiction, with its emphasis on the effect of social institutions on individual psychology, is responsible for this "revolution in the art of the novel" (*English Jacobin*, 19).

17. Austen, *Letters*, 344; Alexander Brunton, "Memoir," 25.

18. Armstrong, "Rise of the Domestic Woman," 109.

19. Alexander Brunton, "Memoir," 25. Katrin R. Burlin concurs with Brunton's self-assessment when she suggests that her "'novel' is a patched-together job, of male and female imaginations bundled indiscriminately into a single composition" ("At the Crossroads," 68). For Burlin, however, the flaw is in the novel's didacticism, rather than its narrative structure. Despite its "clever insights" and "wonderfully comic moments," Burlin argues that *Self-Control* is marred by Brunton's "large-scale idealizations"; her propensity to foreground moral and religious concerns is the source of the novel's "real aesthetic and critical weaknesses" (68). Burlin's assessment accepts the post-Romantic antididacticism that worked to exclude writers like Brunton and More from the canon of the British novel, and devalues what Brunton saw as the most important element in her novel: its "usefulness." Jane Austen's reading of the novel as lacking in "Nature" and "Probability" coincides with Burlin's, and marks the shift in aesthetic priorities that was occurring during this period. With characteristic irony, she notes of this episode: "I declare I do not know whether Laura's passage down the American River, is not the most natural, possible, everyday thing she ever does" (*Letters*, 344).

20. Watson, "Purloined Letters," 186; Krueger, *Reader's Repentance*, 32.

21. Smith, "Men, Women, and Money," 53.

22. Alexander Brunton, "Memoir," 16; Brunton, *Discipline*, 368; Alexander Brunton, 28.

Chapter 7. Historicizing the Domestic Subject

1. Porter, *Scottish Chiefs*, 2:33. Subsequent quotations from this work are cited parenthetically in the text.

2. Batchelor, "Rise and Fall," 366.

3. West, *Loyalists*, 2:39. Subsequent quotations from this work are cited parenthetically in the text.

4. West, *Advantages of Education*, 1:iii; More, *Coelebs*, 2:183. Christine Krueger reads More's construction of domestic heroism as feminist, because its foregrounding of feminine characteristics disrupts conventional gender categories that figure "heroism" as masculine (*Reader's Repentance*, 106).

5. West, *Letters to a Young Lady*, 1:35, 1:57, 1:46, 1:105, West's emphasis.

6. West, *Advantages of Education*, 1:ii; *Gossip's Story*, 2:1, 1:xii.

7. West, *Letters to a Young Lady*, 1:19; *Gossip's Story*, 1:47.

8. London, "Novel and History," 73.

9. West, *Alicia de Lacy*, 1:v. Subsequent quotations from this work are cited parenthetically in the text.

10. West, *Advantages of Education*, 1:ii; *Gossip's Story*, 1:ii.

11. Favret, "Telling Tales about Genre," 289; *British Critic* 2 (November 1814): 549; *Gentleman's Magazine* 84 (August 1814): 137; London, "Novel and History," 73.

12. Walter Scott appends his own historical notes to the end of *Waverley*, published in the same year. Yet April London argues that by the time *Waverley* was published history and romance are "[n]o longer rendered problematic through convergence or

opposition," and that in *Waverley* they are "imagined in terms that make the congruence of private life and public event the special province of the novel" ("Novel and History," 81). Novelistic development is uneven, of course, and what was no longer problematic for Scott remained a concern for West and the reviewers of conservative journals, with their focus on transmitting a moral and political message.

13. *British Critic* 2 (November 1814): 550.

14. West, *Letters to a Young Lady*, 1:19.

15. Langbauer, *Women and Romance*, 92.

16. The Rev. Charles Buck, in the 1833 edition of his *Theological Dictionary*, defines the term "militant" as follows: "from *militans*, fighting; a term applied to the Church on earth, as engaged in a warfare with the world, sin, and the devil; in distinction from the Church *triumphant* in heaven." Modern theological dictionaries define the word in precisely the same terms.

17. Batchelor, "Rise and Fall," 356.

18. Krueger, *Reader's Repentance*, 32–33.

19. West, letter to Bishop Percy, 18 November 1810, in Nichols, *Illustrations*, 8:425; Kelly, *English Fiction*, 100; West, *Letters to a Young Lady*, 1:263.

20. Lukács, *The Historical Novel*, 54, 33, 49, 52, 53.

21. *British Critic* 2 (November 1814): 552; West, *Ringrove*, 2:272–73, 1:2.

22. Davis, "Anglican Evangelicalism," 96; Alexander Brunton, "Memoir," 51.

Postscript

1. West, letter to Miss Henrietta; *Blackwood's* 4 (January 1819): 394–95; More, *Coelebs*, 2:6; Austen, *Northanger Abbey*, 58.

2. Pickering, "Hannah More's *Coelebs*."

3. Davis, "Anglican Evangelicalism," 144; Tonna, *Helen Fleetwood*, 236, 398.

4. Armstrong and Tennenhouse, introduction to *Ideology of Conduct*, 1, 10–14; Langland, *Nobody's Angels*, 8.

5. Lurie, *Unsettled Subjects*, 1.

Works Cited

Primary Texts:

Austen, Jane. *Jane Austen's Letters to her Sister Cassandra and Others*. Ed. R. W. Chapman. 2d ed. London: Oxford University Press, 1964.

———. *Northanger Abbey*. 1818. Ed. Anne Henry Ehrenpreis. Penguin Classics. London: Penguin, 1985.

———. *Pride and Prejudice*. 1813. Ed. James Kinsley. World's Classics. Oxford: Oxford University Press, 1990.

———. *Sense and Sensibility*. 1811. Ed. Tony Tanner. Penguin Classics. London: Penguin, 1988.

Bage, Robert. *Hermsprong; or, Man as He Is Not*. 1796. Ed. Stuart Tave. University Park: Pennsylvania State University Press, 1982.

Brunton, Alexander. "Memoir [of Mary Brunton]." In *Discipline*, by Mary Brunton, 3–56. Standard Novels. London: Bentley, 1849.

Brunton, Mary. *Discipline*. 1814. Standard Novels. London: Bentley, 1849.

———. *Self-Control*. 1810. Standard Novels. London: Bentley, 1849.

Burke, Edmund. *Reflections on the Revolution in France*. 1790. London: Dent; New York: Dutton, 1955.

Collier, Jeremy. *A Short View of the Immorality and Prophaneness of the English Stage*. 1698. Ed. Benjamin Hellinger. Satire and Sense series. New York: Garland, 1987.

D'Israeli, Isaac. *Vaurien; Or, Sketches of the Times: Exhibiting Views of the Philosophies, Religions, Politics, Literature, and Manners of the Age*. 2 vols. London: Cadell and Davies; J. Murray and S. Highley, 1797.

Gaskell, Elizabeth. *Cranford*. 1853. Ed. Elizabeth Porges Watson. World's Classics. Oxford: Oxford University Press, 1980.

Godwin, William. *Caleb Williams; Or, Things As They Are*. 1794. Ed. David McCracken. World's Classics. Oxford: Oxford University Press, 1982.

———. *Memoirs of the Author of "The Rights of Woman"*. 1798. *"A Short Residence in Sweden" and "Memoirs of the Author of 'The Rights of Woman'"*. Ed. Richard Holmes. Penguin Classics. London: Penguin, 1987.

Hamilton, Elizabeth. *The Cottagers of Glenburnie; A Tale for the Farmer's Ingle-Nook*. 1808. Edinburgh: Stirling, Kenney, 1837.

———. *Memoirs of Modern Philosophers*. 1800. 4th ed. 3 vols. London: G. and J. Robinson, 1804.

Hawkins, Laetitia Matilda. *The Countess and Gertrude; Or, Modes of Discipline*. 4 vols. London: F. C. and J. Rivington, 1811.

———. *Letters on the Female Mind, Its Powers and Pursuits*. London: Hookham and Carpenter, 1793.

Hays, Mary. *Memoirs of Emma Courtney*. 1796. Mothers of the Novel series. London: Pandora, 1987.

James, Henry. "The Art of Fiction." 1884. In *Criticism: The Major Statements*, ed. Charles Kaplan, 386–404. 2d ed. New York: St. Martin's, 1986.

Le Noir, Elizabeth. *Village Anecdotes*. 3 vols. London: Vernor and Hood, 1804.

Lillo, George. *The London Merchant; Or, The History of George Barnwell and Fatal Curiosity*. 1731. Ed. Adolphus William Ward. Boston: Heath, 1906.

Lucas, Charles. *The Infernal Quixote. A Tale of the Day*. 4 vols. London: Lane, Minerva Press, 1801.

More, Hannah. "Betty Brown, the St. Giles Orange Girl." In *The Works of Hannah More*, 2:167–80. London: Henry G. Bohn, 1853.

———. Selected Cheap Repository Tracts. 1795–98.

———. *Coelebs in Search of a Wife: Comprehending Observations on Domestic Habits and Manners, Religion and Morals*. 1808. 7th ed. 2 vols. London: Cadell and Davies, 1809.

———. *Hints Towards Forming the Character of a Young Princess*. 1805. Vol. 4, *The Works of Hannah More*. London: Henry G. Bohn, 1853.

———. *Strictures on the Modern System of Female Education With a View of the Principles and Conduct Prevalent Among Women of Rank and Fortune*. 4th ed. 2 vols. London: Cadell and Davies, 1799.

———. "The Sunday School." In *The Works of Hannah More*, 1:183–96. London: Henry G. Bohn, 1853.

———. *The Works of Hannah More*. 11 vols. London: Henry G. Bohn, 1853.

Nichols, John Bowyer. *Illustrations of the Literary History of the Eighteenth-Century. Consisting of Authentic Memoirs and Original Letters of Eminent Persons. To Which Are Appended Additions to the Literary Anecdotes and Literary Illustrations*. 8 vols. London: J. B. Nichols and Sons, 1817–58.

Parsons, Eliza. *Ellen and Julia*. 2 vols. London: Lane, Minerva Press, 1793.

———. *The Mysterious Warning*. 1796. The Northanger Set of Jane Austen Horrid Novels. London: Folio Press, 1968.

———. *Woman As She Should Be; Or, Memoirs of Mrs. Menville*. 4 vols. London: Lane, Minerva Press, 1793.

———. *Women As They Are*. London: Lane, Minerva Press, 1796.

Poe, Edgar Allan. "The Poetic Principle." 1850. In *Edgar Allan Poe: Essays and Reviews*, ed. G. R. Thompson, 71–94. New York: Library of America, 1984.

Polwhele, Richard. *The Unsex'd Females: A Poem*. 1798. New York: Garland, 1974.

Porter, Anna Maria. *Walsh Colville; Or, A Young Man's First Entrance Into Life*. 1797. New York: Garland, 1974.

Porter, Jane. *The Scottish Chiefs*. 1810. Rev. ed. New York: Crowell, n.d.

Scott, Walter. *Waverley*. 1814. Ed. Andrew Hook. Harmondsworth, England: Penguin, 1972.

Seward, Anna. *The Swan of Lichfield, Being a Selection from the Correspondence of Anna Seward*. Ed. Hesketh Pearson. London: Hamish Hamilton, 1936.

Shelley, Mary. *Frankenstein; Or, The Modern Prometheus*. 1818, rev. 1831. Ed. Maurice Hindle. Penguin Classics. London: Penguin, 1992.

Sheridan, Frances. *The Memoirs of Miss Sidney Bidulph*. 1761. Mothers of the Novel series. London: Pandora, 1987.

Steele, Richard. *The Conscious Lovers*. 1722. In *Restoration and Eighteenth-Century Comedy*, 219–76. Ed. Scott McMillin. New York: Norton, 1973.

Swift, Jonathan. *"Gulliver's Travels" and Other Writings*. Ed. Louis A. Landa. Riverside Editions, no. 25. Boston: Houghton Mifflin, 1960.

"Thoughts on Novel Writing." *Blackwood's Edinburgh Magazine* 4, no. 22 (January 1819): 394–96.

[Tonna], Charlotte Elizabeth. *Helen Fleetwood*. London: Seeley, 1841.

Walpole, Horace. *The Yale Edition of Horace Walpole's Correspondence*. Ed. W. S. Lewis. 48 vols. New Haven: Yale University Press, 1961–84.

West, Jane. *The Advantages of Education; or, The History of Maria Williams*. 2 vols. London: Lane, 1793.

———. *Alicia de Lacy: An Historical Romance*. 4 vols. London: Longman, Hurst, Rees, Orme, and Brown, 1814.

———. *Elegy on the Death of the Right Honourable Edmund Burke*. London: Longman, 1797.

———. *A Gossip's Story and a Legendary Tale*. 1796. 5th ed. 2 vols. London: Longman, 1804.

———. *The Infidel Father*. 3 vols. London: Longman and Rees, 1802.

———. Letter to Miss Henrietta. 11 July 1834. Ms. Add. 41567.f.63. British Library, London.

———. *Letters Addressed to a Young Man On His First Entrance Into Life, and Adapted to the Peculiar Circumstances of the Present Times*. 1801. 2d ed. 3 vols. London: Longman and Rees, 1802.

———. *Letters to a Young Lady: In Which the Duties and Character of Women are Considered Chiefly With a Reference to Prevailing Opinions*. 2d ed. 3 vols. London: Longman, 1806.

———. *The Loyalists: An Historical Novel*. 3 vols. London: Longman and Rees, 1812.

———. *The Refusal*. 3 vols. London: Longman, Hurst, Rees, and Orme, 1810.

———. *Ringrove; Or, Old Fashioned Notions*. 2 vols. London: Longman, Rees, Orme, Brown, and Green, 1827.

———. *The Sorrows of Selfishness; Or, The History of Miss Richmore*. 1802. 4th ed. London: J. Harris, 1812.

———. *A Tale of the Times*. 2d ed. 3 vols. London: Longman, 1799.

Obituary of Jane West. *Gentleman's Magazine* 38 (July 1852): 99–101.

Wilberforce, William. *A Practical View of the Prevailing Religious System of Professed Christians*. 1797. London: Davis, 1834.

Wollstonecraft, Mary. *Maria; Or, The Wrongs of Woman*. 1798. New York: Norton, 1975.

———. *A Vindication of the Rights of Woman*. 1792. Ed. Miriam Brody. Penguin Classics. London: Penguin, 1992.

Wordsworth, William. "Preface." 1800. In *Lyrical Ballads*, ed. W. J. B. Owen, 153–79. 2d ed. Oxford: Oxford University Press, 1969.

Periodicals:

Anti-Jacobin Review and Magazine
Blackwood's Edinburgh Magazine
British Critic
Christian Observer
European Magazine
Gentleman's Magazine; and Historical Chronicle
Lady's Monthly Museum
The Mirror (Edinburgh)
Monthly Review
Quarterly Review

Secondary Texts:

Adburgham, Alison. *Women in Print: Writing Women and Women's Magazines from the Restoration to the Accession of Victoria*. London: Allen and Unwin, 1972.

Althusser, Louis. "Ideology and Ideological State Apparatuses (Notes Towards an Investigation)." In *Lenin and Philosophy and Other Essays*, 127–86. Trans. Ben Brewster. New York and London: Monthly Review Press, 1971.

Altick, Richard D. *The English Common Reader: A Social History of the Mass Reading Public, 1800–1900*. Chicago: University of Chicago Press, 1957.

Anderson, Benedict. *Imagined Communities: Reflections on the Origin and Spread of Nationalism*. London: Verso, 1983.

Andrew, Donna. *Philanthropy and Police: London Charity in the Eighteenth Century*. Princeton: Princeton University Press, 1989.

———. "Reading the Demi-Rep: *The Town and Country Magazine* 1769–1795." Unpublished paper.

Armstrong, Nancy. *Desire and Domestic Fiction: A Political History of the Novel*. Oxford and New York: Oxford University Press, 1987.

———. "The Rise of the Domestic Woman." In *The Ideology of Conduct: Essays on Literature and the History of Sexuality*, ed. Nancy Armstrong and Leonard Tennenhouse, 96–141. New York and London: Methuen, 1987.

Armstrong, Nancy, and Leonard Tennenhouse. Introduction to *The Ideology of Conduct: Essays on Literature and the History of Sexuality*, ed. Nancy Armstrong and Leonard Tennenhouse. New York and London: Methuen, 1987.

Ashmun, Margaret. *The Singing Swan: An Account of Anna Seward and Her Acquaintance with Dr Johnson, Boswell, and Others of their Time*. New Haven: Yale University Press, 1931.

Bakhtin, M. M. *The Dialogic Imagination: Four Essays*. Ed. Michael Holquist, trans. Caryl Emerson and Michael Holquist. Austin: University of Texas Press, 1981.

Bannet, Eve Tavor. *The Domestic Revolution: Enlightenment Feminisms and the Novel*. Baltimore and London: Johns Hopkins University Press, 2000.

Barker, Gerard A. *Grandison's Heirs: The Paragon's Progress in the Late Eighteenth-Century English Novel*. Newark: University of Delaware Press, 1985.

Barker-Benfield, G. J. *The Culture of Sensibility: Sex and Society in Eighteenth-Century Britain*. Chicago: University of Chicago Press, 1992.

Batchelor, Rhonda. "The Rise and Fall of the Eighteenth Century's Authentic Feminine Voice." *Eighteenth-Century Fiction* 6, no. 4 (July 1994): 347–68.

Beaujour, Michel. "Exemplary Pornography: Barrès, Loyola, and the Novel." In *The Reader in the Text: Essays on Audience and Interpretation*, ed. Susan R. Suleiman and Inge Crosman, 325–49. Princeton: Princeton University Press, 1980.

Bebbington, D. W. *Evangelicalism in Modern Britain: A History from the 1730s to the 1980s*. London: Unwin Hyman, 1989.

Binhammer, Katherine. "The Sex Wars of the 1790s: Gender and Sexuality in English Jacobin Women's Writing." Ph.D. diss., York University, 1995.

Blee, Kathleen. *Women of the Klan: Racism and Gender in the 1920s*. Berkeley and Los Angeles: University of California Press, 1991.

Booth, Wayne. *The Rhetoric of Fiction*. Chicago and London: University of Chicago Press, 1961.

Bradbrook, Frank W. *Jane Austen and Her Predecessors*. Cambridge: Cambridge University Press, 1966.

Braude, Ann. "Women's History *Is* American Religious History." In *Retelling U. S. Religious History*, ed. Thomas A. Tweed, 87–107. Berkeley and Los Angeles: University of California Press, 1997.

Breen, Jennifer, ed. *Women Romantic Poets, 1785–1832*. London: Dent; Rutland, Vermont: Tuttle, 1992.

Brody, Miriam. "Mary Wollstonecraft: Sexuality and Women's Rights." In *Feminist Theorists: Three Centuries of Women's Intellectual Traditions*, ed. Dale Spender, 40–59. London: Women's Press, 1983.

Brown, Ford K. *Fathers of the Victorians: The Age of Wilberforce*. Cambridge: Cambridge University Press, 1961.

Brown, Laura. *Ends of Empire: Women and Ideology in Early Eighteenth-Century English Literature*. Ithaca: Cornell University Press, 1993.

Burlin, Katrin R. "'At the Crossroads': Sister Authors and the Sister Arts." In *Fetter'd or Free? British Women Novelists, 1670–1815*, ed. Mary Anne Schofield and Cecilia Macheski, 60–84. Athens: Ohio University Press, 1986.

Butler, Marilyn. *Jane Austen and the War of Ideas*. Oxford: Clarendon, 1975.

———. *Romantics, Rebels and Reactionaries: English Literature and its Background 1760–1830*. Oxford: Oxford University Press, 1981.

Case, Alison. *Gender and Narration in the Eighteenth- and Nineteenth-Century British Novel*. Charlottesville: University of Virginia Press, 1999.

Castle, Terry. *Masquerade and Civilization: The Carnivalesque in Eighteenth-Century Culture and Fiction*. Stanford: Stanford University Press, 1986.

Cheyne, A. C. *The Transforming of the Kirk: Victorian Scotland's Religious Revolution*. Edinburgh: St. Andrew Press, 1983.

Childers, Joseph W. *Novel Possibilities: Fiction and the Formation of Early Victorian Culture*. New Cultural Studies series. Philadelphia: University of Pennsylvania Press, 1995.

Cohen, Michèle. *Fashioning Masculinity: National Identity and Language in the Eighteenth Century*. London: Routledge, 1996.

Cohen, Ralph. "History and Genre." *New Literary History: A Journal of Theory and Interpretation* 17, no. 2 (winter 1986): 203–18.

Colby, Robert A. *Fiction with a Purpose: Major and Minor Nineteenth-Century Novels*. Bloomington: Indiana University Press, 1967.

Cole, Lucinda. "(Anti)Feminist Sympathies: The Politics of Relationship in Smith, Wollstonecraft, and More." *English Literary History* 58, no. 1 (1991): 107–40.

Colley, Linda. *Britons: Forging the Nation, 1707–1837*. New Haven: Yale University Press, 1992.

Conniff, James. *The Useful Cobbler: Edmund Burke and the Politics of Progress*. Albany: SUNY Press, 1994.

Davidoff, Leonore, and Catherine Hall. *Family Fortunes: Men and Women of the English Middle Class, 1780–1850*. London: Hutchinson, 1987.

Davis, Robin Reed. "Anglican Evangelicalism and the Feminine Literary Tradition: From Hannah More to Charlotte Brontë." Ph.D. diss., Duke University, 1982.

Duncan, Ian. *Modern Romance and the Transformations of the Novel: The Gothic, Scott, Dickens*. Cambridge: Cambridge University Press, 1992.

Durant, W. Clark. Introduction to *Memoirs of Mary Wollstonecraft*, by William Godwin. New York: Haskell House, 1969.

Easthope, Antony. *Poetry as Discourse*. London and New York: Methuen, 1983.

Erwin, Lorna. "Neoconservatism and the Canadian Pro-Family Movement." *Canadian Review of Sociology and Anthropology* 30 (August 1993): 401–20.

Evans, Eric J. *The Forging of the Modern State: Early Industrial Britain 1783–1870*. London: Longman, 1983.

Evans, M. J. Crossley. "The English Evangelicals and the Enlightenment: The Case of Hannah More." *Studies on Voltaire and the Eighteenth Century* 303 (1992): 458–62.

Favret, Mary A. "Telling Tales About Genre: Poetry in the Romantic Novel." *Studies in the Novel* 26 (fall 1994): 281–300.

Favret, Mary A., and Nicola J. Watson, eds. *At the Limits of Romanticism: Essays in Cultural, Feminist, and Materialist Criticism*. Bloomington: Indiana University Press, 1994.

Feldman, Paula R., and Theresa M. Kelley, eds. *Romantic Women Writers: Voices and Countervoices*. Hanover, N. H.: University Press of New England, 1995.

Ferguson, Moira. *First Feminists: British Women Writers, 1578–1799*. Bloomington: Indiana University Press, 1985.

———. *Subject to Others: British Women Writers and Colonial Slavery, 1670–1834*. New York: Routledge, 1992.

Figes, Eva. *Sex and Subterfuge: Women Novelists to 1850*. London: Macmillan, 1982.

Finke, Laurie A. *Feminist Theory, Women's Writing*. Ithaca and London: Cornell University Press, 1992.

Ford, Susan Allen. "Tales of the Times: Family and Nation in Charlotte Smith and Jane West." In *Family Matters in the British and American Novel*, ed. Andrea O'Reilly Herrera, Elizabeth Mahn Nollen, and Sheila Reitzel Foor, 15–29. Bowling Green, Ohio: Bowling Green State University Popular Press, 1997.

Foucault, Michel. *Discipline and Punish: The Birth of the Prison*. Trans. Alan Sheridan. New York: Vintage, 1979.

Frohnen, Bruce. *Virtue and the Promise of Conservatism*. Wichita: University Press of Kansas, 1993.

Fulford, Tim, and Debbie Lee. "The Jenneration of Disease: Vaccination, Romanticism, and Revolution." *Studies in Romanticism* 39 (spring 2000): 139–63.

Genette, Gérard. *Narrative Discourse: An Essay in Method*. Trans. Jane E. Lewin. Ithaca: Cornell University Press, 1993.

Gilbert, A. D. *Religion and Society in Industrial England: Church, Chapel, and Social Change, 1740–1914*. London: Longman, 1976.

Graham, Kenneth W. "Intercultural Conflicts: Godwin and his Counter-Revolutionary Reviewers." In *Intercultural Encounters: Studies in English Literatures*, ed. Heinz Antor and Kevin Cope, 211–57. Heidelberg, Germany: Carl Winter, 1999.

Harland, Richard. *Literary Theory from Plato to Barthes: An Introductory History*. New York: St. Martin's, 1999.

Hay, Douglas, and Nicholas Rogers. *Eighteenth-Century English Society*. Oxford: Oxford University Press, 1997.

Hilton, Boyd. *The Age of Atonement: The Influence of Evangelicalism on Social and Economic Thought, 1795–1865*. Oxford: Clarendon, 1987.

Hook, A. D. "Jane Porter, Sir Walter Scott, and the Historical Novel." *Clio* 5, no. 2 (1976): 181–92.

Hubert, Judd D. "A Reactionary Feminist Novelist: Gabrielle de Villeneuve." *L'Esprit Createur* 29, no. 3 (fall 1989): 65–75.

Hunter, J. Paul. *Before Novels: the Cultural Contexts of Eighteenth-Century English Fiction*. New York: Norton, 1990.

Iser, Wolfgang. *The Implied Reader: Patterns of Communication in Prose Fiction from Bunyan to Beckett*. Baltimore: Johns Hopkins University Press, 1974.

Jameson, Fredric. *The Political Unconscious: Narrative as a Socially Symbolic Act*. Ithaca: Cornell University Press, 1981.

Johnson, Claudia L. *Equivocal Beings: Politics, Gender, and Sentimentality in the 1790s: Wollstonecraft, Radcliffe, Burney, Austen*. Chicago: University of Chicago Press, 1995.

———. *Jane Austen: Women, Politics, and the Novel*. Chicago: University of Chicago Press, 1988.

Jones, Ann H. *Ideas and Innovations: Best Sellers of Jane Austen's Age*. AMS Studies in the Nineteenth-Century, no. 4. New York: AMS Press, 1986.

Jones, M. G. *Hannah More*. Cambridge: Cambridge University Press, 1952.

Kadish, Doris Y. *Politicizing Gender: Narrative Strategies in the Aftermath of the French Revolution*. New Brunswick: Rutgers University Press, 1991.

Kelly, Gary. *English Fiction of the Romantic Period, 1789–1830*. London: Longman, 1989.

———. *The English Jacobin Novel, 1780–1805*. Oxford: Clarendon, 1976.

———. "Jane Austen and the English Novel of the 1790s." In *Fetter'd or Free? British Women Novelists, 1670–1815*, ed. Mary Anne Schofield and Cecilia Macheski, 285–306. Athens: Ohio University Press, 1986.

———. *Women, Writing, and Revolution, 1790–1827*. Oxford: Clarendon, 1993.

Koonz, Claudia. *Mothers in the Fatherland: Women, the Family, and Nazi Politics*. New York: St. Martin's, 1987.

Kowaleski-Wallace, Beth. "Home Economics: Domestic Ideology in Maria Edgeworth's *Belinda*." *The Eighteenth Century* 29 (1988): 242–43.

———. *Their Fathers' Daughters: Hannah More, Maria Edgeworth, and Patriarchal Complicity*. New York: Oxford University Press, 1991.

Kramnick, Isaac. "Children's Literature and Bourgeois Ideology: Observations on Culture and Industrial Capitalism in the Later Eighteenth Century." *Studies in Eighteenth-Century Culture* 12 (1983): 11–44.

Krueger, Christine. *The Reader's Repentance: Women Preachers, Women Writers, and Nineteenth-Century Social Discourse*. Chicago: University of Chicago Press, 1992.

Langbauer, Laurie. *Women and Romance: The Consolations of Gender in the English Novel*. Ithaca: Cornell University Press, 1990.

Langford, Paul. *A Polite and Commercial People: England, 1727–1783*. Oxford: Clarendon, 1989.

Langland, Elizabeth. *Nobody's Angels: Middle-Class Women and Domestic Ideology in Victorian Culture*. Ithaca: Cornell University Press, 1995.

Lanser, Susan Sniader. *Fictions of Authority: Woman Writers and Narrative Voice*. Ithaca: Cornell University Press, 1992.

———. *The Narrative Act: Point of View in Prose Fiction*. Princeton: Princeton University Press, 1981.

———. "Toward a Feminist Narratology." *Style* 20, no. 3 (fall 1986): 341–63.

———. "Writing Women into Romanticism." Review Essay. *Feminist Studies* 23, no. 1 (spring 1997): 167–90.

Leranbaum, Miriam. "'Mistresses of Orthodoxy': Education in the Lives and Writings of Late Eighteenth-Century English Women Writers." *Proceedings of the American Philosophical Society* 121, no. 4 (August 1977): 281–301.

Lloyd, Pamela. "Some New Information on Jane West." *Notes and Queries* 31, no. 4 (229) (1984): 469–70.

London, April. "Jane West and the Politics of Reading." In *Tradition in Transition: Women Writers, Marginal Texts, and the Eighteenth-Century Canon*, ed. Alvaro Ribeiro and James G. Basker, 56–74. Oxford: Clarendon, 1996.

———. "Novel and History in Anti-Jacobin Satire." *The Yearbook of English Studies* 30 (2000): 71–81.

———. *Women and Property in the Eighteenth-Century English Novel*. Cambridge: Cambridge University Press, 1999.

———. Review of *The Young Philosopher*, by Charlotte Smith, ed. Elizabeth Kraft, and *Translations of the Letters of a Hindoo Rajah*, by Elizabeth Hamilton, ed. Pamela Perkins and Shannon Russell. *Eighteenth-Century Fiction* 13, no. 1 (October 2000): 98–99.

Lonsdale, Roger, ed. *Eighteenth-Century Women Poets*. Oxford: Oxford University Press, 1989.

Lukács, Georg. *The Historical Novel*. Trans. Hannah and Stanley Mitchell. London: Merlin, 1962.

Lurie, Susan. *Unsettled Subjects: Restoring Feminist Politics to Poststructuralist Critique*. Durham: Duke University Press, 1997.

McGann, Jerome. *The Romantic Ideology: A Critical Investigation*. Chicago: University of Chicago Press, 1983.

McKeon, Michael. *The Origins of the English Novel, 1600–1740*. Baltimore: Johns Hopkins University Press, 1987.

Melander, Martin. "An Unknown Source of Jane Austen's *Sense and Sensibility*." *Studia Neophilologica* 22 (1949–50):146–70.

Mellor, Anne K., ed. *Romanticism and Feminism*. Bloomington: Indiana University Press, 1988.

———. *Romanticism and Gender*. New York: Routledge, 1993.

Mellor, Anne K., and Richard E. Matlak, eds. *British Literature, 1780–1830*. Fort Worth: Harcourt Brace, 1996.

Mezei, Kathy. "Contextualizing Feminist Narratology." In *Ambiguous Discourse: Feminist Narratology and British Women Writers*, ed. Kathy Mezei, 1–20. Chapel Hill and London: University of North Carolina Press, 1996.

Michasiw, Kim Ian. "Zeugma and Ideology." *English Studies in Canada* 21, no. 1 (March 1995): 21–39.

Miller, D. A. *The Novel and the Police*. Berkeley and Los Angeles: University of California Press, 1988.

Moler, Kenneth L. "*Sense and Sensibility* and Its Sources." *Review of English Studies* n.s. 17 (1966): 413–19.

Montluzin, Emily Lorraine de. *The Anti-Jacobins 1798–1800: The Early Contributors to the Anti-Jacobin Review*. Houndmills, U.K.: Macmillan, 1988.

Myer, Valerie Grosvenor. "'Caro Sposo' at the Ball: Jane West and Jane Austen's *Emma*." *Notes and Queries* 29, no. 3 (227) (1982): 208.

Myers, Mitzi. "Hannah More's Tracts for the Times: Social Fiction and Female Ideology." In *Fetter'd or Free? British Women Novelists, 1670–1815*, ed. Mary Anne Schofield and Cecilia Macheski, 264–84. Athens: Ohio University Press, 1986.

———. "'A Peculiar Protection': Hannah More and the Cultural Politics of the Blagdon Controversy." In *History, Gender and Eighteenth-Century Literature*, ed. Beth Fowkes Tobin, 227–57. Athens: University of Georgia Press, 1994.

———. "Reform or Ruin: 'A Revolution in Female Manners.'" *Studies in Eighteenth-Century Culture* 11 (1982): 199–216.

Nelson, Bonnie. "The Visions of Jane West and John Keats: Another Source for 'Ode to a Nightengale.'" *Keats Shelley Journal* 43 (1994): 34–38.

Newman, Gerald. *The Rise of English Nationalism: A Cultural History, 1740–1830*. New York: St. Martin's, 1987.

Nickson, Elizabeth. "Behold, the Bible Belles." *The Globe and Mail* (27 February 1999): D1.

Orr, Clarissa Campbell. "Introduction: Cross-Channel Perspectives." In *Wollstonecraft's Daughters: Womanhood in England and France, 1780–1920*, ed. Clarissa Campbell Orr, 1–42. Manchester: Manchester University Press, 1996.

Pederson, Susan. "Hannah More Meets Simple Simon: Tracts, Chapbooks, and Popular Culture in Late Eighteenth-Century England." *Journal of British Studies* 25 (1986): 84–113.

Pedley, Colin. "'The Inward Dispositions of the Heart': Jane Austen and Jane West." *Notes and Queries* 36, no. 2 (234) (1989): 169–71.

Pickering, Samuel F., Jr. "Hannah More's *Coelebs in Search of a Wife* and the Respectability of the Novel in the Nineteenth Century." *Neuphilologische Mitteilungen* 78, no. 1 (1977): 78–85.

———. *Moral Instruction and Fiction for Children, 1749–1820*. Athens: University of Georgia Press, 1993.

Plumb, J. H. *England in the Eighteenth Century*. Pelican History of England, no. 7. Harmondsworth, England: Penguin, 1960.

Poovey, Mary. *The Proper Lady and the Woman Writer: Ideology as Style in the Works of Mary Wollstonecraft, Mary Shelley, and Jane Austen*. Chicago: University of Chicago Press, 1984.

Prochaska, F. K. *Women and Philanthropy in Nineteenth-Century England*. Oxford: Clarendon, 1980.

Rendall, Jane. *The Origins of Modern Feminism: Women in Britain, France, and the United States, 1780–1860*. Chicago: Lyceum, 1985.

———. "Writing History for British Women: Elizabeth Hamilton and the *Memoirs of Agrippina*." In *Wollstonecraft's Daughters: Womanhood in England and France, 1780–1920*, ed. Clarissa Campbell Orr, 79–93. Manchester: Manchester University Press, 1996.

Rogers, Katharine M. *Feminism in Eighteenth-Century England*. Urbana: University of Illinois Press, 1982.

Ruderman, Anne Crippen. *The Pleasures of Virtue*. Lanham, Maryland: Rowman and Littlefield, 1995.

Sarkar, Tanika, and Urvashi Butalia, eds. *Women and Right-Wing Movements: Indian Experiences*. London: Zed Books, 1995.

Simpson, David. *Romanticism, Nationalism, and the Revolt Against Theory*. Chicago and London: University of Chicago Press, 1993.

Smith, Sarah W. R. "Men, Women, and Money: The Case of Mary Brunton." In *Fetter'd or Free? British Women Novelists, 1670–1815*, ed. Mary Anne Schofield and Cecilia Macheski, 40–58. Athens: Ohio University Press, 1986.

Snook, Edith. "Eve and More: The Citation of *Paradise Lost* in Hannah More's *Coelebs in Search of a Wife*." *English Studies in Canada* 26 (2000): 127–54.

Spacks, Patricia Meyer. *Gossip*. Chicago: University of Chicago Press, 1986.

———. "Sisters." In *Fetter'd or Free? British Women Novelists, 1670–1815*, ed. Mary Anne Schofield and Cecilia Macheski, 136–51. Athens: Ohio University Press, 1986.

Spender, Dale. *Mothers of the Novel: 100 Good Women Writers Before Jane Austen*. London: Pandora, 1986.

Stanton, Judith Phillips. "Statistical Profile of Women Writing in English from 1660 to 1800." In *Eighteenth-Century Women and the Arts*, ed. Frederick M. Keener and Susan E. Lorsch, 247–54. New York: Greenwood, 1988.

Staves, Susan. *Married Women's Separate Property in England, 1660–1833*. Cambridge: Harvard University Press, 1990.

Stone, Lawrence. *The Family, Sex and Marriage in England 1500–1800*. Harmondsworth, England: Penguin, Peregrine, 1979.

Suleiman, Susan Rubin. *Authoritarian Fictions: The Ideological Novel as a Literary Genre.* Princeton: Princeton University Press, 1993.

Tobin, Beth Fowkes. *Superintending the Poor: Charitable Ladies and Paternal Landlords in British Fiction, 1770–1860.* New Haven: Yale University Press, 1993.

Todd, Janet, ed. *A Dictionary of British and American Women Writers, 1660–1800.* Totowa, New Jersey: Rowman and Allanheld, 1985.

———. *The Sign of Angellica: Women, Writing and Fiction, 1660–1800.* New York: Columbia University Press, 1989.

Todorov, Tzvetan. *Genres in Discourse.* Trans. Catherine Porter. Cambridge: Cambridge University Press, 1990.

Tompkins, J. M. S. "Elinor and Marianne." *Review of English Studies* 14 (1940).

———. *The Popular Novel in England, 1770–1800.* London: Methuen, 1961.

Trumbach, Randolph. *The Rise of the Egalitarian Family: Aristocratic Kinship and Domestic Relations in Eighteenth-Century England.* New York: Academic Press, 1978.

Ty, Eleanor. *Empowering the Feminine: The Narratives of Mary Robinson, Jane West, and Amelia Opie, 1796–1812.* Toronto: University of Toronto Press, 1998.

———. "Female Philosophy Refunctioned: Elizabeth Hamilton's Parodic Novel." *Ariel* 22, no. 4 (October 1991): 111–29.

———. "Jane West's Feminine Ideals of the 1790s." In *1650–1850: Ideas Aesthetics, and Inquiries in the Early Modern Era*, ed. Kevin L. Cope, 137–55. New York: AMS Press, 1994.

———. *Unsex'd Revolutionaries: Five Women Novelists of the 1790s.* Toronto: University of Toronto Press, 1993.

Vallone, Lynne. *Disciplines of Virtue: Girls' Culture in the Eighteenth and Nineteenth Centuries.* New Haven: Yale University Press, 1995.

Van Sant, Ann Jessie. *Eighteenth-Century Sensibility and the Novel: the Senses in a Social Context.* Cambridge: Cambridge University Press, 1993.

Varma, Devendra P. Introduction to *The Mysterious Warning*, by Eliza Parsons. The Northanger Set of Jane Austen Horrid Novels. London: Folio Press, 1968.

Vaughan, William. *Romanticism and Art.* Rev. ed. London: Thames and Hudson, 1994.

Ward, William S. *Literary Reviews and British Periodicals, 1789–1797.* New York: Garland, 1979.

———. *Literary Reviews in British Periodicals, 1798–1820.* 2 vols. New York: Garland, 1972.

Warhol, Robyn R. *Gendered Interventions: Narrative Discourse in the Victorian Novel.* New Brunswick: Rutgers University Press, 1989.

Watson, George. "Burke's Conservative Revolution." *Critical Quarterly* 26, no. 1 (1984): 87–99.

Watson, Nicola J. "Purloined Letters: Revolution, Reaction and the Form of the Novel, 1790–1825." Ph.D. diss., Oxford University, 1993.

———. *Revolution and the Form of the British Novel, 1790–1825: Intercepted Letters, Interrupted Seductions.* Oxford: Clarendon, 1994.

Westfall, William. *Two Worlds: The Protestant Culture of Nineteenth-Century Ontario.* McGill-Queen's Studies in the History of Religion, no. 2. Montreal & Kingston: McGill-Queen's University Press, 1989.

Wilde, Oscar. *Oscar Wilde: Plays, Prose and Poems*. Ed. H. Montgomery Hyde. London: McDonald, Black Cat, 1989.

Wilson, Carol Shiner, and Joel Haefner, eds. *Re-Visioning Romanticism: British Women Writers, 1776–1837*. Philadelphia: University of Pennsylvania Press, 1994.

Wood, Lisa. "'This Maze of History and Fiction': Conservatism, Genre, and the Problem of Domestic Freedom in Jane West's *Alicia de Lacy*." *English Studies in Canada* 23, no. 2 (June 1997): 125–40.

Index